Handbook of

alitati...

Handbook of Qualitative Research Methods for Psychology and the Social Sciences

Edited by

John T. E. Richardson

BPS BOOKS   THE BRITISH PSYCHOLOGICAL SOCIETY

First published in 1996 by BPS Books (The British Pyschological Society),
St Andrews House, 48 Princess Road East, Leicester LE1 7DR, UK.

Reprinted 1997

A catalogue record for this book is available from the British Library.

ISBN 1 85433 204 X

Origination by Ralph J. Footring, Derby

Printed by Biddles Ltd., U.K.

Whilst every effort has been made to ensure the accuracy of the contents of this
publication, the publishers and authors expressly disclaim responsibility in law
for negligence or any other cause of action whatsoever.

Contents

Contents

List of contributors

Ken Gilhooly, Department of Psychology, University of Aberdeen, Aberdeen AB9 2UB

Rosalind Gill, Department of Sociology, Goldsmiths College, University of London, New Cross, London SE14 6NW

Caroline Green, Department of Psychology, University of Aberdeen, Aberdeen AB9 2UB

Martyn Hammersley, School of Education, The Open University, Milton Keynes MK7 6AA

Karen L. Henwood, Department of Psychology, University College of North Wales, Bangor, Gwynedd LL57 2DG

Estelle King, Department of Human Sciences, Brunel University, Uxbridge, Middlesex UB8 3PH

Nick Pidgeon, Department of Psychology, University College of North Wales, Bangor, Gwynedd LL57 2DG

Jonathan Potter, Department of Social Sciences, Loughborough University, Loughborough, Leicestershire LE11 3TU

Janet Rachel, Department of Innovation Studies, University of East London, London E15 1EY

John T. E. Richardson, Department of Human Sciences, Brunel University, Uxbridge, Middlesex UB8 3PH

Jonathan A. Smith, Department of Psychology, University of Sheffield, Sheffield S10 2TP

Christina Toren, Department of Human Sciences, Brunel University, Uxbridge, Middlesex UB8 3PH

Steve Woolgar, Centre for Research into Innovation, Culture and Technology, Brunel University, Uxbridge, Middlesex UB8 3PH

Part I

Introducing qualitative research methods

Chapter 1

Introduction

John T. E. Richardson

Since the 1960s, there has been a considerable growth of interest in the use of qualitative research methods in the social sciences, although in some disciplines the use of qualitative methods goes back a great deal further (in the case of social anthropology, to its very origins in the earliest years of the 20th century). These developments have culminated in the publication of Denzin and Lincoln's (1994a) *Handbook of Qualitative Research*, which provides an encyclopaedic account of the application of qualitative methods in a wide variety of disciplines, including sociology, education, cultural studies, anthropology and policy studies. They have had a very significant influence on the current practice of social science research in North America, in the UK and elsewhere in Europe. As an example, the UK government's Economic and Social Research Council (1992) declared in its corporate plan for 1992–97 that it intended to diversify its work on research methods by 'giving equal attention to qualitative and quantitative methods and seeking to promote appropriate methodological development in all social science disciplines' (p. 28).

Until the 1990s, however, these developments had little impact within psychology. In the UK, one or two early attempts were made to promote qualitative methods (for instance, Bannister and Mair, 1968; Harré and Secord, 1972), but at the time these did not prompt any major shift in research practice. It is true that these incorporated some robust (though not entirely unwarranted) criticisms of psychological theorizing, as Karen Henwood mentions in Chapter 3, and it is therefore probably not surprising that they encountered resistance and scepticism on the part of a methodologically rather conservative 'establishment'. In retrospect, however, my feeling is that these writings also had little impact because their authors tended to disparage more traditional, quantitative research and failed to engage in any constructive manner with the broad mainstream of the discipline. Consequently, they tended to be dismissed as a rather eccentric fringe, and their ideas had little influence even upon those who might otherwise have been more receptive to alternative ways of conducting and conceptualizing psychological research. When, later, during the 1980s, British psychologists began to pay more attention to qualitative methods, often this was less the result of rediscovering these earlier sources than a consequence of the importation of fresh ideas from cognate disciplines.

Qualitative research methods for psychologists

In 1991, a report commissioned by the Scientific Affairs Board of the British Psychological Society recognized that there was a growing interest in many areas of psychology in the potential value of qualitative research methods, and it proposed that the future development of major areas within psychology might be facilitated by a wider use of qualitative approaches in both teaching and research (Nicolson, 1991). However, its author also concluded that 'Psychology departments do not on the whole appear to have the competence and expertise to employ qualitative methods in research or undergraduate and postgraduate teaching' (p. 1). During the discussion of this report at the Scientific Affairs Board, some members expressed a good deal of enthusiasm with regard to learning about the possible contribution of qualitative methods in psychology, but other members expressed a degree of scepticism and suspicion, comparing qualitative approaches unfavourably with more traditional, 'scientific' methods. (Remarks of this sort often assume a view of 'science' which is not in fact manifested in the natural sciences, as Steve Woolgar and Jonathan Smith point out in Chapters 2 and 14 of this volume.)

As someone who witnessed that discussion, the latter reaction struck me as especially odd, even though I regarded myself as an unreconstructed cognitive psychologist who was more comfortable with the language and the methods of traditional experimental research. This was because I had for many years been a member of the academic staff in the Department of Human Sciences at Brunel University, where I was daily working with sociologists and social anthropologists who took it for granted that ethnographic and other qualitative methods were a wholly appropriate way of studying human activities and who had special expertise in their use. More recently, as their Head of Department, I had been greatly impressed at their excellent appreciation of the aims of psychological inquiry and of the needs and sensitivities of psychologists who might wish to develop their own skills or those of their students in using qualitative methods. This had in turn helped to foster the growth of a team of psychologists in the Department who routinely used such methods in investigating issues in cultural, developmental and social psychology.

Nevertheless, there did appear to be an urgent need for training in the use of qualitative research methods on the part of psychologists, and it occurred to me that the expertise of my colleagues could be put to use to begin to meet this need. Along with colleagues from other institutions of higher education, we therefore planned a two-day training workshop that had the aims of introducing teachers, researchers and research students to the range of qualitative methods being employed in the social sciences, and of illustrating their application to psychological problems. Our proposal was endorsed by the Scientific Affairs Board of the British Psychological Society and subsequently sponsored by the Training Board of the Economic and Social Research Council. The workshop took place at Cumberland Lodge in the Great Park at Windsor on 30–31 March 1992.

It became clear to us at a fairly early stage that the workshop was going to be most successful. Many participants expressed their gratitude for having at least some opportunity to engage in structured training in qualitative research methods, as well as concern that opportunities should be made available in the future, both to themselves and to others. There did appear to remain a considerable unsatisfied demand from psychologists for training in qualitative research methods, as evidenced by a long list of applicants whom we were unable to accommodate at the workshop. There was also a considerable demand from those who did attend the workshop for additional training activities at a more advanced level. Accordingly, the original introductory workshop was repeated in March 1993 and March 1994, and a more advanced workshop was also held in both those years, in each case with financial support from the Economic and Social Research Council. In total, 160 participants attended the three introductory workshops, and 75 participants attended the two advanced workshops.

In the meantime, there were a number of other positive developments that served to enhance the profile of qualitative research methods among British psychologists. In 1992, a review paper by Karen Henwood and Nick Pidgeon, entitled 'Qualitative Research and Psychological Theorising', was published by the *British Journal of Psychology*. Apart from the fact that this article served a valuable tutorial function, it was one of the first papers on qualitative research methods to be accepted for publication in a mainstream psychology journal in the UK. Later that year, a symposium on qualitative research methods was sponsored by the Scientific Affairs Board at the London Conference of the British Psychological Society. This gave rise in turn to a special issue of *The Psychologist* (previously known as the *Bulletin of the British Psychological Society*) devoted to qualitative research (Henwood and Nicolson, 1995b). Other journals have also devoted special issues or sections to this topic, as Jonathan Smith points out in Chapter 14.

Unmet needs of qualitative researchers in psychology

Together with these other activities and publications, our five workshops could certainly be said to have helped to raise the profile of qualitative methods in the development of psychological research. However, they also highlighted a number of specific problems. Two of these were raised by many of the postgraduate students who attended the workshops, and they relate to the training of research students and the assessment of research students.

With regard to the former, it would appear that, in many cases where students were engaged in research that involved qualitative methods, their supervisors did not possess the experience or expertise to train them in the use of such methods. Indeed, it was apparent that in some cases the appointed supervisors showed little or no appreciation of the contribution of qualitative methods to psychological research. This was certainly an undesirable situation from the students' point of view. The departments and institutions concerned were clearly falling well below the generally accepted standards of good practice in research training and supervision, as laid down, for example, in the Economic and Social Research Council's *Postgraduate Training Guidelines*. Nevertheless, this was not simply the result of poor organization being reflected in an inappropriate allocation of research supervisors, but more often a matter of the research culture that prevailed within the departments themselves. Many students attending the workshops reported that the use of qualitative methods had not been covered in the degree courses that they had taken as undergraduate students and that it was generally discouraged in their postgraduate work. One reason given for this was that departments seemed to be assuming that qualitative research would be looked upon less favourably in the forthcoming (1996) research assessment exercise being carried out by the UK Higher Education Funding Councils. (At the time of writing, no evidence exists to judge whether or not such assumptions were justified.)

With regard to the assessment of research students, many of those who attended our workshops expressed concern at the apparent lack of senior figures in the community of psychologists in the UK who were competent to examine doctoral theses that employed qualitative methods. This might mean that they would be assessed by external examiners who were of lesser academic status, which might affect the credibility and reputation of their doctoral degrees. Alternatively, given the (at best) ambivalent attitude of academic departments towards qualitative research, it would be more likely to mean that they would be assessed by external examiners who were more senior but less competent. Many students were genuinely worried that as a consequence they would be assessed unfairly by examiners who did not recognize the value of qualitative methods. (Analogous problems might also arise, of course, in the peer assessment of psychological research in connection with academic publication and with national research assessment exercises.) This, too, conflicts with commonly accepted standards of good practice. For example, Sloboda and Newstead (1995) remarked that doctoral projects might require both quantitative and qualitative methods and analytical techniques, and they proposed that 'an external examiner should have expertise of direct relevance to the candidate's research' (p. 5).

These issues reflect a much broader need to educate the psychological community about the actual and potential contributions of qualitative methods to psychological research. All the participants at our workshops, teachers, practitioners and students alike, complained at the lack of any suitable resources in the form of appropriate textbooks that could be used both by individual researchers in carrying out their work and by teachers in training their students in the use of qualitative research methods. To be sure, there are ample numbers of textbooks in cognate disciplines, most obviously the extensive list produced by Sage Publications. However, as Ashworth (1995) recently pointed out when reviewing a number of new books on qualitative methods, 'It is a great shame that the texts on qualitative methods currently available are almost all sociological in disciplinary orientation' (p. 81). This clearly does not help psychologists and their students to acquire a very good knowledge and appreciation of qualitative research methods. Perhaps more fundamentally, as Ashworth noted, it also creates 'a serious difficulty in securing a rightful place for qualitative methods in the standard psychology syllabus' (p. 82). The present volume has been written to address this need for a text on qualitative research methods that can be used specifically by psychologists and their students.

Aims and structure of this book

The aims of this book are essentially those of our workshops. In the 13 chapters that follow, a team of psychologists, sociologists and social anthropologists will introduce the reader to some of the main qualitative research methods currently used in the social sciences and will illustrate the application of these methods to problems in psychology. Half of these contributors have been associated with the Department of Human Sciences at Brunel University, and have used qualitative methods in their own teaching and research there; the others are colleagues with similar experience from other institutions of higher education in the UK. To ensure a proper disciplinary focus, more than half of the contributors have a background in psychology; nevertheless, all of the contributors are sensitive to the needs and interests of psychologists who want to develop their own skills or those of their students in using qualitative methods. All of the contributors participated in the workshops at Cumberland Lodge, and so they have a good first-hand knowledge of the needs of psychologists in this area. Most have based their contributions on formal presentations or informal tutorial guidance given at the workshops, but I must emphasize that this book is far more than just a conventional volume of proceedings.

What we have sought to do in this book is to discuss the principles, the applications and the implications of qualitative research methods in a supportive yet self-critical manner. We want to provide psychologists and other social scientists who have embarked on qualitative research with the opportunity to develop and refine their skills. We want to provide those who at the moment may have only a general interest in qualitative methods with the self-confidence to use those methods in their own research. We want to provide those who are responsible for the design and the delivery of training courses on research methods or for the supervision of research students with a clear understanding of the strengths, the limitations and the hazards of using qualitative research methods. And we want to provide students who have chosen to examine research issues for which qualitative methods are appropriate or even essential with a sound basis for planning, implementing and evaluating their practical work.

In Part I of the book, two chapters by Steve Woolgar and by Karen Henwood will help the reader to locate qualitative research methods within the broader context of current debates about scientific methods and scientific knowledge. Karen will also describe the principal strands that are to be found in qualitative psychology. Part II is very much the 'core' of the book, which reflects its origins in the practical workshops at Cumberland Lodge. Eight chapters will describe four important types of qualitative research method, selected on the basis that they are likely to be of particular interest and relevance to psychologists. In each case, one chapter will be devoted to the theoretical background of the approach, and a second chapter will be devoted to its practical implementation. Ken Gilhooly and Caroline Green will consider protocol analysis; Nick Pidgeon and Karen Henwood will consider grounded theory; Christina Toren and Janet Rachel will consider ethnography; while Jonathan Potter and Rosalind Gill will consider discourse analysis and other constructionist approaches. In Part III, evaluative chapters by Martyn Hammersley, Estelle King and Jonathan Smith will reflect upon the strengths and the limitations of qualitative methods in contemporary psychological research.

In short, this book is intended as a major resource for teachers of psychology in colleges and universities, for researchers and practitioners who might be interested in using qualitative methods in their professional work, and particularly for students taking undergraduate or postgraduate programmes in psychology. However, we feel that it can also be read with benefit by teachers, researchers and students in other social sciences and by students who are taking psychology as an option in degree programmes in other disciplines. All the authors are based in the UK, and indeed the development of qualitative research methods is an area in which British psychologists have made a distinctive contribution. Nevertheless, the book will be of considerable interest to readers in many other countries, not least in Continental Europe and North America.

Incidentally, when this project was first put forward to an American publisher, a reviewer who had been asked to comment on our proposal made the following (anonymous) response: 'In my opinion such a textbook would have a very limited market in the US. Here there is much discussion about positivism and its limitations, but almost everything that is done uses positivist, quantitative methodologies.' I suspect that this statement exaggerates the true situation in North America, and that there may well be people there (not necessarily located in psychology departments) who use qualitative methods in psychological research. However, they do not seem to represent a coordinated movement, nor do they have access to mainstream psychological journals or (evidently!) to major publishers.

Clearly, therefore, there is a great deal of scope for psychologists in North America to catch up with their counterparts in the UK and with their compatriots in the other social sciences in terms of their understanding and appreciation of qualitative research methods. In fact, I learned towards the end of 1995 that the subsystem of the American Psychological Association that is concerned with the psychology of women (Division 35) had commissioned a task force to investigate opportunities for teaching and training in qualitative research methods. I hope very much that the present volume will inform our colleagues on the task force and that it will help more generally to bring qualitative research methods to the attention of psychologists in North America and elsewhere.

Some health warnings

I want to conclude this introduction by making some general observations, perhaps in the way of a few 'health warnings' about qualitative research. The first is: *qualitative research need not exclude quantitative research*. This book is not a diatribe against the use of quantitative methods in the conduct of psychological investigations, though in Chapter 2 Steve Woolgar criticizes the view of science that often lies behind attempts to defend the use of quantitative methods and resist the use of qualitative methods. Indeed, some of the contributors explicitly conclude that quantitative and qualitative approaches should be regarded as having complementary (though possibly different) roles in psychological research. However, at the same time we would not agree with Watts (1992), who argued:

> I believe the case that needs to be made for qualitative methods in psychology is essentially a pragmatic one rather than an ideological one. Too many enthusiasts for qualitative methods see an issue of principle involved, and present essentially ideological and philosophical arguments in favour of qualitative methods.
>
> (p. 492)

There are genuine differences of principle that separate quantitative and qualitative methods, just as there are differences of principle between different quantitative methods and between different qualitative methods, as Martyn Hammersley makes abundantly clear in Chapter 12. Like Ashworth (1995), we would suggest that Watts placed an inappropriate value upon a naïve pragmatism to the detriment of a proper appreciation of the theoretical, epistemological and sometimes ethical assumptions that differentiate various methodologies in psychology and the social sciences. I hope that in the light of this book readers will be able to make their own choice of research methods in each specific research context, properly informed by *both* philosophical *and* pragmatic considerations.

The second point is that *qualitative research has its own language*. This will strike the reader fairly quickly on reading this book. Like any new area of expertise, there will be problems in accommodating the specialist jargon. The problems are compounded when the relevant jargon is not used in a consistent way, even by skilled practitioners. The contributors are aware of this problem and address issues of definition and explanation at various points in their discussion. As in the case of many other rapidly developing areas of academic discourse, however, there is genuine debate about the categories and concepts that are to define future research, and a degree of licence has to be tolerated among the parties to that debate. Nevertheless, the issue of language goes far deeper, because qualitative researchers tend to question the conventions within which research has traditionally been reported and discussed. Accordingly, the reader will find many alternative styles of writing among these contributions.

The third point is that *qualitative research is not easy research*. One of my own academic responsibilities is to teach statistics to undergraduate students in psychology, and I know how painful for them this sometimes can be. I also know

9

that some students turn to qualitative methods in relief, believing that this will release them from such chores as having to carry out a three-way analysis of variance. Sooner or later, they realize that this is a mistaken assumption. To be sure, the use of qualitative methods does not demand familiarity with statistical packages such as SPSS, but it does involve a whole range of other problems, many of which do not typically arise within traditional quantitative research, and most of which will be discussed at some length in this book.

Some of these problems are technical or technological, perhaps to do with the very real problem of making sense of large amounts of qualitative data. However, some of these problems are much deeper: they have to do with the very point of conducting psychological research, the role of researchers and the proper conduct of their relationships with the research participants. Examples of problems of an ethical or personal nature that can arise in using qualitative research methods are given by Janet Rachel and by Estelle King in Chapters 9 and 13. So, my final point is that *qualitative research needs proper training and supervision.* The role of proper training in enabling the researcher to address such problems is fairly self-evident, but proper supervision is just as important. Indeed, for the research students who participated in our workshops at Cumberland Lodge, the latter appears to have been the crucial component that was most often lacking in their formal training. However, adequate supervision is equally important whether one is carrying out a qualitative project as an introductory student or as an experienced researcher in the closing years of an eminent career. In short, as a perfectly general observation, the significance of an effective and sensitive supervisor–student relationship cannot be emphasized too strongly in the conduct of qualitative research.

Acknowledgements

I am grateful to the Scientific Affairs Board of the British Psychological Society for its encouragement over several years and the Training Board of the Economic and Social Research Council for its financial support of the workshops on qualitative research methods for psychologists. The success of the workshops themselves owed a good deal to the delightful ambience of Cumberland Lodge and the warm hospitality of its staff.

In producing this chapter, I am grateful for the comments (both positive and negative) that were made by the workshop participants and especially for the contribution of David Foxcroft. I am also grateful to Karen Henwood, Estelle King and Jonathan Smith for their comments on a preliminary draft of this chapter.

In editing this book as a whole, I have much appreciated the assistance of the technicians in the Department of Human Sciences at Brunel University in converting the different contributions from a variety of disk formats and software. Finally, I am grateful to all the colleagues who served as speakers and tutors at the workshops on qualitative research methods for psychologists, including those who have not contributed explicitly to this volume but who all played some part in bringing this project to fruition.

Chapter 2

Psychology, qualitative methods and the ideas of science

Steve Woolgar

Assessments of the value, relevance and purpose of different research methods in the social sciences often depend upon various ideas (usually left implicit) concerning the nature of science and the methods of the natural sciences. Not surprisingly, this reflects the fact that debates about methods tend to be infused with the assumption that science is the prime locale for the most reliable use and operation of methods. Within and beyond academic debate, 'scientific method' is frequently asserted to be the best kind of method to deploy. The social sciences, in particular, are relative newcomers to debates about the adequacy of scientific method, and they have had to operate against a legacy of apparent success in the natural sciences. Since the time of Auguste Comte, a strong tradition in the social sciences has maintained that a natural evolution of research would consist in emulating the methods and procedures of natural science.

Although the emergence of qualitative methods and the debates that are associated with them have a fairly long history in anthropology (for example, Geertz, 1973) and sociology (for example, Becker *et al.*, 1961; Cicourel, 1964; Whyte, 1967), they are relatively new in psychology, as John Richardson pointed out in Chapter 1. It is only in recent years that psychologists have advocated ethogenic methods (Harré and Secord, 1972; Harré, 1992a), discourse analysis (Potter and Wetherell, 1987; Edwards and Potter, 1992; Parker, 1992), grounded theory (Henwood and Pidgeon, 1995a) and reflexive inquiry (Curt, 1994; Parker, 1994). Several recent edited collections of papers have advocated the adoption of qualitative research methods on the part of psychologists (Antaki, 1988; Harré, 1992a; Burman and Parker, 1993), while other researchers have discussed their impact on psychology in general (Henwood and Pidgeon, 1992).

Entirely in line with the way in which the same debate raged within sociology and anthropology some years ago, there is a considerable range of opinion about the best form of advocacy of qualitative methods. Thus, while they are largely united against 'traditional' psychology and against the apparent hegemony of 'quantitative' research traditions, advocates of qualitative methods disagree about the relative merits of each method and about the extent to which a pluralistic stance is admissible. In certain quarters, in particular, 'qualitative' methods appear to be regarded as a radical alternative to a dominant orthodoxy, in much the same way that ethnomethodology and allied qualitative perspectives were enrolled as part of a 'new direction' in sociology during the 1970s (see, for example, Filmer *et al.*, 1973). For instance, as we found at the workshops on qualitative research methods for psychologists that were described in Chapter 1, research students tend to be intrigued and attracted by this new subversion, but also fearful that the research supervisors who are available will take at best a dim view of what they regard as merely an errant flirtation with fashionable and ultimately unreliable methods.

The aim of this chapter is to explicate and to challenge some of the assumptions underlying these debates. I shall introduce and discuss the results of recent research into the character of 'science' and 'scientific method', drawing in particular on recent social studies of science. This field is sometimes referred to as the 'sociology of scientific knowledge' and sometimes simply as part of the wider field of science and technology studies. In the space available, I will not be able to do justice to the range and depth of scholarship in this field. However, for introductions and more extensive overviews of the work on which I shall draw, I commend the books by Pickering (1992), Lynch (1993) and Jasanoff *et al.* (1995).

My argument is that this body of work has three main implications for current debates about qualitative methods in psychology. First, one major upshot of this research has been to challenge prevailing conceptions of science. It is, in particular, no longer appropriate to rely upon canonical versions of 'science', because it turns out that ('successful') scientists themselves only rarely conform to them. Scientific practice involves much more than just straightforward application of technical method. Second, it follows that rather more profound issues underpin the apparently innocent choice between quantitative and qualitative methods. Social studies of science unearth a form of scepticism that suggests that merely choosing between qualitative and quantitative methods (or a combination of the two) misses an important epistemological point about the adequacy of representations. (In this chapter, I use 'representation' in the general sense, whereby a sign or symbol for language stands for some underlying reality, rather than in the particular sense of 'cognitive representation' that is more familiar to psychologists.) To put this differently, the choice of qualitative methods in a framework of representational realism misses the significance of the critique of quantitative methods. Third, the same scepticism raises considerable doubt about the appropriate unit of analysis for psychological research. In line with some recent proposals (which themselves happen to advocate the use of qualitative methods in psychology), I shall conclude that one should reconceptualize the dominant image of the cognizing individual.

Alternatives to the 'received view' of science

Most recent work in social studies of science (sometimes also described as 'post-Kuhnian' or 'social-constructivist' science studies) is couched as a critique of the 'received', 'standard' or 'traditional' view of science. The 'received view' of science is the description of science that is often found in textbooks or popular accounts of scientific method and in public declarations concerning the supposed virtues of science. Typically, the 'received view' involves four main assumptions:

(1) Objects in the natural world are objective and real, and they enjoy an existence independent of human beings. Human agency is basically incidental to the objective character of the world 'out there'.

(2) It follows from this that scientific knowledge is determined by the actual character of the physical world.

(3) Science comprises a unitary set of methods and procedures, concerning which there is, by and large, a consensus.

(4) Science is an activity that is individualistic and mentalistic. (The latter is sometimes expressed as 'cognitive'.)

These central assumptions of the 'received view' have been challenged in a number of different ways.

Variations in definitions of science

First, it turns out that the central defining characteristics of science are not timeless. They have indeed been the focus of considerable debate and discussion, by scientists themselves and by academics and scholars, since the idea of natural science was invented in the 17th century (see Shapin and Schaffer, 1985; Shapin, 1994). Since that time, it is evident, for example, that the organization of science has changed markedly. As a very rough approximation, the gentleman amateurs of the 17th century gave way eventually to the growth of 'pure' academic science up to around 1940, but since then science has been increasingly oriented to (and funded by) industrial concerns. Philosophical discussions about science have also generated a wide variety of versions of what is to count as 'scientific'. For example, the notion that a defining feature of scientific questions was that they dealt in facts rather than opinions gave way to the notion that a statement was scientific only if it was provable. Famously, this criterion was subsequently overturned by Popper's (1934/1959) notion that a defining characteristic of a scientific theory was its falsifiability.

Second, the source of variation is not only historical. It turns out that the conceptions of scientists and others about the location and site of science are also highly localized and contingent. In the experience of sociologists and anthropologists, attempts to gain access to laboratories for the purpose of conducting observation or participant observation often involve discussions with practising scientists concerning whether or not a particular site is typical of 'science'. Is science really going on here? Where, and in what sense, are the activities of this particular laboratory exemplary of science? Would not the prospective observer be better off visiting some other laboratory at the University of X? *That's* where one could say that real science was going on.

A response of this sort is by no means peculiar to the interactions between intending ethnographers and scientists in the modern day. In the anthropological literature, it is often reported that observers' efforts to locate the essence of a certain tribe or people or of a particular way of life are met with similar uncertainty about the location of the essence sought by the newcomer. For example, Moerman (1974) reported that his attempts to locate the Lue met with a series of redirections ('down the river', 'over the hill') as each respondent in turn proffered a deferred site for the 'essence of the Lue'. There is an important sense in which 'science', like 'the Lue', is always somewhere else. (An instructive exercise is to apply the same approach to 'psychology'. Is 'psychology' happening here? Now? If not, where exactly is 'psychology' to be found?) More exactly, this suggests that science is not an objective set of activities and practices that are readily available and straightforwardly identifiable, even if in some textbooks and for some occasions it is treated that way. The problem of identifying the essence of 'science' is as undecidable and debatable for the natives (in this case, for scientists) as it is for their observers, whether they be psychologists, sociologists or anthropologists (Sharrock and Anderson, 1982).

One way to deal with the elusive character of the essence of science is to note the distinction frequently made between idealized versions of 'science' and science in practice, for instance between the accounts of 'science' that are often displayed in a Nobel prize acceptance speech or in a grant proposal, on the one hand, and the portrayals of scientific practice that emerge from prolonged periods of participant observation in the laboratory, on the other. The former, 'evaluative' repertoire of descriptions of science tends to stress features of 'science' that appear within the 'received' or 'traditional' view. The latter, 'contingent' repertoire, by contrast, includes mention of human and social factors, the localized indeterminacy of laboratory decisions and so on (Collins and Pinch, 1982; Gilbert and Mulkay, 1984). This distinction is frequently made both by observers and by scientists themselves, and it casts further doubt upon the utility of the idea that there is one unitary phenomenon that is called 'science'. (It is worth stressing that this distinction is *not* between what scientists say about science and what others say. Both scientists and non-scientists switch between the contingent and evaluative repertoires in describing their own activities and those of other people.)

Laboratory studies

The work of Kuhn (1970) is celebrated for its argument that scientific knowledge does not develop through the progressive linear accretion of findings. His alternative model, of scientific growth proceeding through quasi-cyclical revolution, challenged the accepted orthodoxy. However, it was left to a subsequent generation of sociologists to challenge aspects of the 'received view' dealing specifically with the nature of scientific activity and method. This later tradition, which is sometimes referred to as 'laboratory studies', involved the conduct of ethnographic studies of scientific practice using intensive and sustained periods of participant observation of the day-to-day activities of laboratory work (for example, Knorr Cetina, 1981; Lynch, 1985; Latour and Woolgar, 1986; Traweek, 1988).

For present purposes, the significant findings of this research are threefold. First, the authors of these studies noted the extreme disorder and messiness of laboratory practice. This may seem surprising, precisely because the ideal, clinical, 'men-in-white-coats' image of science is so pervasive outside the laboratory.

Second, it is evident that idealized accounts (in other words, the evaluative repertoire) have little place in the cut and thrust of daily scientific work. For example, scientists have in practice little opportunity or inclination to reflect on the 'truth' or otherwise of a particular result. Instead, theirs is a highly pragmatic attitude: they tend to get excited by a published result, not because it reveals 'truth', but because it enables the setting up of another, perhaps decisive, experiment.

Third, decisions about the kinds of experiment to run, the types of instrument to use or the sorts of interpretation that are most appropriate are highly dependent on local conditions, circumstances and opportunities. (The following is based on the account given in Woolgar, 1988c, pp. 87ff.) Here, again, we find an instrumentalism that supports the conclusion that scientific activity is better termed 'constructive' than 'descriptive', to use Knorr Cetina's (1981) terms. Scientists are not engaged merely in the passive description of pre-existing facts about the world, but are engaged in actively formulating or constructing the character of that world. This is fairly obvious from the reading and writing activities of scientists: they can be found constructing drafts, memos, e-mails, letters, articles, computer print-outs, charts, line graphs and so on. It is perhaps less obvious that a whole series of assessments and decisions is imbued in the so-called 'raw' materials of the laboratory. The sample metals that are investigated are chosen from among a variety of sources, the animals for testing are carefully selected and bred, the water used in experiments is purified according to a selected procedure, and so on.

Similar findings emerge with regard to the instruments and apparatus in the laboratory. These have a rhetorical neutrality in the sense that they are thought of as being merely 'used' or 'applied' to the materials or organisms in question; but, of course, the selection and use of 'mere' machines (instruments or apparatus) inevitably involves humans and hence depends upon processes of interpretation. Many laboratory mechanisms are designed according to principles that have been established as the result of previous laboratory investigations. For example, the nuclear magnetic resonance spectrometer is not a neutral 'black box' but the embodiment of some 20 years of physics research. By merely 'using' the device, scientists invoke as 'neutral' a mechanism which in fact draws upon and is shaped by a whole multitude of previous decisions, interventions and selections by previous communities of scientists.

These three findings from laboratory studies reinforce the point that scientific practice is much more creative and contingent than is portrayed by idealized versions of 'science' (the objectivist philosophy). For our particular purposes, the last finding is of especial importance. The fact that the instruments and apparatus are imbued with a history of selections and decisions can apply equally well to methods in psychological research. In choosing a method in psychology, therefore, one is not merely making a selection among neutral tools. Instead, one is effectively 'buying into' a whole series of choices, perspectives and, importantly, epistemological commitments that are embodied in that method. Psychological methods too may have a rhetorical neutrality, in the sense that they are thought of as being merely 'used' or 'applied to' data. But this once again invokes as 'neutral' a mechanism that draws upon and is shaped by a multitude of previous decisions, interventions and selections by previous communities of social scientists. (For an elaboration of the stronger argument that instruments, apparatus and, by extension, methods constitute the phenomena of scientific investigation, see Woolgar, 1988c, pp. 88ff.)

Representations and objects

This last criticism (here articulated in terms of the problems that are associated with the rhetorical treatment of methods as 'neutral') belies a more extensive critique of the epistemological realism found in idealized versions of 'science'. Put most simply, 'traditional' or 'received' views of science operate upon the assumption that the world can be imagined to comprise representations, on the one hand, and underlying objects, on the other hand. The 'ideology of representation' is the set of beliefs and practices stemming from the idea that various entities (meanings, motives, things, essences, reality, underlying patterns, cause, what is signified, intention, meaning, facts, objects and so on) underlie or pre-exist their surface representations (documents, appearances, signs, images, actions, behaviour, language, knowledge and so on). In science, as elsewhere, the main business is to establish and justify connections between the surface representations and the underlying entities; following Mannheim, Garfinkel (1967) described this as the 'documentary method of interpretation'. On this view, the essential difference between science and ordinary everyday activity is that science is able to effect such connections more reliably and more accurately. The 'scientific method' is said to be precisely that which enables the most effective connections between representation and underlying reality.

Needless to say, by the same token it is possible to develop a series of arguments that attest to the impossibility in principle of effectively making connections between representations and underlying reality. I have elsewhere described these as the 'methodological horrors' (Woolgar, 1988c, ch. 2). While it is not clear that such 'horrors' are necessarily endemic to routine scientific practice (Lynch, 1993, p. 194), it is nevertheless true that they are available as 'troubles' to be invoked on any occasion when the effectiveness of scientific method is brought into question. In fact, it is possible to sketch three distinct views of the epistemological relationship between representation and underlying object. The first is the *naïve reflection* view. This is the view that representations in the world derive in a more or less straightforward way from the corresponding underlying reality. While this position is denoted 'naïve' when advanced as an authentic account of the operation of scientific method, it is also clear that it is a realist epistemology that many are happy to portray as characteristic of everyday activity.

The second position is the *mediative* view. This takes the view that the relationship between object and representation is imperfect. In other words, appropriate connections between object and representation can be distorted or deflected by intervening circumstances. The latter can take various forms. At an early stage in the development of the sociology of science, they were identified with 'distorting' social factors. Thus, if an incorrect representation arose, it was imagined that social factors (such as competition, greed or ambition) must have interceded to deflect the course of the true connection. More recently, however, sociologists of science have asserted the need for a more symmetrical approach, one which recognizes that 'social factors' are involved in the generation of knowledge and beliefs (or 'representations'), regardless of whether or not these come to be viewed as true. On this variant of the mediative view, social factors always and inevitably intercede, and it is the aim of the sociology of science to sort out which kinds of factors can give rise to different kinds of knowledge.

The third, *constitutive* view inverts the central assumption of the naïve reflection and mediative positions, that representations derive from underlying objects. Instead, it holds that objects are constituted or created by virtue of the manipulation of representations. If, for the naïve reflection position or the mediative position, one pictures the connection between object and representation in terms of an arrow flowing from the former to the latter, then this alternative position reverses the direction of the arrow: in the constitutive position the arrow flows from representation to object. This is one possible consequence of a wholesale scepticism with regard to the adequacy of connections between object and representation. Why should one assume that objects have any kind of prior existence? This position represents a more extreme ontological relativism compared with the mild-mannered epistemological relativism of the second, mediative, position. Its curiously counterintuitive quality is perhaps indicative of the extent to which we are ourselves members of a culture that is committed to the ideology of representation. (Of course, I am suggesting here that apprehensions of the anti-intuitive character of this argument should themselves be taken as a *representation* of an *underlying* commitment to an ideology. . . .)

This schematic portrayal of different views of the relation between representation and object underscores the point that idealized versions of that connection offer too focused and narrow a view of what science can be about. In order to examine the sense and consequences of these different positions on the relation between representation and object, I shall now consider the example of scientific discovery.

Discovery

The idea of discovery is central to popular conceptions of science. It is the one activity above all others that one most commonly associates with scientific activity. The metaphor of scientific discovery, the notion of 'dis-covering', is precisely that of revealing something that has been there all along: one removes the covers and thereby exposes the thing for what it is; one pulls back the curtains on the facts. The crucial aspect of this metaphor is the presumed prior existence of the discovered object. In other words, an assumption central to the idea of discovery is that the discovered object is antecedent and that it enjoyed an existence before any discoverers happened to come across it. The rhetoric of this ontology portrays the objects of discovery as being fixed and permanent, but the agents of discovery as merely transient.

Clearly, this conception of scientific discovery fits the first (and, to some extent, the second) of the three accounts of representation–object relationships mentioned above. But to what extent does this picture match the findings of investigations of 'discovery' that have been undertaken in social studies of science? The close analysis of particular episodes of scientific discovery suggests that, contrary to the popular 'Eureka' image of discovery as a sudden occurrence, it is better construed as a *process* (see, for example, Brannigan, 1981; Woolgar, 1988c, ch. 4). This process extends in time both before and after the initial announcement of a claim. There is often a protracted uncertainty on the part of the participants themselves over what has been discovered and when it was discovered. It is only subsequently that the episode is rewritten to nominate a specific point or date of discovery. Once this has been done, once the discovery has been celebrated and the discoverers honoured, certainly once the event has been institutionalized in a nation's history, it is often very difficult to re-establish the contingency and uncertainty of the discovery process. (Coincidentally, I am writing this passage on Columbus Day during a visit to the United States.)

This contingency about the date of the discovery is accompanied by a contingency about the nature of the discovered object. For it turns out that whether or not there is (or was) an object and what kind of object it is can also vary during the discovery process. As with the question of the timing of the discovery, the actual character of the discovered object tends to get rewritten. However, during the process of discovery itself, the nature of the object or possible non-object changes according to the kinds of social networks that are brought to bear on it. In the discovery of pulsars, for example, as different and larger groups of researchers were gradually added to the investigating team, and as new equipment was deployed, so the nature of the putative object changed (see Woolgar, 1988c, ch. 4). Significantly, this suggests that the process of discovery is better characterized as the active, contingent constitution of the object and its nature than as the straightforward reflection of an object with a pre-existing character. However, as I have already hinted, the aftermath of this process of constitution involves a rewriting, such that the (now) known transcendent character of the object is said to have been there all along.

The received view replaced

In sum, the main burden of research in social studies of science is that the 'received view' of science is at best an inaccurate and at worst a positively misleading description of how science gets done. Specifically:

(1)   It is misleading to posit a straightforwardly realist ontology of the objects of the natural world. A rather better account of the details of the scientific process emphasizes the ways in which science comprises the constitution of its objects within the context of changing social relations and changing configurations of both equipment and method.

(2)   It follows that scientific knowledge is determined not by 'the actual character of the physical world' but instead by the social relations, beliefs and value systems that pertain within scientific communities. The apposite slogan in social studies of science is that 'what counts as successful scientific knowledge is a social construct'. However, note that this is not the same as claiming that scientific knowledge is *merely* a social construct. 'Social construct' is here intended in a purely technical sense that connotes no assessment of the veracity or truth of the relevant scientific knowledge. The epithet 'merely' (or 'just') is mistakenly introduced by those who caricature social studies of science as a form of epistemological nihilism.

(3)   Science can be considered to be neither a unitary set of methods and procedures nor a universal practice. What counts as 'science' varies over time (philosophically, historically and sociologically) and is elusive. It is more useful to understand 'scientific method' as an evaluative repertoire than as an universal procedure.

(4)   Science is not primarily an individualistic and mentalistic activity. Instead, it is a social process that takes place within a language community and hence is responsive to the prevalent values, beliefs and expectations of that community.

Before considering the implications of this revision of the 'received view' of science for the debate about qualitative methods, I must briefly look at research in social studies of science that bears in particular on this last assumption: the notion of agency. (For a more extended account, see Woolgar, 1994.)

The critique of the cognizing agent

As I have just mentioned, a key element of the 'received view' of science construes the working scientist as an individual cognizer, as someone who is engaged in mentalistic acts of reasoning, thinking, learning, problem solving and so on. As one would expect, the ethnographic study of science has to resist this assumption if only on methodological grounds. To adopt the view that scientific knowledge was the upshot of cognitive processes would be to buy into a central precept of the natives before even setting foot in the field. It would be to 'go native' before the study had even begun. This is one reason why social studies of science have to adopt an ethnographic sensibility. They have to attempt a critical distance on (or an inversion of) the central assumptions of scientific culture (or, more exactly, the central assumptions in accounts of scientific culture of the 'received view' variety given by philosophers and other commentators).

This is a wide-ranging prescription. It means, of course, that the basic 'cognitive' discourse associated with scientific practice must be treated sceptically. In other words, all the perlocutions such as 'he had an idea . . .', 'she reasoned that . . .' and so on should be investigated analytically, as the product of particular conceptions of agency and action that make sense under the rubric of the 'received view' of science. On this account, the precepts of 'cognitive processes' are not the resource for social science investigation but rather its topic. The central question to be addressed is: what sustains the cognitivist image of scientific practice?

Several kinds of criticism of the 'cognizing individual' concept of agency have arisen in recent social studies of science. One concerns the nature of the activity in which the cognizing agent is supposedly engaged. Writers such as Coulter (1979, 1983, 1989; Coulter and Parsons, 1991) and Lynch and Bogen (in press-b) have proposed a reconceptualization of the various detailed practical activities that are construed as 'cognitive'. This is crucial, Lynch and Bogen argue, since these practical activities provide the basis not only for how we talk about or interpret 'cognitive practices', but also for how we conceptualize the 'cognitive practices' of ourselves and other people. Instead of proposing that all the myriad and diverse practical activities that are associated with 'perception' or 'memory' (say) are constituted by a single cognitive process, we need to focus upon the 'situated grammar of practice' (Coulter, 1983), the practical activities in which 'perception' and 'memory' become embedded within the discursive surface of a particular linguistic performance (see Lynch and Bogen, in press-a).

The argument that we need to be sceptical of using an agent's actions as indicative of (or, worse, as deriving from) certain underlying events and processes (especially those that are called 'mental' or 'cognitive') is redoubled if we question our ability straightforwardly to identify and define the character of the agent allegedly responsible for these actions. The second criticism of the notion of the 'cognizing agent' challenges the assumption that actions can be most profitably assigned to single entities that are biologically bounded. Instead, in a similar way to that in which the notion of discursive surface was invoked by Lynch and Bogen, it is argued that practical actions and language constitute and reaffirm a moral order of representation in which both the existence and the identity of separate (cognizing) entities come to have force.

In other words, the basic assumption that 'individuals' are somehow responsible for 'thoughts', 'reasons', 'motives' and so on (and, at a different level of aggregation, that specific physical parts of human individuals are responsible for these) is achieved and displayed through the discursive actions that organize our practical activities. The fact that these attributions of origins of action are essentially arbitrary is implied by the classical debates between contending social theories (and between the competing political philosophies that are brought to bear in response to societal problems). In crude terms, do characteristics reside in particular entities or are they only attributed to particular entities? Are human actions to be understood primarily as emanating from within the individual or as arising from forces outside and beyond their control (and hence outside their responsibility). The notion of cognizing agent tends to support the former position; current forms of (post-modern) scepticism support the latter view.

While the first two criticisms of the notion of the 'cognizing agent' focus upon the presumed nature of agency and upon its boundedness and its attributes, the third criticism originates in attempts to interrogate the presumed distribution of attributes between human and non-human agents. As I mentioned earlier, one pervasive feature of the moral order of representation corresponding to most realist discourse is that attributes are assumed to be distributed between humans, animals and things. Each is presumed to have differential rights and obligations, and in consequence each requires a normatively sanctioned mode of acting on another. In the particular case of the action we call 'explanation', for example, certain conventions make available what can be known by whom about which entities, what they do or do not feel, and so on. In some recent social studies of science, these presumptions have been explored and tested by attempting to (re)write accounts of action and behaviour that effectively invert conventional assumptions about the entities involved.

For instance, in an account of usability testing in a company making personal computers (see Woolgar, 1991), I raised the possibility that the machines might themselves have had a motive for helping to bring about a particular outcome. Or, more precisely, my objective was to examine which features of the conventions of description and explanation helped to sustain a particular distribution of attributes between the agents (both human and non-human). Ashmore (1993) similarly, though delightfully, explored the consequences of changing conventional assumptions concerning agency for our explanations of behaviour. He used as an example a touching domestic drama that involved attempts by a human to persuade a cat to use a form of technology – to enter and exit through a cat-flap. Ashmore constructed and compared several different narratives in which the same (apparently) three central characters interchanged their roles. The upshot of this exercise is that the differential plausibility of these various narratives seems to depend not simply upon the 'correct' assignment of a portfolio of attributes to each character, but rather upon the narrative organization and structure of the description of interaction among the characters. This, of course, is consistent with the whole thrust of the criticism of agency by social studies of science, that attributes are not inherent in entities.

Implications for qualitative methods in psychology

What then are the implications of this discussion for the role and status of qualitative research methods in psychology?

First, it is clear that one should be wary of arguments about the supposed relative merits of different methods that are couched in terms of their scientific value. Social studies of science suggest that practising scientists themselves only rarely conform to the received view of science. In effect, scientific practice is itself not 'scientific' in the canonical or 'received' view. It follows that one would be unwise to emulate those portrayals of scientific procedure and method that are enshrined in the 'received view'. One philosopher of science even argued that, in order to ensure scientific progress, scientists should actively seek to flaunt the canonical 'rules' of scientific procedure (Feyerabend, 1975). This means, in particular, that a choice between methods should not be based on their claimed relative scientificity, at least not without some careful scrutiny of the notion of 'science' that is being mobilized. Hence, efforts in the social sciences to emulate 'science' may well be misguided, since successful science in practice itself rarely pursues the idealized form of scientific method. In particular, in the case of debates concerning quantitative and qualitative methods, it is no longer persuasive to claim that quantitative methods are more scientific than qualitative ones.

Second, it follows from my earlier arguments that one can no longer accept that representation in science is essentially any different from representation in other spheres of human activity. The discourses of both social and natural science, on the one hand, and of everyday life, on the other, tend to be based on the assumption of a realist ontology. In other words, all these discourses are organized to establish a rhetorical 'distance' between the observer and the observed, and to establish the antecedence of the latter. In this way, the ideology of representation is pervasive. It simply reaches its most celebrated form in one particular social institution (that is, science) which has, at least until recently, been highly valued and well funded. (The recent relative decline in the popularity of the natural sciences – as evinced in the UK, for example, in the numbers of university applicants – may have much to do with problems in the 'public understanding of science'. On the basis of the present analysis, one key problem may be that the persistence of the 'received view' succeeds in deterring would-be recruits.) Insofar as the use of quantitative methods is associated with aspirations to be scientific, it follows that qualitative methods are no more and no less scientific than quantitative methods. At the same time, of course, quantitative methods continue to be credited with greater reliability, greater accuracy and so forth. The difference, it would seem, is one of resources, not one of methodological superiority. In short, there is nothing special at the epistemological or methodological level about quantitative methods. What, then, accounts for their greater standing?

Integral to the ideology of representation is the assumption that the world is populated by entities of different kinds and that these entities stand in certain defined relationships to one another. Indeed, the very notion that representation is possible depends upon assumptions about the nature and character of the representing and the represented entities. In particular, it is important to preserve a rhetorical distance between the observer and the observed. In the natural sciences, this requirement is fulfilled through a discourse that makes marked distinctions between the scientist as observer and the nature of the observed objects. Electrons are not people. The distribution of attributes is defined and sustained through discourses about what is proper and legitimate in different kinds of relations. Thus, the moral order of representation (see Woolgar, 1989) encourages and sustains the notion that, whereas we can 'find out about' electrons, they cannot do the same about us.

This rhetorical difference is important for 'acting at a distance', which, as social studies of science have shown, is crucial to the success of any account that aspires to the status of an explanation (Latour, 1988, 1990; Woolgar, 1988b). An excessive reduction of the rhetorical distance between the observer and the observed tends to weaken the strength of the explanation because it compromises the ability to act at a distance. Of course, this is precisely the classical problem for any field of social inquiry that aspires to be a natural science. The more we admit to the idea that people are not like electrons, the more difficult it becomes to sustain a natural-scientific account of their behaviour. In other words, quantitative methods have the effect of increasing the rhetorical distance between the actions of ourselves as observers and the actions of others.

Third, the sceptical epistemological argument that is promoted by some social studies of science makes it clear that many of the problems associated with the use of quantitative methods in psychology are not to be solved merely by opting for qualitative methods instead. For at issue here is a problem with what we assume about the nature of representation. If we accept that a deeper problem is with the ideology of representation itself rather than the particular method by which we enact that ideology, we need to modify our reliance on the assumption that there are truths (or perhaps just objects) out there that are merely waiting to be detected (that is, represented) by whichever is the best methodological tool that comes to hand. On this argument, qualitative methods hold no particular advantage over quantitative methods.

It follows that the proponents of qualitative methods should beware of the danger that their scepticism about quantitative methods and their reaction against such methods will lead them to believe that they have a more reliable means of tapping into 'the way things really are'. It seems to me that a productive implication of criticisms of quantitative methods is that these methods obscure important questions concerning the relation between ourselves and our participants: that qualitative methods at least have the potential to draw attention to the extent to which we share with our participants all the problems and possibilities of making sense of the world. This potential is severely diminished if we think of qualitative methods as simply a better, alternative tool for unearthing 'the facts'.

Finally, I have noted the emergence of a powerful critique of agency that suggests that the cognizing individual is not the most appropriate unit of analysis for psychological research. One way forward would be to investigate how conceptions of agency are generated and sustained, and how different assumptions about agency are embedded in different conventions about reporting, description, explanation and other forms of accounting practice. For example, one could examine different types of narrative organization for the presumptions about agency and attribution that they encourage. To follow this path would seem to imply the use of qualitative methods rather than quantitative methods, albeit with the caveat expressed at the end of the previous paragraph.

Conclusions

In this chapter, I have attempted to expose and challenge a number of the assumptions underlying current debates concerning the use of qualitative methods in psychology. If the previous debates in allied disciplines (and especially in sociology) are anything to go by, discussion in psychology is never likely to resolve the issue of the relative merits of qualitative and quantitative methods. Nor is a climate of permissive pluralism, one promoting the liberal principle of combining qualitative and quantitative methods, very likely to dispel the basic antipathies that exist.

However, these debates do serve to unearth a deeper problem: that of the extent of our reliance upon an ideology of representation that is entrenched in our conventional apprehension and use of any method at all. It is evident from the research in social studies of science that I have reviewed in this chapter that critiques of the basic notions of science, representation and agency may eventually require the respecification of psychological method. In the meantime, I can at least recommend that much greater reflexive attention be paid to the implicit assumptions that are invoked when considerations of method take place.

Chapter 3

Qualitative inquiry: perspectives, methods and psychology

Karen L. Henwood

Denzin and Lincoln (1994b) state that qualitative research 'is a field of inquiry in its own right' that is surrounded by a 'complex, interconnected family of terms, concepts, and assumptions' (p. 1). They go on to note that this complex – and at times contradictory – family has arisen because qualitative research is informed by a variety of intellectual traditions. The latter include those associated with and those opposing several major approaches within the social sciences: *positivism*, which views scientific method as a way of producing knowledge that reflects an objectively present empirical world; *post-structuralism*, which stresses the indeterminacy of language and meaning; and *interpretative studies* of culture, symbolism and texts. One useful further addition to this list is critical studies (and, in particular, feminist studies) as they have reflected on the philosophy and methodology of the social sciences (for example, Bowles and Duelli Klein, 1983; Harding, 1991; Reinharz, 1992). By bringing this particular configuration of traditions together, the field of qualitative inquiry has extended the analytical scope and range of practices available to social researchers, and it has also rendered more accessible to them complex understandings of the nature, role and implications of science itself.

Psychologists are becoming increasingly aware that the gathering and the analysis of qualitative data is not only an inevitable feature of professional practice (for example, in clinical or counselling interviews), but also constitutes one of the competences needed to conduct research. However, there has been no sustained interrelationship between the discipline of psychology and the general field of qualitative inquiry. This is due, in some large part, to psychology's long-standing commitment to experimentation and investment in a particular understanding of scientific method, an understanding that is now highly contestable, as Steve Woolgar demonstrated in Chapter 2.

Much stands to be gained by questioning this apparent exclusion of qualitative research from psychology (Henwood and Pidgeon, 1992; Banister *et al.*, 1994; Henwood and Parker, 1994a; Henwood and Nicolson, 1995a) and, indeed, the apparent exclusion of psychology from qualitative research. Already, the engagement of psychologists with perspectives and methods in interpretative, cultural and critical studies has led to the development of innovative lines of theorizing and empirical research on topics that are of concern not only to psychologists, but to other social scientists as well (see, for instance, Hollway, 1989; Wetherell and Potter, 1992). As a part of this endeavour, psychologists have also begun to contribute to debates concerning the social and ideological conditions of knowledge production (Griffin and Phoenix, 1994), sometimes criticizing (Henriques *et al.*, 1984) and on other occasions bolstering (Henwood and Pidgeon, 1995a, 1995b) the view that psychological researchers can potentially lay claim to practising 'good science'.

Accordingly, the aims of this chapter are: first, to introduce the concerns of qualitative inquiry to a broad audience in psychology and in the social sciences more generally; and, second, to consider some of the various qualitative perspectives and methods that have been developed by psychologists or that are currently in the process of being taken up by psychologists from other disciplines in the social sciences. I will argue for the usefulness of the rubric of qualitative inquiry (both within and beyond psychology), while seeking to undermine any assumption that there is a necessary or an absolute distinction to be drawn between qualitative and quantitative research. I shall also reflect upon the use of simple organizational schemas to classify, discuss or appraise qualitative approaches and methods.

Qualitative research as paradigm and as method

To some extent, all discussions of methodology in the human and social sciences, not just in psychology, are influenced by the esteem afforded to detachment, objectivity and rationality – the guiding principles of Western science – in industrialized democracies. These principles are viewed not only as requirements for sound research, but also as having underpinned those societies' achievements, success and development. Few scientists would dispute that there is a need for additional traditions of academic scholarship, social criticism and cultural analysis. There is nevertheless always the likelihood that their processes and products will be brought under the conventional scientific gaze because of the implicit acceptance of binary oppositions that value nature over culture, objectivity over subjectivity, and 'hard' forms of research (that is, relatively precise, and typically numerical) over 'soft' forms (relatively imprecise, and typically qualitative). Within such a belief system, the idea almost inevitably emerges that qualitative research exists as something *other* than quantitative research, both in the sense of being different from the (statistical) norm, and in the sense of being research of a lesser order (in terms of delivering less accurate accounts).

The method of deconstruction associated with post-structuralism looks for meanings that are taken for granted, hidden and suppressed (Derrida, 1978; Parker, 1988, 1989; Sampson, 1989). Using this method, one can see that privileging quantity over its supposed opposite, quality, contains within it the seeds of subversion and change. The quantity–quality debate has been an important feature of discussions of social science methodology in the mid and late 20th century, and it has both challenged and relativized the assumptions of so-called positivist science (Bryman, 1988). As the result of addressing wide-ranging issues as they bear upon the quantity–quality distinction (such as the problem of assuming a dichotomy between subject and object, and the politics and ethics of asserting a supposedly neutral relationship between researcher and researched), it has appeared that quantitative and qualitative research could be viewed as manifestations of two contrary research *paradigms* (Lincoln and Guba, 1985).

From this frame of reference, quantitative research becomes just one approach to science: manipulating, measuring and specifying relationships between specific variables in order to test hypotheses about causal laws. On the other hand, qualitative research lays down its claim to acceptance by arguing for the importance of understanding the meaning of experience, actions and events as these are interpreted through the eyes of particular participants, researchers and (sub)cultures, and for a sensitivity to the complexities of behaviour and meaning in the contexts where they typically or 'naturally' occur (Dilthey, 1894/1977; Blumer, 1969b; Harré and Secord, 1972). Accordingly, interchangeable labels for the qualitative paradigm are 'interpretative', 'contextual' and 'naturalistic' inquiry.

In social anthropology, which has always been a largely qualitative discipline, the aim of such detailed, contextually sensitive, meaningful research has been described as 'thick description' (see Geertz, 1979), in contrast to the generalized, abstracted explanations of causal analysis. Sociologists attached to the phenomenological and symbolic interactionist traditions have similarly advocated the generation of theory that is well *grounded* in analyses of unstructured material, local contexts and specific problem domains (Glaser and Strauss, 1967). Subsequently, qualitative researchers aligned with post-structuralism distanced themselves from the naturalism that is implicit in contextualist approaches. They argued for a more complete break with empiricism by the adoption of the metaphor of science (and all forms of social life) as a *text* (Weeden, 1987; Denzin, 1994). This view has also been taken by a number of psychologists (Potter and Wetherell, 1987; Parker, 1992; Wetherell and Potter, 1992). It has strengthened one of the key features of the qualitative paradigm, that researchers construct versions of the world through their activities as social and political subjects, and do not merely reflect facts with a self-evident objective reality; this position is known as epistemological 'constructionism' or epistemological 'constructivism' (see Box 3.1).

Qualitative *methods* are privileged within the qualitative paradigm, because they are thought to meet a number of reservations concerning the uncritical use of quantification; in particular, they address the problem of inappropriately fixing meanings where these are variable and renegotiable in relation to their contexts of use. In addition, using such methods can help to avoid the problem of over-writing internally structured subjectivities with *a priori* systems of meaning (as occurs, for example, with standard survey instruments). Qualitative methods have also been adopted in cooperative forms of inquiry, such as the 'new paradigm' approach of Reason and Rowan (1981), because they can act as a vehicle for

---

Box 3.1 Constructionism and constructivism

In this chapter, the term 'constructionism' is mainly used, for the purpose of standardization. Where the term 'constructivism' is used, this is in order to convey the following additional nuances: that meaningful versions are necessarily incomplete, pluralistic and contradictory; and that this insight can be used as an analytical device to take apart (or deconstruct) socially constructed facts. See Chapter 14 by Jonathan Smith for further discussion of the issues involved, and see Chapter 10 by Jonathan Potter on other uses of 'constructionism' and 'constructivism' in the social sciences.

---

bringing the relationship between researcher and researched into view (for example, through the documentation of the processes of interpretation and joint negotiations over systems of meaning). This latter point reinforces the way that arguments for a qualitative paradigm are simultaneously part of the criticism of subject–object dualism in the philosophy and practice of science (see Westcott, 1979; Fox-Keller, 1985; Stanley and Wise, 1993). Analysis of symbols, discourses or texts is, of course, qualitative almost by definition, and has given emphasis to the impossibility of ever capturing completely the meaning of experience, conduct and events.

Bryman (1988) suggested that there was both a minimalist version and a maximalist version of the quantity–quality debate, which he described as the 'technical' and the 'epistemological', respectively. This provides a useful simplifying gloss on the quantity–quality issue (see Figure 3.1). According to the technical version of the debate, the choice of numerical methods or non-numerical methods is based purely upon pragmatic considerations. These include, for example, the scope for and constraints upon operationalizing particular 'variables'; the availability of time and resources (for example, to conduct and analyse extensive interviews rather than using the more 'pre-programmed' methods provided by questionnaires); and the compromises involved in making decisions about sampling (that will almost inevitably fall short of achieving what can plausibly be considered a representative sample). According to the epistemological version of the debate, the gathering, analysis and interpretation of data are always carried out within some broader understanding of what constitutes legitimate inquiry and warrantable knowledge. It is this latter version of the quantity–quality debate that leads to two (apparently) mutually exclusive, paradigmatic positions: the quantitative view (experimental, hypothetico-deductive, positivist and realist); and the qualitative view (naturalistic, contextual, interpretative and constructionist).

In the 1990s, two of the original advocates of a qualitative paradigm in the social sciences expressed a preference for viewing discussions of the

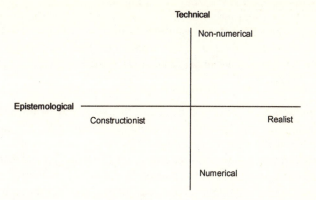

Fɪɢ. 3.1 *Technical and epistemological versions of the quantity–quality debate (after Bryman, 1988).*

methodological aspects of qualitative techniques as being secondary to the epistemological, paradigmatic concerns (Guba and Lincoln, 1994). This clearly prioritizes the epistemological version over the technical version of the quantity–quality debate. However, this prioritization may be questioned because technical and epistemological considerations have never been wholly independent determinants of a researcher's choices about approaches and methods (see Henwood and Pidgeon, 1994). The technical version coexists most readily within a positivist framework, and thus it is rather less agnostic on the question of epistemology than might first appear. For this reason it also holds few surprises for psychology. The danger of these technical arguments is that they often implicitly assume that one would always carry out controlled experiments and use precise measures of the relevant variables, if only one could do so (as when a researcher uses qualitative 'pilot' studies before the main quantitative study). Accordingly, they tend to undervalue the potential of qualitative research in its own right. Researchers who adopt a more open, interpretative, constructionist (or deconstructionist) stance have a clear affinity for qualitative research (which in psychology has been signalled by labels such as 'discourse analysis', as I will point out in a moment), plus a strong conviction that choice of method is liberated and informed by the position one takes within the epistemological debate.

Theorizing links between epistemology, methodology and method

The conventional distinction between quantitative and qualitative research paradigms is currently useful for psychologists because it links issues of research practice and method with wider epistemological questions, as well as with the social and political dimensions of scientific inquiry (Henwood and Nicolson, 1995a). This has proved a productive strategy in other human sciences and social sciences, in that it has led to a greater diversity of approaches and methods, along with a critical awareness of their relative strengths and weaknesses (Bryman, 1988; Hammersley, 1989; Silverman, 1993; Denzin and Lincoln, 1994a). The case that has been made for a qualitative paradigm has also provided a rich foundation for new ways of defining questions and conducting inquiry (Henwood and Pidgeon, 1992).

However, accepting the value of the distinction between quantitative and qualitative paradigms should not be taken to imply that quantitative and qualitative perspectives and methods are mutually exclusive, or that there is a one-to-one relationship between 'quantity' and epistemological realism, on the one hand, and 'quality' and constructionism, on the other. Researchers often wish to argue for a principled mixture of quantitative and qualitative methods (see Silverman, 1985), a position that has been advocated by some psychologists in a number of discussions of the use of qualitative approaches and methods (Griffin and Phoenix, 1994; Reicher, 1994; Smith, 1994b, 1995; Green, 1995; Griffin, 1995).

One reason for this has to do with the appraisal and funding of research. The process of making one's ideas or analyses persuasive inevitably means that researchers (including even epistemological constructionists) engage in a dialogue with people and agencies that remain entirely or mainly committed to the view that greater precision, value and validity accrue to research that gathers and analyses quantitative data, uses representative samples and seeks to support or refute hypothesized relationships between empirical phenomena or events (Griffin and Phoenix, 1994). One cannot just assume that a qualitative, reflexive approach to research will attain recognition in psychology, for instance, since this is still by and large a non-reflexive discipline (Henwood and Pidgeon, 1995b).

A non-dualistic understanding of the numerical and the non-numerical also follows from the position of radical epistemological constructionism. The possibility of a verifiable connection between epistemology (knowing) and ontology (being) is here specifically denied. Consistent with this, *both* the numerical and the non-numerical (particularly text) are explored as inter-changeable ways of re-representing the lack of structure, mobility and complexity (Latour, 1987; Woolgar, 1988c). In this way, the poles of Bryman's (1988) technical and epistemological dimensions of the quantity–quality debate are collapsed together. However, too many potential gains would be lost to psychology if these complications were allowed to stymie the emergent enthusiasm that now exists for extending research issues, questions and practices beyond their traditional confines. It would be premature, at the very least, to ignore the full potential of pursuing the two differing approaches to representation (number *and* text) that we have. For instance, it would merely reassert the privileging of the frequent over the transient or fleeting (where the latter may be important or meaningful), the present over the absent, and the powerfully spoken over the silent or the silenced (Opie, 1992; Henwood and Pidgeon, 1995b).

In endeavouring to legitimate a domain of qualitative inquiry, it is important not to obscure the differences that exist within the qualitative paradigm. As I have already implied, unitary accounts of qualitative methods, such as those provided by Reason and Rowan (1981) and Lincoln and Guba (1985), gloss over very real differences of emphasis and implication. One way to counteract this tendency, which I considered above, would be to analyse the different intellectual traditions that inform qualitative research as a complex historical field. Another would be to draw upon an argument advanced by Harding (1987), a feminist philosopher, with regard to the need to theorize the relationship between epistemology, methodology and method. A third would be to consider different aetiologies, concerns and practices that are associated with a range of perspectives and methods in qualitative social science and psychology; I will discuss this strategy in the following section.

Harding argued that, although the term 'method' tends to be used as a catch-all phrase, one should distinguish one's *epistemological position* (assumptions about the basis for knowledge) from one's research *methodology* (a theoretical analysis defining a research problem and how research should proceed) and in turn from any specific *method* (that is, the strategy or technique that is actually adopted). This framework can be used to demonstrate how different *theoretical choices* link particular epistemologies, methodologies and methods, and thus go beyond the simple technical and epistemological versions of the quantity–quality debate. In Table 3.1, I have given a slightly amended version of a previous attempt to identify three different strands within the emerging tradition of qualitative psychology (see Henwood and Pidgeon, 1994). Table 3.1 fixes what is in reality a fluid set of possibilities, but identifying the three strands is useful in drawing attention to the different sets of priorities to be found in the conduct of qualitative research.

Each of the rows in Table 3.1 represents a paradigmatically linked strand of inquiry. The first column differentiates these strands in terms of how each seeks to justify qualitative research, making it explicit that there are various ways in which researchers have attempted to address this important issue. Three different approaches to warranting are identified: appraising research by means of standardized analogues of the criteria of reliability and validity (strand I); generating new theory that is at the same time firmly grounded in participants' own accounts and in substantive domains (strand II); and focusing analytically on the reflexive functions of language, which construct representations of 'objects' in the world and which have material-discursive effects (strand III). The second column traces shifts in epistemological position from empiricism to contextualism and finally to constructivism. The third column expresses the way that research questions and analytical principles are intertwined.

In the remainder of this chapter, I shall consider the three strands in more detail by providing fairly introductory pointers to some of their illustrative methods, which are listed in the fourth column of Table 3.1. Because of the intimate links between epistemological, methodological and strategic or technical concerns in qualitative research, I have not tried to standardize these accounts in terms of the kinds of issues addressed. Rather, my discussion will reflect a concern for broad perspectives (both epistemological and methodological) as well as for particular methods.

TABLE 3.1. *Three strands of qualitative inquiry (after Henwood and Pidgeon, 1994)*

Broad strand	Epistemology	Methodological principles	Methods and examples
Strand I Reliability and validity	Empiricism	Discovery of valid representations (using induction)	'Data display' model (Miles and Huberman, 1984, 1994) Content analysis (Krippendorf, 1980) Protocol analysis (Ericsson and Simon, 1980)
Strand II Generativity and grounding	Contextualism	Construction of intersubjective meaning (or *Verstehen*)	Grounded theory (Glaser and Strauss, 1967; Strauss and Corbin, 1990) Ethogenics (Harré and Secord, 1972)
Strand III Discursive and reflexive	Constructivism	Interpretative analysis (highlighting deconstruction of texts)	Discourse analysis (Potter and Wetherell, 1987; Edwards and Potter, 1992; Burman and Parker, 1993) Narrative analysis (Gergen, 1988, 1992; Gergen and Gergen, 1993; Riessman, 1993)

Perspectives and methods in qualitative social science and psychology

Miles and Huberman's 'data display' approach

Miles and Huberman's (1984, 1994) widely read source book of strategies for doing qualitative research, *Qualitative Data Analysis*, is an accessible text for psychologists, because it focuses upon one of the main problems established by positivistic science – that of how simultaneously to ensure reliability and validity – and transposes this problem into a discussion concerning qualitative research. The strength of qualitative research for Miles and Huberman is thus its move towards a greater realism (and hence validity), but counterbalanced against this are the attendant dangers of poor reliability (see also Kirk and Miller, 1986). Their book documents practical strategies for ensuring that checks can be made on reliability without compromising analytical gains in terms of flexibility, contextual sensitivity or external validity.

The authors' epistemological stance is that 'social phenomena exist not only in the mind but also in the objective world – and that there are some lawful and reasonably stable relationships to be found among them' (Miles and Huberman, 1994, p. 4), which locates them straightforwardly within a realist, empirical (and empiricist) framework. In the first edition of their book, Miles and Huberman (1984) described themselves as 'soft-nosed logical positivists' (p. 19). However, in keeping with the increased complexities of the modern quantity–quality debate, they subsequently adopted the term 'transcendental realism' (Miles and Huberman, 1994, p. 4; see also Harré and Secord, 1972). Their methodology follows from this epistemological position. In particular, they have advocated the broadly inductivist view that initial representation of social relationships can be discovered from detailed qualitative observations made in relatively unstructured situations of the kind that are found in the field.

This work is invaluable for demystifying the operations at the heart of all qualitative analysis that takes a broadly empiricist, inductivist stance, and hence for debunking the myth that expertise in this area can be gained only through patronage or contact with long-established (mainly ethnographic) schools of thought. It also makes explicit the link between the process of analysis and that of communicating the final product in a publishable (and hence publicly warrantable) form. However, as Miles and Huberman (1994, p. 277) acknowledged in the second edition of their book, the tactics and methods that are recommended do not in themselves stand as evaluative criteria for the purpose of justifying the goodness of conclusions in qualitative research.

Content analysis

Content analysis emerged relatively early in the 20th century in the human sciences, initially in studies that sought to describe the messages conveyed in the mass media. Nevertheless, it has undergone considerable development over the years, so that it came to be defined by Krippendorf (1980) as an approach to the study of the entire range of communicative and symbolic media, including verbal dialogues, films, advertisements, cartoons, theatre and political speeches. From these, researchers seek to make inferences about other phenomena that are of interest.

Some of the changes in content analysis reflect a greater awareness of a range of theoretical perspectives on the functional aspects of words and images as representational, signifying or discursive practices, as I shall discuss later in this chapter. Developments beyond the mainly descriptive, empirical approach were encouraged for practical reasons too, as researchers became aware of the importance of investigating both latent and manifest meanings. For example, research by the Western allies into media broadcasts in Germany during World War II sought to gauge the level of support for government policies, and this required looking beneath the surface propaganda.

However, the continued refinements to content analysis have occurred mainly with regard to the strategies and procedures available for ensuring the accurate coding, sampling and handling of unstructured data as a basis for making reliable and valid inferences about the phenomena of interest. For example, Krippendorf's (1980) much-used text includes chapters that are concerned with: schemes for breaking up the flow of message content into discrete, self-contained, information-giving units (unitization); achieving a representative sample of the whole universe of data (sampling); and assigning units to exhaustive and mutually exclusive coding categories (recording; data languages). Strategies for arranging and organizing the data into meaningful patterns and arrays and for making logically sound links between these arrangements and the relevant phenomena (constructs for inference; analytical techniques) are also covered by Krippendorf.

Protocol analysis

Protocol analysis is similar to content analysis insofar as its primary task is to ensure the validity of inferences made from unstructured qualitative data to some other aspect of 'reality' to which those data are deemed to refer. In this case, however, the data in question are verbal protocols: that is, people's accounts of their thought processes as they perform a cognitive task, such as solving anagrams. The specific purpose of protocol analysis is to make inferences about the cognitive processes that underlie the performance of the task. The background and techniques of protocol analysis are described by Ken Gilhooly and Caroline Green in Chapters 4 and 5.

To date, the insights that have been gleaned about the conditions for generating valid verbal protocols have been confined almost exclusively to the field of cognitive psychology, though verbal protocols have been used in other domains of psychology (see, for example, Condor, 1986). However, there is no reason in principle why these insights should not be applied more widely to the analysis of people's accounts of their own experiences, thoughts and actions in any area of psychology that is content to accept a reflective, realist view of the relationship between verbal accounts and aspects of psychological reality. For instance, verbal protocols could be an obvious complement to the use of standard quantitative instruments when seeking to measure personality structure. Equally, the concerns expressed in the field of protocol analysis with regard to the validity of relating verbal commentaries to psychological processes could also be relevant to the interpretation of psychotherapeutic and research interviews.

Grounded theory

'Grounded theory' was the label chosen by two sociologists, Barney Glaser and Anselm Strauss, originally in a book, *The Discovery of Grounded Theory* (1967), to describe an approach and a method that reflect many of the quintessential features of the older-style, naturalistic, contextual or qualitative paradigm. As an approach, grounded theory specifies that new developments in both substantive and formal theorizing can be facilitated by the close and detailed (or, in other words, well grounded) inspection of particular problem domains, participants' accounts and the associated phenomenal and social worlds. This was advocated as a way of breaking out of the confines of research that had been narrowly preoccupied with the testing of 'grand' theory. Accordingly (and usefully for psychology), grounded theorists focus attention upon the way in which scientific work is also necessarily concerned with issues of discovery or 'generativity'. The background and techniques of grounded theory are described by Nick Pidgeon and myself in Chapters 6 and 7.

Since the publication of Glaser and Strauss's (1967) original book, many texts and articles have been published that describe the method of grounded theory in more detail (for instance, Turner, 1981; Strauss and Corbin, 1990). As in the case of the work of Miles and Huberman (1984), these are valuable in making explicit much of what is often left implicit in many varieties of qualitative research that seek to promote conceptual development. In epistemological terms, generativity and grounding flow from a concern with the contextual specificity of meanings, sometimes described as 'contextualism' (see Jaeger and Rosnow, 1988). The aim of qualitative analysis then becomes the production of a meaningful account that knits together the multiplicities, variations and complexities of participants' worlds. In Table 3.1, this is referred to as seeking to construct intersubjective meaning, or *Verstehen*.

Ethogenics

The second example of contextual inquiry shown in Table 3.1 is that of ethogenics. The origins of this approach lie in Harré and Secord's (1972) book, *The Explanation of Social Behaviour*. With the exception of Marsh *et al*.'s (1978) *The Rules of Disorder*, it is difficult to find any properly documented, published reports of ethogenic investigations. However, Harré and Secord's book holds an important place in the history of qualitative research in psychology, because it provided a critical commentary (both analytical and methodological) on the influence which behaviourism has had upon the discipline. In addition, a number of the arguments used by Harré and Secord in making the case for their ethogenic psychology originated in ethnographers' advocacy of 'thick description' and participant observation (see, for instance, Chapters 8 and 9, by Christina Toren and Janet Rachel) and in the strong affinity which phenomenologists and symbolic interactionists have for qualitative approaches and methods.

In general terms, *The Explanation of Social Behaviour* provides a concerted conceptual attack on theoretical perspectives in psychology (especially stimulus–response psychology) that neglect the meaning of human action as this occurs in socially structured events and contexts. In this book, the authors began by taking the (humanistic) stance that hypothesizing mechanical links between environmental stimuli and their behavioural effects merely serves to ignore those very qualities with which people are endowed in everyday language, such as intentionality and volition. One of their other main arguments was that this sort of approach mistakenly conceptualized the psychologist's object of inquiry in purely physical terms. How human physiologists and psychologists might be expected to differ in their explanations of two people shaking hands gives a useful illustration here. One might expect a physiologist's explanation to be given in terms of the processes responsible for the sequence of physical movements involved in lifting an arm and grasping an object. However, the way that such movements function as meaningful social acts (for instance, as a greeting or as a means of sealing an agreement) is likely to be of far more interest to psychologists, along with other social scientists.

Harré and Secord's methodological criticism of experimental behavioural science for its narrow approach to explanation (referring to efficient causes or chronologically preceding events) is also significant in this respect. Here, their argument was that this misreads the approach of natural science, in which it is commonplace to try to develop iconic models of the mechanisms responsible for generating observed regularities. For example, Gregor Mendel explained the pattern of inheritance of physical characteristics in terms of dominant and recessive genes, a useful structural model rather than an explanation in terms of preceding efficient causes.

Accordingly, Harré and Secord proposed that the regular and patterned features of human social behaviour could be explained by using a model of generative social roles and rules. In this respect, their claims closely mirror some of the most distinctive features of structuralist anthropology, such as that of Lévi-Strauss (1949/1969). Harré and Secord's suggestion was that one important task, for social psychology at least, was that of determining the roles and rules on which people can choose to act or not to act. In addition, they were quite unequivocal that this would require a new package of methods, which included the observation of human conduct in its natural habitat and asking people themselves and others to account for such conduct (in other words, a form of participant observation with a special place for interviewing). Ethogenicists would also at times need to relate these accounts to wider systems of meaning within particular social groups or within society at large. In this way, although their approach leaned towards assuming the veracity of the participants' deeds and words, these would not always be taken wholly at their face value.

Harré and Secord's methodological prescriptions would clearly locate them at the qualitative end of Bryman's (1988) technical dimension in the quantity–quality debate, together with the approach of grounded theory. However, the fact that the goal of such research is to discover the real structural determinants of patterns of human conduct in the form of social roles and rules means that this approach is ambivalent in its commitment to a constructionist epistemology (Potter and Wetherell, 1987; Parker, 1989). Subsequently, advocates of the ethogenic approach began to forge links with meta-theory in discourse analysis (see below). Nevertheless, at the same time, discussion continued on the constraints that the material world could place upon the interpretation of data (see, for example, Harré, 1992a, 1993; Gillett, 1995).

Discourse analysis

The approach of discourse analysis, which includes specific methods for interrogating discourses or texts, appears as a general strand of inquiry in psychology, following the wider cultural and social science trends that are associated with post-structuralist and post-modernist theorizing. The two latter terms are often used interchangeably, and when distinctions are made these vary and can be contradictory. One possible differentiation is to view post-structuralism as a movement that is concerned with the study of language and meaning, and to view post-modernism as a perspective upon cultural and societal organization and development; however, the two foci are thoroughly intertwined. A core idea of the two in combination is that knowledge and identities lack firm foundations in fissured and fractured societies. Their portrayal of science as a grand meta-narrative (to be read alongside psychoanalysis, for example) is a way of questioning the simple equation of science with progress.

Discourse analysts have made significant attempts to render both the approach and its associated methods accessible as a new methodology. As a part of this, they have typically stressed that users must be prepared to ask new kinds of questions (see, for example, Potter and Wetherell, 1987, 1994; Wetherell and Potter, 1988; Wooffitt, 1992a, 1992b; Burman and Parker, 1993; Coyle, 1995). Simplistically, such research could be described as both non-numeric and constructionist in terms of Bryman's technical and epistemological dimensions, although, predictably given the intricacies of the quantity–quality debate, anomalies can be found. For example, one discourse analytic study has used a standard questionnaire approach to study the various meanings attached to community care (see Potter and Collie, 1989). In order to understand the theorized links between epistemology, methodology and method in discourse work, it is necessary to grasp its many nuances as an identifiable but differentiated research tradition. Jonathan Potter will discuss the theoretical background of discourse analysis and other constructionist approaches in more detail in Chapter 10, and Rosalind Gill will describe the practical implementation of discourse analysis in Chapter 11.

Narrative analysis

One point of fracture within the field of discourse analysis relates to the issue of subjectivity and whether it is given adequate coverage in all lines of work. At one level, the issue is of universal importance, because a scepticism about objectivity and its replacement with the view that subjectivity and objectivity are interdependent moments in a unified process of power/knowledge relations represent the starting point for all work on discourse. Nevertheless, dramatic differences are to be found. Diagnosing a lack of concern for the suppressed, unconscious aspects of personal 'experience', some discourse analysts have drawn (critically) on psychoanalytic theory to fill this gap (Henriques *et al.*, 1984; Hollway, 1989; Parker, 1992; Madill and Doherty, 1994). The term 'subjectivity' is then typically preferred to that of 'experience' to signify that multiple, fragmented, shifting and contradictory meanings inevitably constitute the psychic domain (Squire, 1994; cf. Bhavnani and Phoenix, 1994). The need to provide further theorization of the idea of subjectivity has been disputed (Widdicombe, 1992). In addition, other possibilities have been suggested, including the idea that aspects of biography become 'sedimented' in order to explain people's psychological and emotional investments in particular ways of interpreting the world (Wetherell, 1994).

Where a researcher's specific topical focus is upon aspects of what psychologists would normally call 'the self', 'personality' or 'identity', another strategy has been to study the stories or narratives people tell about their lives, since this constitutes their subjectivity (Shotter and Gergen, 1989; Gergen, 1994a, 1994b). This development is part of a wider move to include 'narrative analysis' (Riessman, 1993; see also Gergen, 1988, 1992; Gergen and Gergen 1993) as part of a panoply of options for reflexive method in psychology and social science (Steier, 1991). In clinical and therapeutic psychology, where narrative analysis has obvious relevance, discussion has suggested that research and therapeutic encounters can be seen as textual productions which have *both* referential and performative aspects (Burck and Frosh, 1994). This point suggests complications in the assumption that discursive approaches and social constructivism (which are identified as strand III in Table 3.1) can be unambiguously differentiated from those interpretative approaches that eschew naïve anti-realism (strand II).

Feminist research

Feminist research does not appear in Table 3.1, as it cannot be assigned to any one strand. Nevertheless, epistemological criticism of subject–object dualism, appreciation of the moral and political dimensions of research, and a consideration of the relevance of qualitative methods have all been part of the development of this distinctive domain of inquiry. Early on, the focus was very much upon the way in which women's *experiences* had been rendered invisible by androcentric biases in the assumptions and practices of science. The more flexible, context-sensitive and meaning-sensitive methods of qualitative research were advocated as one way of better apprehending such experience. Another tactic was to introduce women as scientists and as participants so that their concerns could not so easily be ignored.

This position has been described as 'feminist empiricism', and hence it would fall within strand I in Table 3.1. However, today it coexists with two further feminist epistemologies (see Harding, 1986, 1987, 1991). 'Standpoint epistemology' (which can be roughly equated with strand II) starts from the position that all knowledge is constructed from a specific social location, and that less partial knowledge can result when those who have previously been excluded from the dominant order become involved in the scientific process. 'Feminist post-structuralism' (strand III) is less sanguine about such claims to less distortion and partiality; rather, it emphasizes that judgements about truth and falsity are themselves always socially constructed, because they are informed by moral, political and cultural concerns. It also questions any tendency to view experience and womanhood as pure, unmediated ontological states that precede social and interpretative processes.

Lessons about the changing relationship between quantitative and qualitative research have been promoted by shifts between the different epistemological positions within feminist scholarship, and by discussion of the relevance of such philosophical concerns for politically committed research (Griffin and Phoenix, 1994; Maynard and Purvis, 1994; Griffin, 1995). This has prompted the emergence of the apparently consensual position of methodological pluralism, according to which the researcher should simply choose to adopt either quantitative or qualitative methods, according to which appears best suited to the problem at hand. However, it may be difficult to distinguish this from Bryman's (1988) technical version of the quantity–quality debate. Therefore, arguments have now been put forward for 'remaking the link' between qualitative research and feminist standpoint theory, in the sense of appreciating the possible benefits of exploring specific lines of inquiry connecting epistemology, methodology and method (Henwood and Pidgeon, 1995b).

Conclusions

In this chapter, I have considered the aetiology and changing complexion of arguments for qualitative research in its various guises in psychology and the social sciences. I have been critical of some commonly held assumptions about scientific research, and yet I have also tried to be pluralistic, recognizing that readers will wish to take up a variety of positions within their constructed account or narrative. However, as a counterpoint against such pluralism, I have not assumed that particular methods can always be set within theoretical frames that are compatible with one another.

Those psychologists who enter the maze of qualitative research (and even those who do not but whose research takes place within shared topical domains) are necessarily confronted by complex decisions and choices about how to deal with the crisis of representation, as well as interconnected questions about criteria of legitimation that were previously raised by naturalistic, contextual, inter-pretative researchers. The academic context is now one in which social and cultural theorists can begin to 'refuse the identity of empirical science' (Clough, 1992, p. 135), but, as a corollary of this refusal, they can find themselves entangled in the intricate webs of the 'politics of textuality' (cf. Denzin and Lincoln, 1994b, p. 10).

Part II
Using qualitative research methods

Chapter 4

Protocol analysis: theoretical background

Ken Gilhooly and Caroline Green

In the context of research into human cognition, *protocols* are detailed records of behaviour during a task. This chapter and the one that follows concern *verbal* protocols that result from instructions to think aloud during a task. Verbal protocols are transcriptions that are derived from recordings of the participants' speech while they are carrying out a task under thinking-aloud instructions. The present chapter will focus on the theoretical background underlying thinking aloud and protocol analysis, and any practical matters that we shall discuss (such as whether protocols should be produced during the task or after the task) will be treated from a theoretical viewpoint. The next chapter will deal in more detail with the practicalities of protocol collection, processing and analysis.

We must make clear at the outset what the participants are typically instructed to do when they are thinking aloud (for extensive discussions, see Ericsson and Simon, 1980, 1983, 1993). The instructions are to think aloud during the task, verbalizing overtly all thoughts that (in adult participants, at least) would normally be silent. Note that participants are not asked to explain or justify what they are doing, and they are not asked to report their strategies. The inference of cognitive strategies is the task of the analyst, not of the participants. In everyday terms, the participants are asked to report as continuously as possible what they are aware of as they carry out the target task. Most participants seem to understand readily what is required and generally comply well, especially once they have done a few warm-up tasks involving thinking aloud (see Payne, 1994).

Spontaneous thinking aloud can be observed in adults, particularly when they are on their own and the task is difficult, or if the environment is noisy. Among children, spontaneous thinking aloud is very common when they encounter difficulties in problem solving or understanding. Such overt verbalization in children seems to aid their long-term learning and understanding of new domains (Berk, 1994). In general, then, thinking aloud is not an unnatural process, even if it is not the norm among adults.

The method of thinking aloud as briefly outlined above is distinct from classical *introspection* (Titchener, 1909), which required a highly artificial form of verbal report in the language of elementary sensations (for instance, 'I am aware of a trapezoidal pinkish shape in the upper left visual field' rather than 'I see a red book'). Extensive training in the classical introspective method was required before participants could produce the desired type of report. Wundt is said to have insisted upon up to 10,000 trials before his participants were deemed to be proficient (Boring, 1953). In contrast, current thinking-aloud methodology stresses that participants need use only ordinary, everyday terms and concepts and that they require minimal practice. The many criticisms of classical introspection that led to its demise do not apply to thinking aloud.

The method of verbal production in thinking aloud is also distinct from the methods used in naturalistic studies of discourse, conversation, rhetoric and so on, which are discussed in subsequent chapters. The social element in verbal protocol production during thinking aloud is played down, and reports may well be highly egocentric rather than carefully designed for clear communication. The participants are often encouraged to think aloud as if they were alone, and the researcher typically remains out of view to avoid cueing a conversational mode in the participant. For instance, a puzzled look on the part of the researcher might prompt the participant to provide extra explanations and distort the participant's normal thought processes.

Verbal protocol methods have been found to be useful in both pure and applied research. In pure cognitive psychology, thinking-aloud methods can provide information that supplements response latencies and response frequencies and hence provides further constraints on theorizing. It is not expected that protocols will tell the researcher directly how the participants carried out the task in hand: rather, they are a further source of data to be used in interpretation and model construction. The use of thinking aloud has been widespread in the study of problem solving, from the early research of Claparède (1934), Bulbrook (1936) and Duncker (1945) to Newell and Simon (1972) and Anderson (1993). In applied areas such as knowledge engineering, the collection of protocols may help to supplement other methods of eliciting knowledge (such as repertory grids, sorting, laddering and multidimensional scaling) in order to determine experts' problem-solving procedures and the knowledge that needs to be incorporated into machine expert systems (see Olson and Biolsi, 1991).

Since thinking aloud is an externalization of thought, we shall now discuss some key issues that arise in the study of thinking, such as verbal versus non-verbal thinking, whether there may be unconscious thought streams parallel to the conscious stream, and the depth to which thought processes are reportable.

Thinking and thinking aloud

Thinking is a form of internal symbolic activity that can involve a variety of codes. The verbal code is predominant in most people, but a visuospatial code is also available to most participants. Other codes, such as auditory, tactile, gustatory and olfactory ones, may also be used, and these can be important for some forms of expertise. For example, the olfactory code will be important to a scent designer, while the gustatory code will be important to an innovative chef. Thought that is already in a verbal code should be readily externalized. Indeed, Watson (1920), the founder of behaviourism, argued that thinking was just covert internalized speech, and he advocated the use of thinking-aloud methods to externalize thought so that it could be studied.

Thought in a non-verbal code will require translation into a verbal code for thinking aloud. This suggests that some slowing down can be expected on tasks that predominantly involve a non-verbal code when thinking aloud is required. It is noteworthy that areas of expertise that involve non-verbal codes have evolved specialized vocabularies for verbal communication, such as the jargon of wine-tasters. Thus, for important non-verbal types of skill, verbal codes have been established, and these could be used in thinking aloud in such domains.

Thinking and the cognitive system

Thinking takes place in the context of the overall cognitive system, and so it is appropriate at this point to consider some general frameworks for understanding human information processing within which models of thinking should fit. A number of general frameworks have been proposed, but until the early 1980s certain assumptions had been widely accepted by different theorists (for instance, from Broadbent, 1958, to Anderson, 1983). These common assumptions are incorporated into what might be referred to as the *standard* model for thinking (Simon and Kaplan, 1989).

According to this standard model, individuals have a vast long-term memory but a working memory of limited capacity. Working memory includes the information that is the current focus of attention, plus recently attended material that is highly accessible and that can be returned effortlessly to focal attention. These two memories are supplemented in the overall system by high-capacity but short-lived sensory memories (for instance, see Sperling, 1960), but these are not usually regarded as very important for thinking, and they can be ignored for our present purposes. In the standard model, thinking is regarded as the processing or manipulation of symbols both in working memory itself and between long-term and working memory. The manipulations are assumed to be in accord with rules stored in long-term memory: in other words, a *production system* approach is taken. Anderson's (1983) ACT*, Newell's (1990) SOAR and Holland *et al.*'s (1986) PI models represent variations of this approach.

Production systems contain production rules, which are composed of a condition part and an action part. If the condition of a rule is satisfactorily matched to the contents of working memory, then its action part may be activated, with consequent changes in the contents of working memory, leading to a new rule being activated and so on. The flow of thought is thus represented by the changing contents of working memory as rules are activated. Rules can also add new contents to long-term memory and cause overt actions. Because many different rules may be satisfied at any one time, procedures for conflict resolution have to be built into production systems, to prevent paralysis. Different systems have different methods of conflict resolution and different methods for assessing whether the match is sufficient. In general, at any given time, the rule selected from long-term memory for activation will depend upon the current goals and upon the contents of working memory. It is assumed in the standard model that only one thinking step is taken at a time (the seriality assumption). On the standard model, thinking aloud should externalize the moment-to-moment changes in the contents of working memory.

The standard model of thinking we have just outlined is consistent with many broader frameworks for the whole human information processing system, but it is not consistent with certain other approaches, such as connectionism (Rumelhart *et al.*, 1986a; Quinlan, 1991), in which both the symbol-manipulation assumption and the strict seriality assumption are abandoned. However, the connectionist approach, which seems well suited to applications in memory, learning and pattern recognition, is much less easily applied to sequential thought, as in problem solving and reasoning (Fodor and Pylyshyn, 1988). Intermediate positions have been proposed, in which symbol manipulation is assumed though strict seriality is abandoned (Holland *et al.*, 1986), while hybrid connectionist/symbol-manipulating models have also been proposed (Norman, 1986; Lamberts, 1990; Lamberts and Pfeifer, 1992). The conflict between the standard model and connectionist approaches may be reduced by adopting a proposal made by Rumelhart *et al.* (1986b), that successive states of a connectionist network could represent successive thought contents (or states of consciousness) that last about 500 ms and that follow each other sequentially. Transitions between states take much less time and depend on parallel unconscious, unreportable processes. On this model, verbal reports could be made about the sequence of states but not about the transition processes.

Serial versus parallel thought

Taking as a working assumption the idea that thinking can be reasonably viewed as the manipulation of symbols, the further specification of the standard model, that manipulations are either within working memory (as when rearranging letters to solve a short anagram) or between working memory and long-term memory (as when retrieving an intermediate sum from long-term memory and placing it in working memory in mental arithmetic), discounts the possibility of any manipulations occurring purely within long-term memory. The production system approach requires that matches are made to the contents of working memory, and information in working memory is usually regarded as conscious (or, at least, recently conscious and highly available to be returned to a conscious state).

To have manipulations purely within long-term memory would require the postulation of unconscious working memory or memories, and this does not seem to have been explicitly mooted. The standard model thus clashes with notions of spontaneous activity within long-term memory as proposed by Freud (1900), Neisser (1963b), Singer (1975) and the Gestalt memory theorists (see Baddeley, 1976, ch. 4). Theorists who have postulated activity within long-term memory have usually also considered that this activity occurs in parallel with the main stream of conscious thinking. Since the idea of activity within long-term memory thus clashes with the seriality assumption, too, the latter will now be discussed more fully.

The question of whether thought is serial or could involve parallel streams is, of course, very important for modelling thought, in that the answer chosen influences the model-maker's treatment of many other topics, including the interpretation of phenomena such as 'incubation', intrusive thoughts and goal interruptions. This issue is also very important for the value of verbal thinking-aloud reports. If all thinking is serial, then verbal reports could be useful data on that large portion of thought that is either in a verbal code or readily translatable into verbal terms (Ericsson and Simon, 1980, 1983, 1993). However, if parallel, unconscious streams of thought exist, but if people can report only on the stream that is currently going through working memory, then much thought could not be reported, and less direct methods would be needed to tap the 'underground' parallel thought streams. Wilson (1994) discussed this issue in terms of explicit versus implicit processes. Implicit learning and memory, where the effects of prior experience can be demonstrated without any subjective awareness, appear to be robust phenomena (see Evans, in press), and by definition thinking aloud cannot shed light directly on such processes. However, thinking-aloud methods are very relevant to studies of implicit learning and memory, insofar as discrepancies between the thinking-aloud record and behaviour can suggest the occurrence of implicit processes.

Of course, the seriality assumption is simpler, more parsimonious and more testable than the alternative, and it has the advantage of leading to models for particular tasks that can be readily explored on existing computer systems, which are of course mostly purely serial devices. So, there is much to be said for adopting the seriality assumption as an initial hypothesis. Also, as Newell (1962) argued, an awkward possibility arises when parallel activities are permitted, in that information processing may become like an 'Alice in Wonderland croquet game, with porcupine balls unrolling themselves and wandering off, and flamingo mallets asking questions at inopportune times' (p. 398). Newell was here pointing to the chaotic possibilities of parallel systems; however, other theorists have not been so deterred, and, although some have willingly embraced chaos (for instance, as a potential source of novel ideas), others have striven to show how order and parallel activity can coexist within a single system. Consideration of some of these proposals and of the 'serialist' treatment of the relevant data is now in order.

Early in the development of the information processing approach, Neisser (1963a) argued that information processing models cast in the form of computer programs were overly single minded in seeking relentlessly for a single, top-level goal and also ignored connections between emotion and thought. Simon (1967) replied with suggestions for incorporating certain emotional phenomena and for dealing with multiple goals. In the case of emotion, Simon proposed that emotion is often associated with interruption of the current activity sequence by an urgent stimulus demanding real-time attention (for instance, shouts of 'Fire' while a person is working on an algebra problem). However, to handle interruptions, Simon did allow that a low-level parallel monitoring process might occur, along with the main stream of thought:

> A certain amount of processing must go on continuously or almost continuously, to enable the system to *notice* when conditions have arisen that require ongoing programs to be interrupted. The noticing processes will be substantially in parallel with the ongoing goal attaining program of the total system, although this parallelism may be realized in fact, by the high frequency time sharing of a single serial processor.
>
> (p. 34, italics in original)

Thus, Simon raised the possibility of parallel 'noticing' processes that scanned for 'danger' signals, but he kept open the serialist option of 'time sharing'. The notion of 'time sharing' is simply that the system rapidly switches from one program to another and so gives the appearance of doing two things at once without true simultaneity. Time sharing requires a higher-level program to determine which lower-level program should take over next and for how long. Time sharing is one way in which real computer systems allocate processing to the various jobs that come in and queue for attention, and so it is a method of known utility for serial processing systems.

In short, the anti-serialist points in Neisser's (1963a) paper were acknowledged and largely 'defused' by Simon, but in a second paper in the same year Neisser (1963b) espoused the more radical notion of multiple simultaneous thought processes, and this concept cannot be accommodated within a serial framework. Neisser proposed that a number of more or less independent trains of thought co-occur but that there is a 'main sequence' corresponding to the ordinary flow of consciousness. The main sequence has control over motor activity, except perhaps in pathological cases. Neisser suggested that the unconscious trains of thought might generally follow the rules of Freud's primary process thinking and interact together in a chaotic way. However, when the main sequence was not too demanding, the unconscious sequences might attain high degrees of complexity and do useful 'unconscious work', the results of which could later be made available to consciousness. Accounts of *incubation* and *inspiration* in problem solving (see, for example, Poincaré, 1908; Wallas, 1926) were taken by Neisser to support these ideas. (Incubation involves setting a problem aside and not carrying out any conscious work on the task for a period; inspiration is the spontaneous occurrence of a solution idea in consciousness.) Ohlsson (1992) distinguished sharply between incubation and inspiration (or 'illumination'), and he argued that, although there was some evidence for the benefits of incubation periods, there was no real evidence for inspiration.

Serialist rejoinders to the proponents of incubation and inspiration (Simon, 1966; Ericsson and Simon, 1980, 1983, 1993) have tended to play down the solidity of reports of incubation and inspiration and to propose alternative explanations for any apparent incubation phenomena. So, for instance, Ericsson and Simon (1980, 1983, 1993) pointed out that reports of incubation had frequently been given many years after the supposed events occurred. It could be that the scientists, inventors or artists concerned did start consciously to muse on their problems, but that, on the critical occasion of 'inspiration' or rapid solution, they forgot the details of their own thought processes and then reported the event as one of sudden insight occurring without warning (Woodworth and Schlossberg, 1954). The occurrence of a rapid solution on trial $(n + 1)$ after n failures can be attributed to the beneficial forgetting of misleading sub-goals during the rest period between trial n and trial $(n + 1)$ (Simon, 1966). The topic of 'incubation' is clearly very important for theories of thinking, but unfortunately the supposed phenomenon has turned out to be difficult to capture in the laboratory. Apart from a few published experimental studies (Patrick, 1937; Fulgosi and Guilford, 1968; Murray and Denny, 1969; Dominowski and Jenrick, 1972; Olton and Johnson, 1976), there are only anecdotal data on which to rely. However, at present, the very existence of the phenomenon, let alone its explanation, is uncertain.

The question of 'intrusive' thoughts also arises in connection with the parallelism issue. Antrobus *et al.* (1966) and Becker *et al.* (1973) found experimentally that unwelcome thoughts appeared to intrude into consciousness following exposure to disturbing information. Such intrusive thoughts are a frequent consequence of real-life trauma. This phenomenon is certainly consistent with Neisser's multiple thinking scheme. The rival (serial) position could propose, following Simon's (1967) reply to Neisser (1963a), that goals of assimilating the disturbing information are set up and given high priority. Thus, a time-sharing system could switch from 'external' goals to the 'intrusive' goals quite frequently. It is conceivable that a long-standing, high-level goal is to process disturbing information even if it is painful, and that this goal is not easily ignored.

Wegner (1994; Wegner *et al.*, 1987) developed a model of the intrusions that tend to occur when a person tries to suppress particular thoughts (such as thoughts of food while dieting). He used a paradigm in which thought suppression was required (for example, 'Do not think of a white bear!'), and the participants thought aloud concurrently or pressed a button if the unwanted thought became conscious. It turns out to be remarkably difficult not to think of a white bear if one tries not to do so. Thinking-aloud methods showed quite frequent intrusions, and similar results held up with button pushing as an indicator. Wegner interpreted these data in terms of an 'ironic' model of mental control, in which there is a conscious operating process that seeks states consistent with the goal (such as non-white-bear states) while an unconscious monitor scans consciousness for states that violate the goal (white-bear states). Violations reactivate the operating process. From time to time, especially with fatigue or mental load, the operating process falters and the monitoring goal becomes conscious, causing an intrusion. This model gains some support from intrusions in the thinking-aloud records, where thoughts (of white bears) unrelated to previous thoughts occurred, normally at or after gaps where the participant was apparently searching for a fresh non-white-bear topic (Wegner *et al.*, 1987).

Accuracy and completeness of verbal reports

If the important thought processes involved in problem solving are indeed serial, then it is reasonable to anticipate that verbal reports could be informative about the course of those processes. On the serial processing assumption, thinking aloud involves externalizing the information that goes through working memory. However, if parallel thought streams occur, the best verbal reports can only be very incomplete, being restricted to the main conscious stream that passes through working memory. Thus, the apparent completeness and accuracy of verbal reports on mental processes is relevant to the controversy over serial versus parallel streams of thought. Inaccurate reports or reports that contain marked gaps or discontinuities of content might indicate that unconscious parallel thought processes were playing a role. The question of the accuracy and completeness of verbal reports of mental activity has generated considerable controversy since the era of the introspectionists until the present time. A major critical analysis of verbal reports as a source of information on cognitive processes was presented by Nisbett and Wilson (1977), and their article stimulated replies from Ericsson and Simon (1980, 1983), who attempted to detail the circumstances under which the standard model of thinking would expect verbal reports to be valid. White (1988) also gave a detailed critique of Nisbett and Wilson's assumptions.

Nisbett and Wilson reviewed a dauntingly large collection of studies, mainly from the social psychological literature. The experiments reviewed by Nisbett and Wilson involved such varied topics as participants changing their opinions (Goethals and Reckman, 1973), coming to eat grasshoppers (Zimbardo *et al.*, 1969b), receiving electric shocks (Zimbardo *et al.*, 1969a) and selecting which of four pairs of stockings they preferred (Wilson and Nisbett, 1978). When participants in these various studies were asked about the cognitive processes that had led them to make their responses, their verbal reports did not refer to the stimuli that the experimenters could demonstrate to be influencing their behaviour. In view of the very low accuracy of the verbal reports in these studies, Nisbett and Wilson concluded that reports on cognitive processes are not based on genuine 'privileged' information of a type available only to introspection, but are based rather on implicit and widely held causal theories concerning which stimuli could cause particular responses.

This latter point draws its support from studies in which control subjects are asked to say which factors they think will be effective in particular experiments. The control subjects' predictive judgements of the effectiveness of experimental variables were highly correlated with the experimental subjects' judgements – but both sets of judgements were equally inaccurate. Nisbett and Wilson qualified their condemnation of verbal reports and allowed that such reports may be accurate if confined to mental contents (such as the contents of focal attention, current sensations and plans), but they maintained that verbal reports would be woefully inaccurate regarding mental processes. In short, they claimed that the most important processes underlying behaviour in a variety of tasks were unavailable to consciousness and that the conscious thought stream was largely epiphenomenal.

Even if Nisbett and Wilson's conclusions are accepted, a serial model could still be tenable, if the unreportable processes were seen not as using working memory, but as being run off in a 'ballistic' or 'compiled' mode, such as has been postulated in the case of highly practised actions (for example, by Anderson, 1983). Ericsson and Simon (1980, 1983, 1993) took a different approach, and on the basis of the standard serial model they proposed conditions under which accurate verbal reports should and should not occur. In particular, they suggested that verbalization could be expected to be accurate only if the report was made concurrently with the task-related cognitive activity. Furthermore, for maximum validity the report should be made in a free manner (that is, in the participant's own words) and not confined to some experimenter-defined categories, which might not match the participant's own representational schemes.

The basic notion put forward by Ericsson and Simon was that only the information in focal attention can be verbalized. This principle limits 'verbalizable' information to that which is in working memory, and it further predicts that information about the inputs and outputs of current mental processes will receive priority in free concurrent verbal reports. Ericsson and Simon pointed out that almost all the studies discussed by Nisbett and Wilson had involved retrospective reports, often obtained some considerable time after the relevant behaviour had occurred. The standard serial model would not predict accurate reports in such circumstances, since the contents of working memory during processing are transitory and as a result participants who are asked to give retrospective reports have to fall back on inferences based on their implicit causal theories of behaviour. Under more favourable conditions, as in Newell and Simon's (1972) study of cryptarithmetic problem solving, Ericsson's (1975) studies of eight-puzzle performance and De Groot's (1965) studies of chess play, concurrent verbal reports would be quite consistent with behaviour and would lead to coherent models of underlying processes. In these cases, then, verbal reports were satisfactorily accurate and complete.

From Ericsson and Simon's analysis, it follows that processes that do not use working memory will not be reportable. This would be true for highly practised sequences of operations. Beginners at writing, say, would perhaps be able to report how they wrote a 't', at least to the level of 'draw vertical' then 'put cross-bar through vertical', whereas skilled writers would probably not be able to say with confidence which operation had been carried out first. Highly practised motor sequences become 'automatic' and seem to run off as wholes, without any reference to working memory. This is of course generally a useful development, though it can contribute to accidents since intermediate steps are not monitored and may be based upon assumptions that no longer hold (see, for instance, Reason, 1979, and Norman, 1981, on behavioural slips and accidents). On this view, the depth of detail with which mental processes can be verbally reported will depend on their degree of automaticity. Where subprocesses have not been 'compiled' or automatized into larger wholes, then extensive detail would be expected.

A further point of contention lies in Nisbett and Wilson's claim that, although mental processes can never be reported, mental contents can sometimes be reported. This may be disputed. For example, if one sets people the task of multiplying 11 by 15 while thinking aloud, the labels of various processes are likely to be mentioned, such as 'multiply 5 by 11' or 'add 15 to 150'. Their reports will tend to mention inputs, outputs and process labels. Admittedly, if one asks 'How did you multiply 5 by 11?' the answer will likely be, 'I don't know how; I just know it's 55'. In other words, the relevant 'look-up' or retrieval process from long-term memory is automatized in the practised numerate person. It seems that processes can be reported, but only down to the level of the component subprocesses that have been automatized. Overall then, it seems that much information on mental contents and processes can be accurately reported in the proper conditions up to the point at which automatized subprocesses come into play. The 'proper conditions' include both the conditions of the main task and those of the verbalization task. For accurate reports, the task must not be too highly practised, and free concurrent verbalization should be used, since this will be much more likely to yield valid reports than delayed retrospections to vague or inappropriate probes.

Thus, on the issue of serial versus parallel processing, it appears that the data from studies of the validity of subjective reports are not absolutely decisive. In certain circumstances, detailed by Ericsson and Simon and summarized above, valid reports of the contents of working memory, including process labels, can be given, in accord with the serialist position. That is to say, the parsimonious serial assumption leads to useful analyses of thinking-aloud records when those records have been produced under those conditions that the assumption would predict to be favourable. A parallel model would interpret cases of valid verbal reporting to mean that, in the appropriate circumstances, behaviour is controlled by the reportable main sequence.

What of inaccurate or very incomplete verbal reports? The serialist position could account for many of these cases in terms of delays in reporting the short-lived contents of working memory, leading to gaps and to retrospective rationalizations rather than to valid reports, since the relevant information may have been lost before the query was made. Also, failures to report accurately may be due to the relevant processes being automatized and hence not using working memory. The parallel alternative would propose that the effective processes were unconscious in the case of inaccurate verbal reports and so were never available, even for concurrent reports.

In the face of the controversy over the accuracy of verbal reports, it may be noted that one research possibility is to carry out the relevant experiments reported by Nisbett and Wilson, but to obtain verbal reports in accord with the conditions that Ericsson and Simon deem ideal for valid introspective reports. If the results remained as before (in other words, the reports were inaccurate), the view that important thought processes can be unconscious and parallel to the conscious stream would be upheld. A step in this direction was carried out by White (1989), who found that immediate retrospective reports of reasons given for liking or disliking imaginary characters, presented by questionnaire, were more accurate than delayed retrospections, just as the standard model would predict.

Effects of thinking aloud

Thinking aloud is intended to provide researchers with useful information to aid their inferences about how target tasks are normally carried out when thinking aloud is not required. Hence, it is important to establish whether thinking aloud tends to distort normal processing (in other words, whether it is a reactive method), and, if so, how and under what conditions.

Extensive research, reviewed by Ericsson and Simon (1993), generally indicates that direct concurrent thinking aloud has no significant effect on the quality of performance. For example, no effects of thinking aloud were found when solving anagrams that required the rearrangement of words into sentences (von Borstel, 1982) or when solving N-term series problems (Deffner, 1983, 1984, 1989). Nor were any effects found of concurrent thinking aloud when carrying out Raven's Progressive Matrices (Rhenius and Heydemann, 1984; Heydemann, 1986). Direct concurrent thinking aloud does tend to increase the times required to arrive at a solution compared with silent controls, presumably because of the extra time required to verbalize.

However, Russo *et al.* (1989) found that concurrent thinking aloud was linked to some reduction in accuracy in mental arithmetic but to increased accuracy in choosing between simple gambles (which required the correct multiplication of money amounts by probabilities). No effects on accuracy were found for concurrent thinking aloud on Raven's Progressive Matrices or anagram solving. Retrospective reports had similar effects. Instructions had been given at the start of each task.

Ericsson and Simon (1993) pointed out, among other possible explanations for these results, that the participants had carried out all conditions, and that those who performed the concurrent thinking aloud condition after the retrospective reporting condition may have approached the task in a different way from 'normal' concurrent-only participants. Additionally, all the participants had been trained in both retrospective and concurrent methods of reporting during an initial training period, and this also could have affected their approach to concurrent reporting. Replications and extensions of Russo *et al.*'s study are clearly needed.

However, less direct concurrent reporting, in which the participants are asked to give reasons and explanations, quite often seems to affect processing and hence task performance, as well as learning from repeated tasks. For example, Stinessen (1985) found that stating reasons for moves in the Tower of Hanoi problem reduced the number of incorrect moves, and a similar result was found by Ahlum-Heath and Di Vesta (1986) in the case of participants with no prior practice on the Tower of Hanoi task. Using a complex control task, Berry and Broadbent (1984) found that prior verbal instructions were more effective for a group required to give reasons for each move than for a group not so required. This was presumably because the instructions directed their attention to the relevant task features, and because the reporting requirement kept their attention on the same key features (see Berry, 1990).

Schooler *et al.* (1993) have examined the effects of retrospective and concurrent reporting in the case of insight tasks. An interval of 2 min midway through solution attempts in which participants were required to give retrospective reports interfered with finding the solution in comparison with a silent control condition involving a 2 min interval of unrelated activity. However, the accounts that were requested in this study were for indirect information, such as 'approach and strategies'. It is possible that the intervening recall period rehearsed and strengthened inappropriate directions of working, producing an interference effect. Concurrent reporting, including reports of what was read of the problem statement, also produced interference effects on insight tasks but not on non-insight tasks. Here, it is possible that reading the problem statement strengthened initial incorrect representations in the case of the insight tasks, but strengthened what are usually correct initial representations in the non-insight tasks (Ericsson and Simon, 1993).

Conclusions

Verbal reports of cognitive contents can take many forms in terms of what exactly is to be reported and when the reports are made. Overall, the most useful reports are straightforward verbalizations of ongoing thought as it happens, without either elaboration or explanation. Such direct concurrent reports are generally accurate and reasonably complete, and have little reactive effect beyond some slowing of performance. Delayed (retrospective) reports are likely to be less complete and more likely to contain rationalizations. Indirect reports of strategies or reasons for behaviour, whether retrospective or concurrent, are likely to be both inaccurate and reactive with the main task and hence are not recommended.

Chapter 5

Protocol analysis: practical implementation

Caroline Green and Ken Gilhooly

This chapter sets out to give the intending user of protocol analysis some advice about the practical considerations that need to be borne in mind when planning a research study. Through the use of detailed examples, we shall take the reader through the required sequence of steps involved in undertaking such a study.

Planning and design

The first step in any research study is to design and plan it. This phase is particularly important in the case of research using protocol analysis, because this technique can be resource intensive and the use of available resources needs to be carefully planned. The following points need to be considered before any research study commences.

(1) Consider what resources you have available and plan the study in the light of these. Protocol analysis is a time-consuming exercise (allow ten hours for every hour of protocol material collected), and there is no point in planning a research study that requires extensive resources if these are not likely to be obtainable. Many of the following points should be considered with reference to the resources available.

(2) Consider what is required – what you need to obtain from the protocols – and the aims of your study. For example, do you need very specific details of decision-making processes or merely a broad outline? If you are working in a domain with which you are not very familiar, do ensure that specialist advice on theoretical and practical issues will be available to you when you need it. This is likely to be at the start of the study, when you are devising the experimental set up, but also later on, when you come to examine the protocols in order to devise the coding scheme. Many applied domains have their own 'jargon' and you are likely to need expert advice on the way in which this has been used.

(3) Think about the feasibility of collecting protocols. Does the domain allow for the concurrent recording of thinking-aloud material? Is it feasible to think aloud in the particular domain? For instance, you might be able to get mathematicians to think aloud while they solve a complex problem, but it is not so feasible to get doctors to think aloud when they are examining real patients

and making diagnoses. While it may be possible in principle for protocols to be obtained in the medical domain, it is unlikely to be accepted as wise or ethical for patients to be privy to the doctor's decision-making processes. In such domains, the study may need to be retrospective or performed on a hypothetical case (for example, one where an actor is briefed to simulate a patient: see Elstein *et al.*, 1978). You then have to consider whether this is appropriate for the task that you wish to study.

(4) Consider the practicality of collecting protocols. Is the domain one in which it is possible for you or a research assistant to be physically present and to record the material? If not, can the participants record the material themselves? Will self-recording by participants be sufficient for what is being studied or do you need to be present (for instance, to prompt, to focus the problem solving or to make observations of bodily movements that may be relevant to the analysis)? Where are the protocols to be gathered? If the project is an applied one, and they are to be gathered at multiple sites or in a domain where access cannot always be guaranteed at particular points in time, you must allow for this in the allocation of resources: you may be kept waiting, or appointments may be postponed or missed owing to other priorities of the people involved.

(5) Think about how many protocols are required. How long is each protocol likely to be? The participants may show fatigue, boredom or annoyance if the task is too long. Some applied domains may allow for collection of material for protocol analysis only over short periods of time. The time to analyse the data must also be considered: as noted above, this can be as long as ten hours for each hour of protocol.

(6) Make plans for the data analysis. You are certainly going to need to transcribe the protocols. Make sure that this is done on a word processor at the very least, so that you can make multiple copies and edit and segment while retaining the original transcription. Do you want a degree of automation in the segmenting and coding? If so, you will need to write yourself, to have written or to purchase suitable programs to do this. Most analysis is likely to be carried out on computers, so check that the necessary software and hardware are available, particularly if programs have to be written to automate the analysis.

(7) Think about the equipment that will be needed and the recording methods available. A tape recorder, a supply of tapes and possibly also a video-camera will be required. If you plan to employ a transcriber, check that your recording equipment and tape are compatible with the equipment that the transcriber will use, and also ensure that they are familiar with the domain. Consider the length of time that it will take to do the transcription: check in advance the costs and time that will be involved. Consider whether notes will be needed on bodily movements and gestures. If the task being studied is computerized, consider the idea of collecting key-press data. Additional data of this sort may be useful if the participants' reports do not make it clear what information or part of the task they have been attending to. Nevertheless, such additional data should not replace the verbal report: they merely enable you to clarify what has actually been going on.

(8) Ensure the cooperation and motivation of the participants. If the participants are not motivated in some way, then it is difficult to collect 'rich' data: they may not be bothered to report all that they are thinking. Consider how you may motivate them. It may be possible to pay them, or to offer them access to the results of the study if they are likely to be of use or interest to them, or to indicate (truly, of course) that their cooperation will be looked upon favourably by their superiors. Likewise, if they are tired or in a hurry to complete the task, they may also give an incomplete account of their thoughts as they undertake the task. Do not (for example) try to take busy doctors away when they are planning to start a ward round shortly. They may say that they can spare a few minutes, but they are likely to start looking at their watches once their perception of 'a few minutes' is up. It is much better to ascertain exactly what time is available and to plan accordingly.

(9) Note the importance of running a pilot study. This cannot be stressed enough. You will gain much information from a pilot study, and you may need to redesign aspects of the study as a result. Check that your equipment functions properly in the position where you need to use it. In some settings, this position may change. You may need to fix a lapel microphone to the participants if they are mobile during the task. Prepare a checklist of steps and checks to go through before you collect each protocol; for instance, 'Check that the tape recorder is switched on before each participant starts'. This may appear pedantic, but there is nothing worse than knowing that a participant produced some really useful material and then finding that the tape is blank.

Preparation of subjects

You must prepare your participants well; it is very important to make them aware of what they are required to do in order to produce 'rich' verbal reports as opposed to 'poor' or incomplete ones. You may have to describe in some detail what they are required to do and to demonstrate the art of thinking aloud. You should make sure that the participants are made aware that the task you are asking them to perform is the primary task, whereas the thinking aloud is secondary to that task. Your instructions should be very carefully worded and tested on a number of participants to exclude anything that is liable to be misunderstood or open to misinterpretation. On occasion, some researchers request that the participants explain their thoughts as they verbalize them. However, you should note that an instruction to this effect makes additional demands on the participants, since they have to rationalize their thoughts, and this may well alter the way in which the task is performed.

When you have given the instructions to the participants, you should ask them whether these have been understood. It is important to ensure that the participants keep talking and that their speech is loud enough and clear, so that the material collected can be accurately transcribed. You should include instructions to this effect in your preliminary instructions to the participants. You may also need to prompt them during the think-aloud procedure, but this may not be possible if the protocol is applied to a real-life situation or if you are unable to be present. In these circumstances, you may need to devise some kind of prompting mechanism such as a written sign to hold up or a taped reminder to be played to the participants at predetermined intervals. Once again, however, you must ensure that any such device does not interfere with the production of the protocols.

Ericsson and Simon (1993) noted that, if participants fall silent for a period, the instruction 'Keep talking' is less disruptive than the instruction 'Please can you tell me what you are thinking?' You may wish to define in advance the length of time for which you are prepared to allow a participant to remain silent. For example, Gilhooly and Gregory (1989) allowed their participants one minute before asking them to 'keep talking'. Or you may decide to keep this flexible, according to the way that the participant appears to be performing the task. Some participants maintain a period of silence while they engage in thought, but have a very productive period immediately afterwards when they report those thoughts. This cannot really be described as a 'retrospective' report, because the problem-solving task is still going on, but one should be aware that such participants may not be directly thinking aloud but have thought already and then be reporting, so an element of rationalization may have entered their protocol. On occasion, it may be necessary to question them about certain things as they perform the task, for instance asking 'What were you referring to at that point?' Such interventions should however be kept to a minimum: they should be used only to clarify essential issues, and they should be made at a suitable point in order not to interrupt the participants' train of thought.

Your participants will almost certainly need practice, either with a sample of the material that you are using to stimulate the protocols or with 'warm-up' tasks, whichever is more appropriate. Such tasks are used for several reasons. First, they allow the experimenter to clarify any misunderstandings that an individual participant may have about what is required in the procedure. Second, providing that the tasks are relatively simple, so that participants' first experience of thinking aloud is an easy one, they help to ensure that the participants are able to do what is asked of them, and this can relax them if they are nervous about the prospect. A good choice of warm-up task is simple mental arithmetic, appropriately selected to match the participants' apparent mental abilities. Third, a warm-up period for each participant allows the experimenter to check that each will actually think aloud; just occasionally, a participant is too shy or for some other reason finds it almost impossible to speak while performing the primary task. In this situation, the participant can be given more practice until deemed to be satisfactory or, in extreme cases, discarded as a participant. In the latter case, the participant should be thanked for participating so far and told that this has been valuable, but that, as the warm-up task has taken rather longer than expected, he or she is not required to complete any further tasks.

When the participant has completed the warm-up task in a satisfactory manner, it is usual to indicate this explicitly by saying 'Good!' or some other suitable

---

Box 5.1 Recommended thinking-aloud instructions

In this experiment, we are interested in what you think about when you find solutions to some problems I am going to ask you to do. In order to do this, I am going to ask you to THINK ALOUD as you work on the problem you are given. What I mean by 'think aloud' is that I want you to tell me EVERYTHING you are thinking from the time you first see the question until you reach a solution or until I tell you to stop working on the problem. I would like you to talk aloud CONSTANTLY from the time I present each problem until you have given your final answer to it or have been asked to stop. I don't want you to plan out what you say or try to explain to me what you are saying. Just act as if you are alone in the room speaking to yourself. It is most important that you keep talking. If you are silent for any long period of time, I will ask you to talk. Please try to speak as clearly as possible, as I shall be recording you as you speak. Do you understand what I want you to do?

We shall start with a practice problem.

---

expression. This will help to alleviate any residual nervousness the participant has about performing the task ahead. Box 5.1 shows a set of 'best practice' instructions for a thinking-aloud study, based upon our own experience and upon the research findings of Ericsson and Simon (1993) and Gilhooly and Gregory (1989).

Recording of verbal reports

You must ensure that your recording conditions are good. It is important that your recordings and, indeed, the participants' trains of thought are not interrupted by other voices or external disturbances, unless this is unavoidable (as it might be in applied situations: for instance, if the participant were a pilot receiving intermittent information over a radio that was relevant to the particular flying task that you were examining). Consider whether you wish the tape recorder or you yourself to be visible to the participants. Ericsson and Simon (1993) indicated that in some conditions it was better to keep the tape recorder and the experimenter outside the participants' field of view. It is possible that they might be influenced by the facial reactions of the researcher or feel the need to address the researcher and to explain their actions rather than think aloud. The obvious presence of the tape recorder may initially intimidate some participants, although most people seem to be able to disregard this with very little difficulty.

Assuming that the experimenter is present while the participants are generating their protocols (or that the protocol-taking situation has been video-recorded), a check should be made that the verbal protocol parallels the behavioural one. Ericsson and Simon (1993) suggested that, as long as this was the case, the verbal protocol could be validated. It is worth checking this point, since, if the participants are doing something that is clearly different from what they say they are doing, the protocol will not be of much use. In our experience, marked dissociations between their protocols and their behaviour are in practice extremely rare.

Transcription of verbal reports

Each of the protocols will need to be transcribed in order to be analysed. Consider how you intend to do this. In any major study you are likely to need the protocols to be transcribed using a computer. You may need to employ a typist to do this, in which case you will need either to ensure that they are familiar with the terminology of the domain or to check all the typed material against the original recordings, which could be very time consuming. It may be possible to check the transcription for accuracy while you are segmenting the data, if you are planning to do this yourself (see the following section). Some researchers record details of time in the transcript, using markers to indicate the passing of specified time periods. This allows them to determine how much time has been spent on a particular part of a task. You will also need to decide whether you want details of pauses, and so on, to be transcribed. These may be important, depending on the theoretical notions of your coding scheme: for example, if a pause indicates a period of thought, you may wish to record this, as it may influence the coding of the preceding or following segment.

Preparation and coding of the protocols

Once the recorded material has been transcribed, it needs to be segmented and encoded. This is likely to be an iterative process, partly driven by the nature of your hypotheses. In the initial stages, you should take a random sample of approximately 10% of the protocols on which to try out the segmentation strategy and develop the coding categories.

In constructing the task and its theoretical framework, and in the light of the pilot protocols, you should have some idea of how you intend to code your data. You will need to identify a set of coding categories. In doing this, you will need to ensure that they will adequately describe the data collected. Task analysis is a useful initial source of probable codes, and this involves an *a priori* analysis of the kinds of concepts and operations that are likely to be useful to an effective problem solver in the task area. In mental arithmetic, for example, task analysis would expect participants to use number properties, the usual operations of addition, subtraction, multiplication and division, and carrying, plus the storage and retrieval of intermediate sums held in memory. You will also need to be able to define clearly the conditions for the use of each code. A good scheme will be simple and easy to understand, in order that subjective interpretation by the coders is kept to a minimum. If you have too many categories, and particularly if there is a danger of them overlapping, the coders will have difficulty in distinguishing between them, while if there are too few, you are unlikely to be able to extract any useful information from your data, since it will be too general.

Most coding schemes have a 'residual' or 'ragbag' category labelled 'Other'. Try to avoid placing too many segments in this category. If your initial attempts have left a large number of segments in the 'Other' category, consider whether one or more new categories are needed, or whether some of the 'Other' examples might really fit into one of the remaining categories. If you find that you need a new category, check whether some of your previously coded segments do not in fact meet the specifications of the new category better than they did their original category. There will often be a few borderline cases like this: as we noted earlier, protocol analysis is an iterative and very time-consuming process! Time spent at this stage on improving and checking your scheme will pay off at a later date, since the need to revise a scheme once a large body of data has been analysed is even more time consuming and can be disheartening. You may need a few attempts to produce a coding scheme that satisfies you, one that covers most of the segments and produces the information that you require.

When you have devised and revised your scheme, you should prepare a set of instructions for the coding, with examples. Even if you plan to do the coding yourself, you will need to check the reliability of the coding, and so another coder will have to code your protocols. He or she will need to be given explicit instructions in the use of the coding scheme, otherwise the likelihood of a satisfactory level of agreement being reached will be low.

Protocol analysis: a practical example

The following example is provided to illustrate the sequence of events in the generation and analysis of protocols. The protocol in question was in fact generated at a workshop, and the coding scheme was developed by the workshop participants over a very limited period. The problem is the eight-puzzle problem, in which eight numbers are placed in a square that has space for nine numbers, allowing the numbers to be moved one at a time (Fig. 5.1a). The numbers are then moved, perhaps yielding a configuration like that shown in Fig. 5.1b.

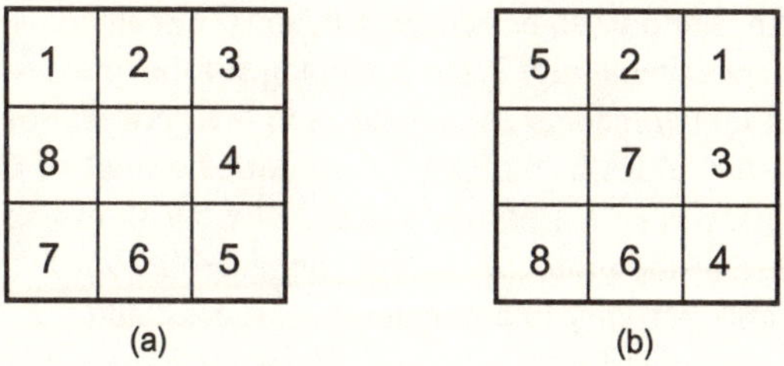

(a)   (b)

FIG. 5.1. *An example of the eight-puzzle problem*

Box 5.2 Example section of a protocol generated with an eight-puzzle problem

Right, I've got to get the one across to the top right, er, seven across, two down, one across, three up, four across, seven across, two down, one across. Now I've got to get the two into the top middle, erm, how can I do that? seven up, two across, six up, eight across, five across, two down, three down, seven across, two up. Now I've got to swap over the three and the seven. Oh dear. (pause) I can get the eight into the right place. (pause) Seven's in completely the wrong place. So, I've got to move that down somehow. . . .

The participant is shown the initial configuration of the numbers and then asked to reconstruct the final configuration, moving one number at a time. Instructions are given along the lines described earlier in this chapter, but including the description of the task. Box 5.2 shows an excerpt from a protocol generated by someone trying to solve this problem.

It is usual for the initial sample of protocols to be segmented and encoded by at least two coders and the intercoder reliability computed, so as to determine the validity of the segmentation and coding schemes. In the segmentation process, it is usual to break the data up (or segment them) into a series of single ideas or statements, perhaps clauses, phrases or sentences, which will later be coded. You may find during the coding that you need to adjust the segmentation in order to allow for a finer- or coarser-grained coding. The intercoder segmentation reliability is the percentage of the total number of segment indicators on which two coders are agreed. Box 5.3 shows an illustration of the method for calculating this in the case of the protocol excerpt in Box 5.2. The intercoder reliability should be at least 85% for the scheme to be considered valid. In the present example, the one disagreement occurred when two segments had been coded into the same category. The first segmenter saw this as one segment, but later agreed that there were two separate ideas here.

Once any discrepancies in segmenting agreement have been discussed, the criteria agreed for the final segmenting and the appropriate level of agreement attained, the entire sample can be segmented, and the protocol is then ready to be coded. The intercoder reliability is the percentage of the total number of segment indicators on which two coders are agreed as to their codes. For instance, if two coders agree on the codes in the case of 60 out of a total of 68 segments, the intercoder reliability is 88% [(60/68) × 100]. Box 5.4 shows an example of the coding in the case of the protocol excerpt contained in Box 5.2.

You may be able partially to automate this process, and you should certainly consider this if the body of data is large. Gilhooly and Green (1989) developed a suite of Spitbol programs to do this. These have now been superseded by more

---

Box 5.3 Segmentation reliability calculation

First segmenter
Right, I've got to get the one across to the top right,/ er,/ seven across, two down, one across, three up, four across, seven across, two down, one across./ Now I've got to get the two into the top middle,/ erm,/ how can I do that?/ seven up, two across, six up, eight across, five across, two down, three down, seven across, two up./ Now I've got to swap over the three and the seven./ Oh dear. (pause)/ I can get the eight into the right place./ (pause) Seven's in completely the wrong place. So, I've got to move that down somehow. . . ./

Second segmenter
Right, I've got to get the one across to the top right,/ er,/ seven across, two down, one across, three up, four across, seven across, two down, one across./ Now I've got to get the two into the top middle,/ erm,/ how can I do that?/ seven up, two across, six up, eight across, five across, two down, three down, seven across, two up./ Now I've got to swap over the three and the seven./ Oh dear. (pause)/ I can get the eight into the right place./ (pause) Seven's in completely the wrong place./ So, I've got to move that down somehow. . . ./

Percentage agreement $= \dfrac{\text{Total number of segment indicators agreeing} \times 100}{\text{Total number of segment indicators}}$

$= (22/23) \times 100 = 96\%$

---

modern text analysis programs. There are various items of software now available for the computer-assisted analysis of text that allow both the segmentation and the coding of text on-line, including Ethnograph, Qualpro, Textbase Alpha and Hyperqual. (For further details, contact Renate Tesch at Qualitative Research Management, PO Box 30070, Santa Barbara, California 93190, USA.) Such systems can decrease bias and increase reliability.

Crutcher *et al.* (1994) described a semi-automatic system in which the entire set of protocol segments obtained in a study are stored in a single file. The program randomly presents coders with individual segments from the file, so that they have no information about the participant, the protocol or the experimental condition in which a particular segment was obtained. This reduces any bias resulting from preconceived ideas that the coder may have about individual participants or conditions, and prevents contextual information from previously coded segments being used in the current coding. However, this is not always practical, since contextual information may be required to decide upon a code for the segment. In contrast, the suite of programs that was devised by Gilhooly

---

Box 5.4 Example of coding

The researchers in this study decided upon a coding scheme containing five categories. They basically wanted to look at the strategies a participant used in attempting to solve the puzzle. The categories they chose to use were: Planning (P); Questioning (Q); Assessment (A); Simple Descriptions of Movement (M); and Filler/Thinking Time (T). The excerpt was coded thus:

Segment	*Code*
Right, I've got to get the one across to the top right	P
er	T
seven across, two down, one across, three up, four across, seven across, two down, one across	M
Now, I've got to get the two into the top middle	P
erm	T
how can I do that	Q
seven up, two across, six up, eight across, five across, two down, three down, seven across, two up	M
Now I've got to swap over the three and the seven	P
Oh dear (pause)	T
I can get the eight into the right place	A
(pause) Seven's in completely the wrong place	A
So, I've got to move that down somehow	P

---

and Green (1989) allowed the segments to be displayed with or without the context, so that the context was available if required. It should be noted that the use of context can increase the subjectivity of coding decisions, and the use of one segment to help code another segment means that the segment used cannot be considered an independent observation. Programs such as the Oxford Concordance Program may be useful in the initial phases of the analysis to allow you to examine the frequency of key words and so on. (For further details, contact Oxford University Computing Service, 13 Banbury Road, Oxford OX2 6NN, UK.)

At this stage in our discussion, it will be useful to describe two studies that exemplify many of the points made in this chapter concerning the application of protocol analysis.

Example 1

Gilhooly *et al.* (1988) used protocol analysis as a means of determining the types of processes used by experts and novices in map reading and in memory for maps. This study was undertaken by a research team consisting of three psychologists (including a research assistant) and a geographer/cartographer. Thus, all of the necessary expertise for planning and analysis was available within the research team itself. The participants were university students studying geography or psychology (or both) within the academic departments where the researchers worked. Thus, they were easy to recruit and contact. They were paid a small honorarium by way of motivation for taking part in the experiment.

Process-tracing techniques (thinking aloud and using pointers) were employed while 10 low-skill subjects and 11 high-skill subjects studied and then recalled topographic contour maps. The resulting process traces were analysed in order to uncover differences in encoding and retrieval between skilled and unskilled map readers. The participants were tested individually. The participant sat at a table on which a map was firmly fixed in the focal plane of an overhead video-camera. Underneath the map was the sheet of paper on which the participant would later try to draw the map from memory, so that the research assistant merely had to remove the map at the appropriate time without having to refocus the camera.

The sequence of administration was as follows. The participants were instructed to think aloud during the entire course of the experiment; that is, to tell the research assistant everything they thought about from the time they first saw the map until they had decided that they had finished. They were requested to talk aloud constantly, not to plan what they were saying or to try to explain it, but to act as if they were totally alone. They were told that it was most important that they should keep talking, and that, if they were silent for any long period of time, they would be prompted. They were asked if they had understood the instructions they had been given.

They were also requested to use a small pointer in order to indicate where on the map they were attending to, at all times during the study period. They were told that the session would be both video- and audio-recorded. They were given two warm-up tasks before the main task, using similar material to the experimental material, in order to familiarize them with the thinking-aloud and pointing procedures. All of the participants were able to complete these satisfactorily. They were not under any extreme time pressures, other than those inherent in the actual experiment. They were told the approximate duration of the experiment, although the exact duration varied according to each participant's ability to recall the material that had been presented.

At each stage of the experiment, the research assistant read out the relevant instructions to the participant and then left the room to follow the participant's progress by means of a remote TV monitor. Among other things, this ensured that the research assistant was thoroughly familiar with the data when transcribing the resulting protocols. Box 5.5 contains an example of a protocol obtained from one of the unskilled participants in this experiment, and Box 5.6 shows the same example segmented into simple statements.

The same research assistant then coded the protocols. Each segment was coded as representing the use of one out of a number of 'procedures'. The coding scheme was devised after discussion and examination of the transcribed protocols by the

Box 5.5 Example protocol from an unskilled participant in the map study

Meeting, Limp, river, must be a river, 700, must be hills, here's a river here, Salt River, 600, must be a cemetery there, seven, Limp, seven, er, I'm not sure what this could be, these lines, that must be the height, the river, Salt River, Tinker, Tinker, Meeting, Tinker, Limp, Tinker, Meeting, cemetery, can't think, that must be hills, river. Meeting, Tinker, Tinker, Meeting, cemetery. Railway, I think, must be a railway up here as well. (pause) Tinker, Meeting, Limp, 700, cemetery, 600. (pause) Tinker (pause) [Experimenter: Can you keep talking, please?] Must be a river that separates these or, I'm not sure. Railway line must stop there, doesn't, doesn't seem to join up to anything. That must be a town. Tinker, Meeting, Limp. (pause) I don't know what all these lines mean. Big area there, must be empty, does not say anything. (pause) Cemetery must be on the road, Moore cemetery.

members of the research team. A number of the procedure categories were taken from a previous study by Thorndyke and Stasz (1980) and represented encoding strategies commonly found in memory studies, such as rehearsal, verbal association and pattern encoding. Other procedure categories were specific to map learning, such as map feature description and inferring height. More detailed descriptions of the procedure categories are contained in Box 5.7, and a coded example of a protocol obtained from one of the unskilled participants in this study is shown in Box 5.8.

Box 5.6 Segmented protocol from an unskilled participant in the map study

Meeting,/ Limp,/ river, must be a river,/ 700,/ must be hills,/ here's a river here,/ Salt River,/ 600,/ must be a cemetery there,/ seven,/ Limp,/ seven,/ er, I'm not sure what this could be,/ these lines,/ that must be the height,/ the river,/ Salt River,/ Tinker,/ Tinker,/ Meeting,/ Tinker,/ Limp,/ Tinker,/ Meeting,/ cemetery,/ can't think,/ that must be hills,/ river./ Meeting,/ Tinker,/ Tinker,/ Meeting,/ cemetery./ Railway, I think,/ must be a railway up here as well./ (pause)/ Tinker,/ Meeting,/ Limp,/ 700,/ cemetery,/ 600./ (pause)/ Tinker/ (pause)/ [Experimenter: Can you keep talking, please?]/ Must be a river that separates these or,/ I'm not sure./ Railway line must stop there,/ doesn't, doesn't seem to join up to anything./ That must be a town./ Tinker,/ Meeting,/ Limp./ (pause)/ I don't know what all these lines mean./ Big area there,/ must be empty,/ does not say anything./ (pause)/ Cemetery must be on the road,/ Moore cemetery./

Box 5.7 Coding scheme for the procedure categories in the map study

Procedure label (code)	Description
Map feature description (MFD)	Describes a surface feature of the map with no interpretation (for example, 'there are some small circles')
Reading names (RNA)	Reads names off the map
Rehearsal (RHL)	Rehearses by repeating names or contour values, etc.
Reading height (RHT)	Reads a height value from the map
Inferring height (IHT)	Infers a height from other features
Schema use (SUS)	Uses a lay schema to describe what he or she sees (for example, 'here are hills')
Specialist schema use (HSU)	Uses a specialist schema (for example, 'interlocking spurs')
Relational encoding (REN)	Encodes one feature in terms of its relation to another
Pattern encoding (PEN)	Encodes a feature in terms of its shape or pattern
Directional encoding (DEN)	Encodes a feature by its relationship to compass directions (N, S, E, W)
Positive evaluation (PVA)	Indicates that he or she is certain of a particular aspect of the map
Negative evaluation (NVA)	Indicates that he or she is unsure of the quality of their knowledge about the map
Verbal association (VAS)	Associates a feature of the map with something unrelated to the map itself
Counting (COU)	Counts certain map features
Meta-cognition (MCN)	Refers to his or her own mental processes (for example, 'I have trouble remembering names')

Coding reliability was checked using an independent judge, who coded protocols from two low-skill participants and two high-skill participants, chosen at random. The judge's coding showed agreement with the research assistant's on 83% of the segments, which was deemed to be satisfactory. The average frequencies of use of each of the procedures, as inferred from the protocols, were computed. The analysis showed certain statistically significant differences between the high-skill and low-skill groups. In particular, the high-skill group made more use of specialized schemata, whereas the two groups did not differ

---

Box 5.8 Coded protocol from an unskilled participant in the map study

Segment	Code
Meeting	RNA
Limp	RNA
river, must be a river	SUS
700	RHT
must be hills	SUS
here's a river here	SUS
Salt River	RNA
600	RHT
must be a cemetery there SUS seven	RHT
Limp	RHL
seven	RHT
er, I'm not sure what this could be	NVA
these lines	MFD
that must be the height	SUS
the river	SUS
Salt River	RHL
Tinker	RNA
Tinker	RHL
Meeting	RHL
Tinker	RHL
Limp	RHL
Tinker	RHL
Meeting	RHL
cemetery	SUS
can't think	MCN
that must be hills	SUS
river	RHL
Meeting	RHL

— Continued —

---

in their use of 'lay' or everyday schemata. The low-skill group spent more time in reading names, and they also expressed more negative evaluations of their state of knowledge.

Thinking-aloud protocols were also obtained from the recall phase, as the participants attempted to draw the map from memory. Segmentation and coding were conducted in the same way. The retrieval procedure categories were mostly related to the corresponding encoding procedure categories and are contained in Box 5.9. Box 5.10 shows a segmented and coded example of a recall protocol, which was in fact obtained from the same participant as the one who produced the study protocol that we discussed earlier.

┌─ *Continued* ─ ─ ─ ─ ─ ─ ─ ─ ─ ─ ─ ─ ─ ─ ─ ─ ─ ─┐

Tinker	RHL
Tinker	RHL
Meeting	RHL
cemetery	RHL
Railway, I think	SUS
must be a railway up here as well	SUS
(pause)	
Tinker	RHL
Meeting	RHL
Limp	RHL
700	RHT
cemetery	RHL
600	RHT
(pause)	
Tinker	RHL
(pause)	
[Experimenter: Can you keep talking, please?]	
Must be a river that separates these or	SUS
I'm not sure	NVA
Railway line must stop there	SUS
doesn't, doesn't seem to join up to anything	REN
That must be a town	SUS
Tinker	RHL
Meeting	RHL
Limp	RHL
(pause)	
I don't know what all these lines mean	NVA
Big area there	MFD
must be empty	SUS
does not say anything	MFD
(pause)	
Cemetery must be on the road	REN
Moore cemetery	RNA

The statistically significant differences that emerged were that the low-skill group spent more time retrieving names, whereas the high-skill group retrieved more in terms of both 'lay' schemata and more specialized schemata; the low-skill group also produced more meta-cognitive statements (mainly of the sort 'I am no good at remembering maps'). The two groups did not differ in terms of the length of their protocols or in terms of the number of different codes per protocol. The researchers considered that these results cohered well with those obtained in the study phase, where the high-skill group made more use of specialized schemata and the low-skill group spent more time reading place names and expressing doubt about their actual or likely performance. It was interesting that, even though

---

Box 5.9 Coding scheme for the recall procedure categories in the map study

Retrieve map feature (RMF)
Name retrieval (NRL)
Retrieve contour value (RCV)
Retrieve spot height (RSH)
Retrieve lay schema (RSC)
Retrieve specialist schema (RSS)
Relational retrieval (RRL)
Directional retrieval (DRL)
Negative evaluation (NVA)
Positive evaluation (PVA)
Self-questioning (SEQ)
Meta-cognition (MCO)

Box 5.10 Coded recall protocol from an unskilled participant in the map study

Segment	*Code*
Can't remember	MCO
There was a Salt River	NRL
up here	RRL
I think it went down	RRL
that way	RRL
There was a Tinker	NRL
here somewhere	RRL
(pause)	
I can't remember the way this came down	MCO
There was a Meeting	NRL
this way	RRL
There was a cemetery	RSC
here	RRL
Moore cemetery	NRL
These were all lots of lines	RMF
near the edge	RRL
so many lines	RMF
700	RCV
I think that said	MCO
um	

— *Continued* —

— — *Continued* — — — — — — — — — — — — — — — —

there was a 600	RCV
and what was it	SEQ
645	RCV
I think it was	MCO
I cannot remember what was at this side	MCO
No that doesn't look, that doesn't look right	NVA
(pause)	
I cannot remember this side at all	MCO
What else was there?	SEQ
Railways, just stopped in the middle of nowhere	RSC
I think there was another railway	RSC
here	RRL
I think that's wrong	NVA
There was blue, blue lines all around	RMF
I was not sure what they were	MCO
How many were there?	SEQ
I cannot remember	MCO
Just can't understand these contours at all	MCO
(pause)	
They were mostly round about 700	RCV
(pause)	
I cannot think of anything else	MCO
I don't think that looks anything like what I saw	NVA
(pause)	
No that's all I can remember	MCO

the two groups made equal use of 'lay' schemata during the study phase, the high-skill group seemed to be able to retrieve the information thus encoded much better than the low-skill group.

This experiment involved both objectively scorable process-tracing data (obtained by plotting pointer and pencil positions) as well as the more subjectively interpreted process-tracing data from thinking aloud. The objectively scorable process-tracing data yielded few statistically significant differences between the two groups, although they did differ in term of their memory performance, both on a questionnaire task and on the contour aspects of their drawn recalls. It was plausible to assume that the groups would differ in their processing activities during the study period, even though their attentional focusing patterns appear to have been similar. The results from verbal protocol analysis mentioned above supported this interpretation, and similar results were obtained for the recall phase. Thus, without the use of verbal protocol analysis in this experiment, it would not have been possible to show why the memory performance between the groups might have differed and how it might have been affected by the participants' study and recall processes.

Example 2

A quite different type of study using protocol analysis was carried out by Gilhooly *et al.* (1995), and this is of interest insofar as the coding of protocols was partially automated. The study was concerned with the use of biomedical knowledge in diagnosis, and the particular diagnostic task involved was that of electrocardio-gram (ECG) interpretation. The value of studies of medical expertise is often circumscribed by the use of small numbers of participants and of a limited range of problems, and so there was a particular concern in this study to use a sufficiently large number of participants to obtain reliable results and a sample of problems of varying difficulty. However, this meant that the volume and the length of the protocols obtained were relatively large, and so partially automated methods were used for data analysis.

The entire research team consisted of four psychologists (including a research fellow and two part-time assistants), two computer scientists and a cardiologist, and so once again all the relevant expertise was available within the research team. Participants, chosen to represent three levels of expertise in ECG inter-pretation, attempted to reach diagnoses for eight cardiographic traces that varied in difficulty. In a subsequent session, the same participants attempted to generate causal explanations for the same traces. The research fellow conducting the study obtained on-line thinking-aloud protocols in both of the sessions, and clear and detailed instructions were given to the participants concerning the nature of the thinking-aloud task.

The protocols were transcribed by the research fellow on a Unix-based computer system. For the first stage of analysis, they were divided into segments consisting of a phrase that could stand alone, corresponding to a simple statement. This process produced 3,496 diagnostic segments and 2,390 causal explanation segments. The reliability of segmentation was assessed using a sample of ten protocols and was found to be satisfactory, with over 90% agreement between the two independent judges. The initial analysis looked at the average numbers of segments as a function both of expertise and of task difficulty. For the diagnosis session, it was found that the number of segments increased with task difficulty, but was not affected by the participants' level of expertise. There was a significant interaction between the effects of level of expertise and task difficulty, such that experts produced more segments than the other two groups when the task was more difficult. For the causal explanation session, more segments were produced in more difficult tasks, the experts produced more segments and the effect of expertise was enhanced in more difficult tasks.

Examination of the protocols led to the identification of three main activities or processes: trace characterization, clinical inferences and biomedical inferences. Owing to the large number of segments to be coded, it was decided to use a keyword method of analysis in order to provide an overview of the segments in an efficient manner. As a first step, a list of all of the words used in the protocols was compiled, using the Oxford Concordance Program. The total number of words per participant and the number of different words per participant were also obtained in this way. Vocabulary measures showed no significant correlations in the case of the diagnostic protocols, but for the causal explanation protocols there was a correlation of 0.54 between the level of expertise and the number of words produced and a correlation of 0.55 between the level of expertise and the number of different words produced, suggesting a larger range of relevant concepts in the more expert participants. In short, this first level of analysis gave rise to some useful results regarding effects of expertise.

A list of technical words was extracted from the total list of words produced, and these were categorized by the cardiologist on the research team into one of the three types of processes that had been identified in the initial examination of the protocols. A residual 'problem' category was added for words that did not fit neatly into one of these three main categories. The words belonging to each category were termed 'keywords' for that category. Once again, because of the large body of data, it was decided that coding these data should be automated, which was made easier by the fact that the research team included two computer scientists. One of these team members wrote computer programs that scanned the segmented protocol files and tagged each segment according to the keywords (if any) that it contained. (It should be noted that any particular segment could fall into more than one category as a result of containing more than one type of keyword.) This analysis then allowed a comparison of the use of different procedures by participants with different levels of expertise. The results showed that both clinical and biomedical forms of processing increased with level of expertise, but that the participants who had an intermediate level of expertise produced more statements concerning the physical characteristics of traces than either the experts or the novices.

Other effects investigated in this study were the chronological order of the different processes and the effects of level of expertise and task difficulty upon the position and frequency of various types of hypothesis statement in the protocols. Hypothesis statements, defined as statements of possible diagnoses, were identified by the cardiologist on the research team and were a subset of the category of clinical statements. However, the identification of these statements could not be automated and thus had to be carried out manually.

Conclusions

The two examples cited above should have given some idea of what may be achieved using techniques of protocol analysis and some idea of how this can be done. For further guidance, particularly if the protocols are intended to be the basis of detailed computer models, readers are advised to consult the book by Ericsson and Simon (1993). To summarize the most important points of this chapter:

(1)　Spend time on the design and planning of your research study, and ensure that you have sufficient resources available to undertake what you have planned: time spent at this stage will pay dividends later.

(2)   Always undertake a pilot study.

(3)   Prepare the participants well using carefully worded instructions and an appropriate warm-up task.

(4)   Check the recording and experimental conditions before you start.

(5)   Once the material has been transcribed, use a sample of protocols drawn at random to try out your segmentation strategy and to develop your coding categories.

(6)   Use an independent segmenter and coder to check the reliability of the segmentation and the coding of the protocols you have obtained.

Chapter 6

Grounded theory: theoretical background

Nick Pidgeon

A distinction in research is between that which is concerned with *verification* and that which is concerned with *discovery*. In the former type, theory serves as a framework to guide verification. In the latter, theory is the 'jottings in the margins of ongoing research', a kind of research in which order is not very immediately attained, a messy, puzzling and intriguing kind of research in which the conclusions are not known before the investigations are carried out.

(Gherardi and Turner, 1987, p. 12)

Generating theory that is 'grounded' in semi-structured interviews, field-work observations, case-study documentation or other forms of textual material is one important principle of much contemporary qualitative research. This principle is often associated with the methodological approach first developed by the sociologists Barney Glaser and Anselm Strauss during their investigation of the institutional care of the terminally ill (1965), which they subsequently termed *grounded theory* (1967). Their approach to qualitative research is particularly suited (though is by no means restricted) to the study of local interactions and meanings as related to the social context in which they actually occur. It therefore has considerable potential for psychologists and has been used in areas as diverse as social psychology (Currie, 1988) and cognitive science (Pidgeon *et al.*, 1991), but particularly by those working within the emerging practitioner disciplines such as health psychology (Charmaz, 1990; Gantt, 1992; Beck, 1993; Gloersen *et al.*, 1993; Wilde *et al.*, 1993), clinical psychology (Rennie *et al.*, 1988; Borrill and Iljon Foreman, in press) and educational psychology (Alton-Lee and Nuthall, 1992; Rottenberg and Searfoss, 1992).

In this chapter, I shall outline the origins and development of the grounded theory approach and place it in the context of wider developments and debates that have taken place within psychology and the human sciences since the 1970s concerning the value and status of qualitative inquiry. In so doing, I hope to make it clear that the issue of grounding involves not simply the appreciation of a particular research technique but also questions of an epistemological nature (that is, questions regarding the assumptions that we make about the very bases for our understanding). In turn, these are part of a wider and highly productive debate about human inquiry and the social generation of scientific knowledge (for instance, see Denzin and Lincoln, 1994a).

In the first part of the chapter, an historical account of grounded theory will be presented that highlights some of the antecedents to the philosophy of this approach. Second, the fundamental analytical commitments of the grounded theorist, constant comparison and theoretical sampling, will be outlined. In the third section, the 'dilemma of qualitative method' will be discussed, and some unresolved critical issues will be identified that bear upon grounded theory and the qualitative paradigm of inquiry. Finally, I shall argue for a constructionist revision of the approach, in order to address the challenges raised by contemporary understandings of science and the research process.

The discovery of grounded theory

The idea of grounded theory, as both a method and a stance regarding the conduct of qualitative research, emerged in the 1960s against the backdrop of long-standing debates in the human sciences about the relative merits of qualitative and quantitative inquiry (see Hammersley, 1989). In their book, *The Discovery of Grounded Theory*, Glaser and Strauss (1967) observed that, at that time, sociological practice was almost exclusively reliant on quantitative methods (for example, survey research) and that the status of qualitative methods was essentially at an all-time low. One particular manifestation of this was a preoccupation with the quantitative testing of propositions derived from a few highly abstract, 'grand' theories (such as structural functionalist accounts). Glaser and Strauss argued that this led to theory that was impoverished, in the sense of having a restricted empirical relevance to any particular 'substantive' content domain. (This argument applies not just to sociology but to contemporary psychology, as well: see Rennie *et al.*, 1988; Henwood and Pidgeon, 1992, 1995a.) Closing this 'embarrassing gap between theory and empirical research' (Glaser and Strauss, 1967, p. vii) therefore required a radical change of philosophy, aimed at generating more local, contextual theory that would as a consequence 'work' and also be of relevance to those being studied.

Glaser and Strauss therefore chose the term 'grounded theory' in order to express the idea of theory that is generated by (or grounded in) an iterative process involving the continual sampling and analysis of qualitative data gathered from concrete settings, such as unstructured data obtained from interviews, participant observation and archival research. As one aspect of the close and detailed inspection of specific problem domains, grounded theory places great emphasis upon an attention to participants' own accounts of social and psychological events and of their associated local phenomenal and social worlds.

There are a number of historical antecedents to this perspective. In psychology, these can be traced back to the work of Wilhelm Dilthey (1894/1977), who, in arguments with the early experimentalists such as Hermann Ebbinghaus, maintained that the human sciences would be mistaken to pursue causal explanation at the expense of establishing understanding (*Verstehen* or 'meaning'). The idea of *Verstehen* subsequently became significant in interpretative phenomenology (see, for example, Schutz, 1962), which orients psychological inquiry towards everyday understandings and human subjectivity, as well as in the idiographic school of 1950s and 1960s psychology. Advocates of the latter, such as Allport (1962), argued that the uniqueness of an individual's 'personality' could not be captured by means of simple scores along abstracted statistical dimensions.

The roots of grounded theory can also be traced back more directly to the symbolic interactionist perspective of Herbert Blumer (1969b) and the case-study approach of the so-called Chicago school of social psychology and sociology in the 1920s and 1930s. Symbolic interactionism sees the individual's social world as enacted and hence as involving the interplay of significant gestures, symbols and systems of meanings embedded within a significant social context. This, in turn, requires the researcher to engage in interpretative work, unravelling the multiple perspectives and common-sense realities of the research participant. As in the case of grounded theory, this leads to a model for research that is flexible, that is carried out in everyday contexts and that has as its goal the (co-)construction of participants' symbolic worlds and social realities.

Analytical commitments: constant comparison and theoretical sampling

The method of grounded theory is suitable for use with almost any form of qualitative material, but, in approaching research without strong prior theory, the researcher is always faced with the analytical task of sorting and making sense of what is likely to be at first highly unstructured. In order to achieve this, Glaser and Strauss (1967) advocated the development of an open-ended indexing system, where a researcher works systematically through a basic data corpus, generating codes to refer both to low-level concepts and to more abstract categories and themes (see Chapter 7, by Karen Henwood and myself). This process can be characterized as one of moving towards a data representation language.

In the early phases of a grounded theory project, the researcher is allowed maximum flexibility in generating new categories from the data. This is a creative process that fully taxes the interpretative powers of the researcher, who is nevertheless disciplined by the requirement that low-level descriptions, in Glaser and Strauss's terms, should *fit* the data well. The aim throughout is to foster theory generation, and here Glaser and Strauss (1967) noted somewhat polemically (but not without good cause) that 'when generating is not clearly recognized as the main goal of a given research, it can be quickly killed by the twin critiques of accurate evidence and verified hypotheses' (p. 28). Hence, their approach was expressly concerned to overcome the tendency for the research process to be sterilized by overly rigid methodological prescriptions.

More recently, Strauss and Corbin (1994) point out that, although coding is a key feature of the method of grounded theory, the tendency by some commentators to identify grounded theory *merely* with a way of coding the content of an unstructured corpus of qualitative data has been misleading. One danger is that the approach risks dilution and becomes identified merely as a form of content analysis, a point echoed by Stern (1994), who comments that 'as a rule of thumb, when researchers present their work as grounded theory and it is something else, the something else is usually content analysis' (p. 214). Like protocol analysis (see Chapters 4 and 5, by Ken Gilhooly and Caroline Green), content analysis typically has a very different goal from that of theory generation, and it emphasizes the criteria of reliability and validity and the counting of instances within a *predefined* set of mutually exclusive and jointly exhaustive categories (see Weber, 1990). Accordingly, it is important to recognize that two fundamental analytical commitments shape the methodological stance adopted by Glaser and Strauss and clearly differentiate grounded theory from traditional content analysis or other forms of thematic analysis. These are the method of *constant comparison* and the use of *theoretical sampling*. Both are advocated primarily as means of generating theory, as well as of building conceptual and theoretical depth of analysis, and both are more than mere procedures for selecting and processing data.

The method of constant comparison defines the principal analytical task as one of continually sifting and comparing elements (such as basic data instances, cases, emergent categories and theoretical propositions) throughout the lifetime of a research project. By making such comparisons the researcher is sensitized to similarities and differences as a part of the exploration of the full range and complexity of a corpus of data, and these are used to promote conceptual and theoretical development. This comparison of basic data instances in an emergent category

> 'very soon starts to generate theoretical properties of the category. The analyst starts thinking in terms of the full range of types or continua of the category, its dimensions, the conditions under which it is pronounced or minimized, its major consequences, its relation to other categories, and its other properties.'
>
> (Glaser and Strauss, 1967, p. 106).

Theoretical sampling, on the other hand, involves the active sampling of new cases as the analysis proceeds. Since the goal of grounded theory is the elaboration of a conceptually rich, dense and contextually grounded account, there is no compunction to sample multiple cases where this would not extend or modify the emerging theory. Accordingly, sampling is often explicitly driven by theoretical concerns, with new cases being selected for their potential for generating new theory by extending or deepening the researcher's emergent understanding (and not merely for *generalizing* the findings of research, as would be the aim with the 'random' sampling more common in experimental and survey research). One consideration in theoretical sampling is so-called negative case analysis (for instance, Kidder, 1981), where the researcher explores cases that do not appear to fit an emerging conceptual system. This is invaluable because it serves to challenge initial assumptions and categories and hence can work as a check against the very real danger, noted by Turner (1981), of building indefensible arguments from a corpus of data. Negative case analysis is also one way in which sampling decisions become a part of the process of constant comparison.

Taken together, the commitments of constant comparison and theoretical sampling involve the researcher in a highly interactive and iterative process in which the traditional distinction between the data collection phase and the data analysis phase of a project often breaks down. Data analysis can (and ideally should) proceed as soon as sufficient material is collected to work on (rather than waiting until a predefined data set has been obtained), and this in turn feeds back into the sampling of new data. Charmaz (1990) commented:

> the 'groundedness' of this approach fundamentally results from these researchers' commitment to analyse what they actually observe in the field or in their data. If they find recurrent themes or issues in the data, then they need to follow up on them, which can, and often does, lead grounded theorists in unanticipated directions.
>
> (p. 1162)

This dynamic relation between data analysis and data collection is a critical characteristic of the whole approach.

Looking back, it is now clear that publication of *The Discovery of Grounded Theory* served a number of very useful purposes for researchers. First, by challenging the view that research in the human sciences should proceed solely by the quantitative testing of prior theory, it became used (and cited) as a manifesto by researchers who wished to break out of the confines of existing types of theory. Second, it pointed the way to more progressive, 'discovery'-based research, by highlighting the role that qualitative methods could play in the neglected activity of generating new ideas. Third, it demonstrated how such qualitative research could be systematic and yet simultaneously help to stimulate highly creative work. Finally, it made the case for valuing detailed, contextually sensitive, interpretative research in its own right and thus countered the frequently expressed view that research of this sort could only have the status of an exploratory investigation or a pilot study.

Nowadays, the term 'grounded theory' has come to mean a number of different things. Not only is it used to describe Glaser and Strauss's *method* for the systematic analysis of unstructured qualitative data (oriented around the principles of theoretical sampling and constant comparison), but it is also commonly used to refer to *theory*, where this is grounded closely in, or arises from, the detailed analysis of qualitative data. Furthermore, since one of Glaser and Strauss's (1967) original aims was to write a text that legitimated careful and systematic qualitative research, it is also no surprise to find the claim that a theory or piece of research is well grounded (for example, in data, in participants' accounts and life-worlds, in multiple subjectivities and so on) occurs frequently within qualitative social science as a rhetorical statement to signify the merits of a piece of work. In this latter sense, the expression 'well grounded' becomes a *warrant*.

The idea that 'grounding' is anything more than just a methodological procedure is bound up with the development of the contemporary debate over quantity versus quality in the human sciences. As Karen Henwood mentioned in Chapter 3, this debate has two interlinked variants, which have been termed the 'technical' and the 'epistemological' (Bryman, 1988). Developing some of the epistemological themes, Lincoln and Guba (1985) argued that a number of disparate theoretical and methodological developments in the human sciences could be brought together under the rubric of a unified qualitative or 'naturalistic' paradigm (see also the discussion of *contextualism* by Jaeger and Rosnow, 1988).

The qualitative paradigm shares a number of characteristics with the approach of grounded theory, including: an emphasis upon the importance of viewing the meaning of experience and behaviour in context and in its full complexity (and the use of qualitative data to 'access' this); a view of the scientific process as generating working hypotheses rather than immutable empirical facts; and an attitude towards theorizing that emphasizes the grounding of concepts in data rather than their imposition in terms of *a priori* theory. Put simply, the naturalistic inquirer:

> prefers to have the guiding substantive theory emerge from (be grounded in) the data because *no* a priori theory could possibly encompass the multiple realities that are likely to be encountered; because believing is seeing and [she] wishes to enter her transactions with respondents as neutrally as possible; because a priori theory is likely to be based on a priori generalizations, which, while they may make nomothetic sense, may nevertheless provide a poor idiographic fit to the situation encountered.
>
> (Lincoln and Guba, 1985, p. 41)

The dilemma of qualitative method

The case that has been made for a qualitative paradigm of inquiry is useful for psychology at the present time because it provides a rich foundation for new ways of defining relevant questions and of carrying out research. However, one immediate problem is that the renewed interest this brings in qualitative research might come to be viewed in *solely* technical terms. Accordingly, Guba and Lincoln (1994) have expressed a preference for viewing the discussion of the methodological aspects of qualitative techniques as being secondary to more paradigmatic concerns, specifically those of constructionism.

A second problem is that the notion of a paradigm simplifies and unifies what may in reality represent rather diverse, and at times incompatible, intellectual strands and positions (Henwood and Pidgeon, 1994; see also Chapter 3, by Karen Henwood). In particular, accounts of the qualitative or naturalistic 'paradigm' tend to gloss over a fundamental tension that Hammersley (1989) referred to as the *dilemma of qualitative method* (see also Chapter 12, by Martyn Hammersley). Put simply, this dilemma arises from a simultaneous commitment, on the one hand to realism and science (by claiming to reflect objectively the participants' accounts and perspectives) and, on the other hand, to constructionism through a recognition of the multiple perspectives and subjectivities inherent both in a symbolic interactionist world view and in the engagement of the researcher in the interpretative work of generating new understandings and theory. Hammersley concluded that there was as yet no qualitative method, including that of grounded theory, that had satisfactorily resolved the challenge involved in accommodating both the 'objective' and the 'subjective' in human sciences research.

The dilemma of qualitative method is writ large in many accounts of grounded theory, which often appeal both to inductivist–empiricist and to phenomenological–constructionist themes (including the present account!). As it was originally conceived, the approach is founded upon a critique of the technical appropriateness of quantification in research in the human sciences (for such things as context stripping, exclusion of meaning and so on) but did not challenge the received view of scientific inquiry in and of itself. These can be referred to as the 'intraparadigm' critiques of quantification (Guba and Lincoln, 1994). Of course, grounded theory was developed before (and hence is not fully sensitive to) the rejection of the scientific method inherent in the strong programme in the sociology of scientific knowledge (see, for example, Woolgar, 1988c), and the subsequent 'turn to text' in psychology and the human sciences that has accompanied this (see Potter and Wetherell, 1987; Gillett, 1995).

Given such a history, therefore, it is no surprise to find that some aspects of grounded theory appear to rest squarely upon a positivist, empiricist epistemology. This is most obviously seen when Glaser and Strauss (1967) talk of the way in which theory is 'discovered from' data: that is, they imply that a set of social or psychological relationships exist objectively in the world, are reflected in qualitative data, and hence are there to be 'captured' by any researcher who should happen to pass by. A first point is that the discovery model implies a somewhat over-determined and static notion of human experience and subjectivity, which contradicts the premises of symbolic interactionism with regard to the mobile and constructed nature of all meaning. The assumption that qualitative researchers can directly access their participants' lived experiences (and with it Glaser and Strauss's own conception of 'fit') is particularly problematic here.

For example, feminist researchers in the human sciences have long recognized the need fully to understand and begin research from the perspectives of women's experiences, in order to counter androcentric biases in mainstream social science theory as well as to give voice to women's lives and concerns (Reinharz, 1992). This has led many feminist researchers to advocate qualitative research, but they have at the same time acknowledged the impossibility of merely holding up a mirror to reality (for instance, Duelli Klein, 1983; Griffin, 1986; Henwood and Pidgeon, 1995b). A more extreme manifestation of this dilemma is to be found in the post-modern insistence that any idea of naturalism should be rejected on the grounds that experience is 'created in the social text written by the researcher' (Denzin and Lincoln, 1994b, p. 11), and that as a result a crisis of representation now confronts the practitioner of 'naturalistic' qualitative research.

Unpacking these arguments a little further, the derivation or discovery of general principles from a set of data or observations relies on acceptance of a classical notion of induction, which has traditionally been held to play a central role in science since its very inception. We should not, however, take a naïve view of it or its role in inquiry. In order to begin analysis, the researcher needs at least *some* theoretical resources to guide the process of interpretation and representation (see Riessman, 1993). Without the orientation provided by the researcher's prior understandings, no sense at all can be made of any data, whether qualitative or quantitative. Although this consideration is present in all forms of research, it becomes quickly apparent with qualitative work, where, as noted earlier, we are invariably faced with the problem of making sense of and organizing an unstructured and often initially 'meaningless' corpus of data. Accordingly, Glaser and Strauss (1967) themselves noted, almost as an aside, that 'the researcher does not approach reality as a tabula rasa' (p. 3), while Strauss and Corbin (1994) admitted that because of the polemical purpose of *The Discovery of Grounded Theory* the critical role played by theory and concepts that sensitize the trained researcher to certain aspects of a data corpus was left largely unexplicated. The latter authors also argued more directly that the qualitative techniques of grounded theory could be used to interrogate, modify and extend existing grounded theories through new data and cases (see, for example, Vaughan, 1992; Turner, 1994).

Constructionist revisions of grounded theory

If legitimate data are necessarily defined through theory, this in turn raises an important question: what grounds grounded theory? In the case of some research projects, it might be simplest to ignore this dilemma. Again, the danger here is that the approach risks being followed as if it were a prescriptive method, a standardized procedure for guaranteeing 'truth'. Indeed, this tendency can be seen to be encouraged by Strauss and Corbin (1990; also Strauss, 1987), who have developed grounded theory to incorporate hypothesis testing explicitly, so much so that Glaser (1992) has argued that their approach is no longer true to the ideals of the original (see also Stern, 1994).

Therefore, a more satisfactory resolution of the problem of grounding in grounded theory is to recognize that it makes no sense to claim that research can proceed *either* from testing prior theory alone *or* from a 'pure' inductive analysis of data. In the case of grounded theory, in particular, what appears to be the 'discovery' or 'emergence' of concepts and theory is in reality the result of a constant interplay between data and the researcher's developing concept-ualizations, a 'flip-flop' between ideas and research experience (Bulmer, 1979). This sort of process is better described as one of *theory generation* (rather than as one of discovery), something which is a central aspect of the social practice of science, as well as use of the grounded theory technique (see Henwood and Pidgeon, 1992). One should also note the critical role played by constant comparison and theoretical sampling in fostering such creative interplay.

Accordingly, some researchers have argued for a constructionist revision of grounded theory (Charmaz, 1990; Layder, 1993; Henwood and Pidgeon, 1995c).

Such a revision would capture more nearly the creative and dynamic character of the research process, and emphasize the active and constitutive analytical process of inserting new discourses into old systems of meaning. In perhaps the best developed account of this, Charmaz (1990) clarified how qualitative researchers need to have a perspective from which they actively seek to build their analyses, without merely 'applying' it to new data, problems or contexts. 'Researcher perspective', in Charmaz's terms, includes substantive interests that guide the questions to be asked, a philosophical stance or a school of thought that provides a store of sensitizing concepts, and the researcher's own personal experiences, priorities and values. Focusing upon the concepts provided by a school of thought, in particular, her description of the stance of grounded theory is that it 'implies a delicate balance between possessing a grounding in the discipline and pushing it further' (p. 1165). Seen from this perspective, the activity of engaging in qualitative research should not leave the data, the theory or the researcher unchanged.

One valid practical criticism of grounded theory is that some researchers (particularly those who are fairly new to the technique) find themselves unable to theorize beyond the everyday phenomenal worlds and local interactional contexts of their basic data and domain of inquiry. Under these circumstances, grounded theory indeed becomes no more than a glorified form of re-description or content analysis. A constructionist revision alerts the researcher to the fact that data should *guide* but certainly not *limit* theorizing (Layder, 1993), and in particular that the 'everyday' can (and often should) be interpreted in terms of wider social contexts and power relations (including the contexts and dynamics involved in the research setting itself: see Gubrium and Silverman, 1989). The constructionist revision also implies a move towards a more discursive form of analysis (see, for example, Potter and Wetherell, 1987; see also Chapter 10, by Jonathan Potter), so that certain elements of the grounded theory method (particularly that of constant comparison, with its emphasis upon exploration of variety and difference in meaning) might potentially serve as a vehicle for a form of deconstructive analysis.

Conclusions

This chapter has not sought to resolve all of the wide-ranging issues and questions raised when we consider the nature of grounding in qualitative psychological and social research. Of course, to some extent the value of grounded theory for psychology will ultimately depend upon the ability of researchers to use it to shed new theoretical light upon interesting and relevant research questions. The same is true of the entire qualitative 'paradigm' of inquiry and the turn to text more generally. One final conceptual issue that should be raised, however (and one that bridges the theoretical and practical aspects of grounded theory) is that of warranting the results of grounded studies. There are several paths that can be trodden here by grounded theorists, depending in part on their epistemological commitments as well as the stance that they take on the dilemma of qualitative method (see Henwood and Pidgeon, 1994).

As I noted earlier, Glaser and Strauss (1967) emphasized that the traditional criteria of 'reliability' and 'validity' could stultify the process of discovery, but they were not entirely clear whether or not grounded theory could be 'true' (and, therefore, in principle at least, subject to evaluation in terms of such criteria). Minimally, and if seen through the positivist–empiricist frame, the whole philosophy of much qualitative research is founded upon an explicit move towards increased validity. In Glaser and Strauss's work, this is captured by the notion that grounded theories should 'work', 'fit', and be recognizable and of relevance to those studied. This in turn implies that some form of validity criterion could be employed (perhaps in concert with checks on the reliability of a theoretical account, too: see, for example, Kirk and Miller, 1986; Strauss and Corbin, 1990; Miles and Huberman, 1994).

In this context, grounded theorists sometimes appeal to the criterion of 'respondent validation': in other words, a researcher's interpretations should subsequently be recognizable when presented to the participants in the study or to others within a similar social and interactional context. This is a technique that I and my colleagues used successfully in carrying out case studies of structural engineering projects that had resulted in disasters (see Pidgeon *et al.*, 1988). If participants agree with the researcher's account, then greater confidence can be attached to it. Unfortunately, there will always be circumstances in which this is inappropriate or impractical (because of the research topic, for ethical reasons, where several participants disagree or where the researcher's perspective is at variance with that of participants). A more fundamental problem arises because, as I noted earlier, we cannot simply hold up a mirror to reality, no matter how well grounded our account. This being so, and also bearing in mind the role that relations of discourse and power play in constituting both researchers' and participants' understandings, validity claims in qualitative research cannot be based solely, or in any simple way, upon appeals to the correspondence between accounts.

A second path, developed primarily by naturalistic researchers, is to argue that it is wholly inappropriate to assess interpretative qualitative research by the standard canons of quantitative research. Rather, radical alternative criteria must be sought that are sensitive to both the epistemology and methodology of qualitative research. Examples listed by Lincoln and Guba (1985) include the ideas of trustworthiness or 'goodness' criteria; the availability of an 'audit trail', so that another person can later check the process of theory generation and interpretation; the use of various checks to over-interpretation, such as negative case analysis; considerations surrounding the potential transferability of the findings of research from the original context of inquiry to other settings; and the extent to which researcher reflexivity is built into the process.

As befits a naturalistic paradigm, however, such criteria once again contain within them the germ of Hammersley's (1989) 'dilemma'. Seen, on the other hand, as guidance for good *scholarship* in qualitative research (rather than as ultimate arbiters of the 'truth') many of Lincoln and Guba's (1985) practical suggestions appear far less problematic. These include their recommendation that a researcher should externalize the analysis and the processes of interpretation (in the form of ongoing written category descriptions, theoretical memos and other representations; see Chapter 7, by Karen Henwood and myself) and the keeping of a 'reflexive journal', including the daily schedule and logistics of the study, methodological decisions as they occur and reflections on the role of the researcher's own values and interests.

In the final analysis, constructionist grounded theorists leave far behind them the false sense of security that comes from a belief in establishing absolute foundations for knowledge in either the rules of method or direct access to the empirical world. Instead, they enter the hermeneutic circle of multiple, partial and competing interpretations. However, this need not lead to a total scepticism with regard to the possibility of arriving at partial warrants for knowledge, since knowing, like seeing, always starts from some embodied, but socially situated, perspective (see Haraway, 1991). Harding (1991), a feminist philosopher, has made the important distinction here between 'weak' and 'strong' objectivity. Weak objectivity in science occurs when the multiple layers of subjectivity and interpretation (such as researcher perspective) are over-written or obscured, as is the case in traditional accounts of scientific practice. In moving towards strong objectivity the researcher makes public the full interpretative processes of knowledge production. The implications of producing strongly objective accounts with grounded theory have yet to be worked through. However, what is clear is that research that genuinely seeks to reveal (rather than to obscure) the social bases for knowledge does indeed have some claim to generate more adequate knowledge.

Acknowledgements

I wish to acknowledge the generous help of the late Barry Turner, who first introduced me to grounded theory and who taught me much about the art and craft of qualitative research. Karen Henwood collaborated in developing a number of the ideas in this chapter.

Chapter 7

Grounded theory: practical implementation

Nick Pidgeon and Karen Henwood

In this chapter, we shall describe some of the more practical aspects of grounded theory, in the gathering, the coding and particularly the analysis of qualitative data. This is an important task in the context of the present volume, because psychologists (perhaps more than any other group of social scientists) tend to expect fairly explicit practical guidelines and precedents on which to model their own research.

We shall not seek to privilege the approach of grounded theory above other existing or developing qualitative approaches or methods. In this respect, we note the rather unfortunate tendency found in some writings to present grounded theory as *the* generic form of qualitative social science. However, grounded theory can in our view play a vital role in encouraging productive psychological work, by laying out a set of flexible procedures for beginning the difficult task of rendering qualitative data meaningful, both in its own terms and in relation to the researcher's theoretical aims and interests (see Rennie *et al.*, 1988; Henwood and Pidgeon, 1992, 1995a; Charmaz, 1995). These procedures are not tantamount to standard tactics or rules which, if followed, could act as guarantees of truth. We would therefore anticipate the possible emergence of other, parallel tactics, and we would expect a degree of selectivity on the part of those who utilize the grounded theory approach. What matters is that we use grounded theory or other tactics in the course of our own research to engage actively in a close and detailed analysis of our research materials, in order that they can both stimulate and discipline the theoretical imagination (Henwood and Pidgeon, 1992).

One aspect of the grounded theory approach that we want to highlight is the requirement to document the analytical process fully. This serves not only as a trace but also as a prompt to further analysis, an important part of which is to force the tacit, the implicit or the subliminal to the surface of awareness (Turner, 1981). This process is not an easy one, and it is therefore helpful to think of grounded theory strategies as offering ways into the maze of a fractured and multiseamed reality that is infused with multiple and often conflicting interpretations and meanings. Indeed, grounded theory strategies and some of the writings on the subject may be of less help in finding ways out of such a maze (see Pidgeon *et al.*, 1991). Achieving this relies upon the researcher's commitment to generating a focused understanding of what led her or him to the particular research problem, together with an (ultimately) coherent account addressing it. In essence, breaking out of *a priori* theorizing using the grounded theory approach should not leave the theory, the data or the researcher unchanged.

We also want to draw attention to the observation that qualitative researchers who approach inquiry without strong or specific hypotheses are faced with the problem of dealing with large amounts of unstructured data. Grounded theory is useful for tackling this problem directly, by embarking on the analysis with a close, systematic inspection of the corpus of data. This will result in the generation of an array of concepts, categories and theoretical observations, which provide the building blocks for subsequent theorizing. As Nick Pidgeon noted in Chapter 6, this typically begins with the development of an open-ended indexing system, in which the researcher works through the basic data transcripts, generating labels to describe low-level features and more abstract concepts that are deemed to be relevant (or, in other words, a 'data representation language').

The grounded theory approach freely generates new categories from the data, particularly in the early phases. This is a creative process that fully taxes the researcher's interpretative powers. Nevertheless, at the same time, one is disciplined by the requirement that emergent categories should, in Glaser and Strauss's (1967) terms, 'fit' the data (or, in other words, provide a recognizable description). Success in generating theory that is well grounded in data therefore depends upon maintaining a balance between the full use of the researcher's own subjective understandings and the requirement of 'fit'. We shall now move on to develop our preliminary discussion with reference to specific strategies that are used in grounded theory work, illustrating these with examples taken from our own and other researchers' projects.

Overview: core steps, iteration and theoretical sampling

Although grounded theorists use maximum flexibility in qualitative data analysis, it is still useful to chart a number of steps in the overall scheme of moving from the collection of unstructured data through to the theoretical outcomes. These are illustrated in Fig. 7.1, but they will be described in greater detail in the following sections. In general terms, they guide a researcher along a path from unstructured materials, to the generation of descriptive codes, on to more developed conceptual understandings or links, and finally to wider theoretical interpretations. In the course of the following discussion, it may appear that these stages are being regarded as discrete steps. However, it is important to stress that analysis proceeds from data to outcomes in only a very loosely linear fashion. Grounded theory is an iterative process, and researchers often move between steps (and the steps merge into one another) as the analysis proceeds. More fundamentally, while many accounts of methodology in the social sciences imply that data collection and data analysis are separate phases, Glaser and Strauss (1967) insisted upon the importance of moving between the two. In particular, as Nick Pidgeon observed in Chapter 6, one might well wish to use early analyses to prompt further data collection by theoretical sampling or by returning to either

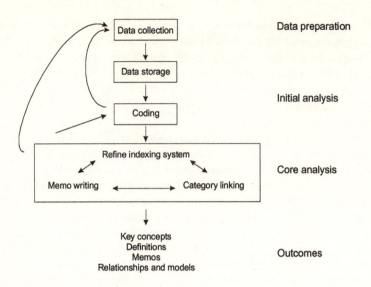

FIG. 7.1. *Grounded theory approach*

the original participants or others to explore aspects of the emerging interpretations further. This iterative stance is one facet of the 'flip-flop' process between the data and the researcher's conceptualizations.

By way of example of theoretical sampling, we can consider Glaser and Strauss's (1967) original methodological writings, which were themselves derived from their qualitative study of the awareness of dying (Glaser and Strauss, 1965). Their emergent theory posited that the 'perceived social value' of patients in hospital wards and the context of awareness in which dying occurred (including the extent of the patients' awareness of death, the expectations of death on the part of staff and patients, and the rate of death) were integral to the nurse–patient relationship and associated treatment regimes. This account had been developed explicitly by sampling different hospital wards, each selected in terms of the various aspects of awareness contexts; they included premature baby services, neurosurgical wards containing comatose patients, hospices for terminally ill patients, and accident and emergency units. Subsequently, this work was extended by cross-national comparisons, as indicated in the following research memo:

> The emphasis is upon extending the comparisons made in America in theoretically relevant ways. The probability of fruitful comparisons is increased very greatly by choosing different and widely contrasting countries. That is, the major unit of comparison is the country, not the type of hospital. . . . The selection of hospitals and services at which I would observe overseas will be guided, as in the current terminal study, by the conceptual framework developed to date. I will want to observe at hospitals, to begin with, where [four important] structural conditions

we have noted are different than in America. I will observe, where possible, in hospitals (or on wards) where all four conditions are maximally different from the usual American conditions; also where three are different, where two are different, and one. I shall also choose wards or services which will maximize some of the specific conditions studied in the United States; namely, wards where dying is predominately expected by staff and others where dying is relatively unexpected; wards where patients tend to know they are dying, and ones where they do not; wards where dying tends to be slow, and wards where [the] predominant mode of dying tends to be relatively rapid. I hope to observe on various of those wards patients who are of high as well as low social value, and will try to visit locales where conditions are such that very many patients tend to be of low social value, as well as where there would tend to be many patients of high social value.

(Glaser and Strauss, 1967, pp. 59–60)

Phases of data collection and the grounded theory approach to interviewing

Sampling considerations are of course interconnected with data collection, which in the grounded theory approach includes both initial and continuing phases. The aim, especially with early data collection, is to generate a 'rich' set of materials. Later on, as we have already indicated, these decisions tend to become more focused. Data sets may be drawn from any relevant source and are not restricted to any one mode of data gathering. Glaser and Strauss (1967) themselves explicitly encouraged the use of archival and other textual materials and a combination of sources and data types. However, in keeping with a commitment to phenomenological and contextual relevance, a common source is the research interview (often combined with some form of participant observation). This commitment leads grounded theorists who use interviews to view them as a 'directed conversation' and not as a closely controlled, monitored and measured pseudo-experiment (see, for example, Lofland and Lofland, 1983; Mishler, 1986).

The need to observe the conversational aspects of interviewing may be beyond question, in the sense that it is necessary to build a rapport with one's respondents. Consequently, research interviews tend to benefit from observing at least some of the 'rules' of politeness of human dialogue and social interaction, as a first step to facilitating a smooth flow or the exchange of information. The issue of direction is, however, quite vexed. In grounded theory terms, the question of 'when' and 'how' to direct (and, equally important, when *not* to do so) becomes framed by the concerns and dilemmas that are associated with the notions of work and fit. Grounded theorists are acutely aware of the potential dangers of overly directive interviewing in cutting off interesting theoretical leads or rich data and in unwittingly loading assumptions into the questions that are asked.

For example, Charmaz (1990, p. 1167) gave the following account of the dangers faced in her grounded theory study of the experiences and self-concepts of people suffering from a serious chronic illness, which was initially based on interviews:

Asking 'How did you decide to have the surgery?' assumes that the respondent decided. In contrast, 'How did you come to have surgery?' leaves things open. 'Who was most helpful to you during the crisis?' assumes that others were involved. 'Tell me what happened when you had the crisis' allows the researcher to piece events and people together before asking about helpful participants.

However, she concludes pragmatically that it would be misleading to view the 'loading' of questions as something that was always or necessarily destructive of the entire research process, since it might have specific purposes and beneficial outcomes in certain circumstances. She goes on to remark (p. 1167) that:

> Loaded questions [such as those above] may prove to be useful, when suitable and when raised in logical sequence, i.e. if the researcher senses that the patient played a part in the decision or already knows that other people were involved in the crisis. If not [such] questions may raise sticky issues at a time the respondent may not be able to face them.

Grounded theorists, then, try to follow an open-ended conversational style in interviewing, while not assuming that this is an unproblematic task. The tension between not losing sight of interesting theoretical issues that might require more directed questioning, and the dangers of becoming constrained by preformulated questioning, is at the heart of grounded theory work. A number of methodological texts in social science provide guidance on the strategies that can be adopted here (for example, Burgess, 1984; Robson, 1993). A wider set of issues flows from the often understated dilemmas posed by the inevitable, but complex, operation of power in the context of field work (see Gubrium and Silverman, 1989; Phoenix, 1990; Banister *et al.*, 1994).

Data preparation: the permanent record

For grounded theory work to proceed, the corpus of data must be assembled in some form of permanent record that allows ready access during analysis. Assuming that it has been desirable and possible to make tape recordings, some researchers prefer to treat these as their record and to conduct the analysis directly from them. Others transcribe the data from interviews and protocols. Transcription from tape is highly labour intensive. As a rule of thumb, it may take eight to ten hours to transcribe the basic content from a one-hour interview tape, although depending on the level of detail more time may be required (for example, if significant paralinguistic features are transcribed in addition: compare Chapters 10 and 11, by Jonathan Potter and Rosalind Gill). Another strategy is to transcribe only those aspects of the tape that feed into the developing analysis.

A frequent next step in handling each discrete data set (that from a single interview session, say) is to provide it with a label (for example, giving the date, the interviewee and the topic). Another is to allocate a numerical reference to the segments of the text. Typically, this involves numbering pages, paragraphs or

---

Box 7.1 Paragraphs from an interview relating to case study concerning hazardous waste

Interview with S., 27 April

Paragraph 8. I don't think there is any doubt that on this job I readily accepted the advice of the civil engineering consultant, L., and didn't have the experience to question that advice adequately. I was not aware of the appropriate site investigation procedure and was more than willing to be seduced by the idea that we could cut corners to save time and money.

Paragraph 9. But L.'s motives were entirely honourable in this respect. He had done a bit of prior work on a site nearby. And his whole approach was based upon the expectation that there would be fairly massive gravel beds lying over the clay valley bottom, and the fundamental question in that area was to establish what depth of piling was required for the factory foundations. He was assuming all along that piling was the problem. And he was not (and he knew he was not) experienced in looking for trouble for roads. His experience said that we merely needed a flight auger test to establish the pile depths.

Source: Architect S., a member of the design team involved in the incident, describing the decision of the civil engineering consultant, L., restricting the scope of the initial site investigation to the question of the need for piled foundations for warehouse units. (From Pidgeon *et al.*, 1988.)

---

lines in the transcription. Box 7.1 shows an example of how data are labelled in this manner. This is taken from a multidisciplinary investigation into the individual and organizational preconditions for accidents and safety failures in the UK construction industry (Pidgeon *et al.*, 1988). The research had taken a retrospective case-study approach, in which we interviewed design teams involved in the events being studied and also obtained relevant documents from them. This particular interview had been carried out with an architect who had been involved, with others, in a failure to predict the presence of hazardous chemical waste on an old industrial site that was being developed.

Initial analysis: coding

Having collected, transcribed (if appropriate) and labelled a sufficient quantity of material, the next task is to construct a second version of these data that will allow sorting and re-representation of the material as the interpretation develops. Some researchers achieve this by first photocopying or word processing the original material and then highlighting, cutting and pasting when similar themes occur. The technique that we describe here involves building an indexing system on file cards. This indexing or coding should proceed as soon as possible after the data collection has begun. A practical implication of this is that the interviewing timetable should ideally allow sufficient space between the sessions for some transcription and analysis.

Coding proceeds by means of the tentative development and labelling of concepts in the text that the researcher considers to be of potential relevance to the problem being studied. That this is a complex procedure (and, as Nick Pidgeon argued in Chapter 6, one that involves a constitutive relationship between the researcher and the text) is clear from the fact that judgement is always involved in this labelling process. The facets of the data that are coded will vary, depending upon how the aims of the research have been presented to the participants, the accounts that are subsequently offered by the participants, and the interpretations of the investigator.

To construct an indexing system, the researcher starts with the first paragraph of the transcript or notes and asks: 'What categories, concepts or labels do I need in order to account for what is of importance to me in this paragraph?' When a label is thought of, it is recorded as the header on a 5-inch by 8-inch file card (although, increasingly, computer packages are used to aid the mechanical tasks of indexing, searching and sorting: see Mangabeira, 1995; and see also Chapter 14, by Jonathan Smith). A précis of the data of interest, together with a reference to the specific transcript and paragraph, is noted on the card, and the latter is then filed in a central record box. This initial entry then serves as the first indicator for the concept described by the card header. The process of coding continues by checking whether further potentially significant aspects of the paragraph suggest new concepts, and this is repeated with subsequent paragraphs.

At this stage, the labels used in categorization may be long winded, ungainly or fanciful, and they may be formulated at any conceptual level that seems to be appropriate. What is crucial is that the terms should, to use Glaser and Strauss's (1967) term, 'fit' the data well, so that they provide a recognizable description of the item, activity or discourse that is under consideration. The active 'flip-flop' between the data and the researcher's developing conceptualizations demands a dynamic process of changing, rechanging and adjustment of the terms used until the fit can be improved.

Developing codes: the method of constant comparison

As coding continues, not only will the list of concepts (and hence file of cards) rapidly expand, but also concepts will begin to recur in subsequent paragraphs or transcripts. Box 7.2 lists the concepts coded from the two paragraphs in Box 7.1. Note that the concept 'experience' occurs in both paragraph 8 and paragraph 9. For the purposes of subsequent analysis, it is important to recognize that the aim is not to record *all* the instances where 'experience' occurs. In this respect, the grounded theory approach is very different from classical protocol analysis

> **Box 7.2 Significant concepts identified within the paragraphs shown in Box 7.1**
>
> Paragraph 8
> Accepting professional advice
> Criticizing other's work
> Cutting corners
> Experience
>
> Paragraph 9
> Knowledge of local conditions
> Selective problem representation obscures wider view
> Experience

(Ericsson and Simon, 1993; see also Chapters 4 and 5, by Ken Gilhooly and Caroline Green) and from content analysis (Weber, 1990; see also Chapter 10, by Jonathan Potter). In the case of the latter methods, the aim is primarily a counting exercise, that of recording how often a predefined concept is observed in the data set. However, the aim of grounded theory is to seek similarities and diversities, collecting a range of indicators that point to the multiple qualitative facets of a potentially significant concept.

The exercise of coding to explore similarities and differences is basic to implementing the method of constant comparison on which grounded theorists rely. In the present example, 'Experience' was first suggested (in paragraph 8 of Box 7.1) by the architect's belief that this is related to the ability to evaluate expert advice that one receives. In contrast, later (paragraph 9) he refers to the level of local knowledge held (in this case, regarding geological conditions). Both together allow a wider view of what the architect means when he is talking about 'experience', and an understanding of this category emerged from the interplay between the researcher's interpretation and variation in the data corpus. This use of constant comparison is integral to theoretical elaboration, which involves further theoretical sampling. The two examples of 'Experience' indicate that there are two somewhat different facets in the development of professional problem-solving expertise: technical knowledge and social evaluations. The question this then poses is: what other facets might there be, and in what other contexts (or samples) might they be manifest?

The success of the initial coding will depend in part on choosing an appropriate level of abstraction for the concepts in question. The use of particular terms ('member categories' or '*in vivo* codes': see Strauss and Corbin, 1990) that are derived directly from the interviewee's discourse (for instance, 'Cutting corners' in Box 7.2) will tie the analysis to the specific context of these data. Other terms (or 'researcher categories') refer to more theoretical ideas that have not been directly raised by the participants (for instance, 'Selective problem representation obscures wider view' in Box 7.2). A particularly difficult judgement for beginners to make here is the level of coding to be adopted: a common trap is to generate mainly member categories, with few researcher categories (or none at all), and this may in turn constrain subsequent theorizing. In this respect, training using seminars and group discussions of coding exercises is particularly beneficial (see also Turner, 1981; Strauss, 1987).

Figure 7.2 illustrates the final file card for the concept 'Selective problem representation obscures wider view', showing five of the entries that were made. The notion of a selective problem representation was an important one for the project, and it emerged in a number of guises, which these five entries illustrate. Once again, this highlights the importance of qualitative variety when coding each concept, in order to facilitate the process of constant comparison. As well as the card number, the concept's label and entries with references to the transcribed data, it is useful to include potential links with other concepts that appear on the cards. (In this example, a link with card 19, 'Perception of simplicity/ complexity of task', was suggested by the researcher's hypothesis that a representation of the problem would need to be appropriately matched to the complexity of the task.) At an early stage of coding, such links will be tentative, but they provide an important resource for the later analysis, particularly if it becomes necessary to specify relationships among significant concepts. It is worth noting that some cards will eventually contain relatively few instances; this need not mean that the relevant concepts are unimportant, but it does provide the researcher with a means of sifting for potentially irrelevant material.

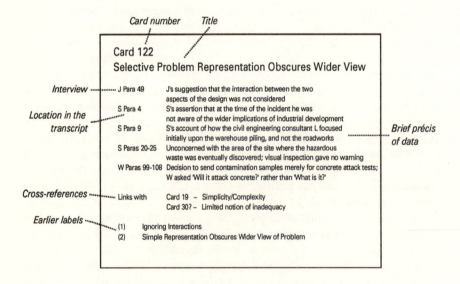

FIG. 7.2. *Example of a concept card from Pidgeon* et al. *(1988)*

Core analysis

The process of coding can be interrupted at any time by the collection of further data. However, as the number of concepts increases, some indexed to many facets of the data and others to few, the analysis involves other operations. The coded concepts must be refined, extended and related to each other as additional material is explored. Activities such as memo writing, refining the indexing system (for instance, by category development and writing definitions) and category integration – which Strauss and Corbin (1990) term 'axial coding' – are all useful for taking the analytical process forward (see Fig. 7.1). We present three examples to highlight these.

Memo writing and category splitting

Theoretical memos are typically generated in parallel to, and are often stimulated by, the coding analytical process. Some researchers build up a separate record system for filing these memos. Their contents are not constrained in any way and can include: hunches; comments on new samples to be checked out; explanations of modifications to categories; emerging theoretical reflections; and links to the literature. It is important to write a memo as soon as the thought has occurred, for, if left unrecorded, it is likely to be forgotten. In addition to externalizing the process of data analysis, the act of writing memos can frequently stimulate further theorizing.

In a study of the relationships between mothers and adult daughters, Karen Henwood (1993) conducted 60 interviews, each lasting one to one and a half hours, with mothers (who were aged from 50 to over 80) and daughters (who were aged between 18 and 49) concerning their relationships with their own mothers or daughters. The initial coding of the interviews led to the development of a long and varied, but highly unwieldy, list of instances under the initial label 'Relational closeness'. The permanent record of the interviews in this study took the form of a more detailed transcription using conventions derived from discourse analysis. (It may be noted, in passing, that guidance on such conventions is not typically provided in thematically based writings on grounded theory.) This type of record makes it possible to explore language either as representation or as action in use, and it can in turn play a role in framing analysis. The grounded theory part of the analysis proceeded by refining the core category 'Relational closeness', at first simply by means of dividing it into two cards, roughly on the lines of positive and negative evaluative themes. A memo concerning this splitting of the concept of closeness is shown in Box 7.3.

The majority of the attributes that had been coded on the original card headed 'Relational closeness' were glossed as attaching global value to the relationship: for instance, feelings of fondness and affection; an ability to confide about personal matters; feeling comfortable as opposed to lacking self-consciousness in each other's company. The features that were coded subsequently indicated a

---

Box 7.3 Example memo from the mothers-and-daughters project

Memorandum: On splitting of relational closeness
(July 1992 by Karen Henwood)

Splitting of this category (Relational closeness) became necessary initially in order to make it more manageable. The splitting also provides a fruitful starting point for reflecting upon the relationship between certain categories: (1) closeness and the 'gender marking' of the mother–daughter bond; and (2) closeness/overcloseness and represent-ations of the good/bad mother. Not uncommonly, ascriptions of valued mother–daughter closeness are also associated with the assumption that women share a special feminine gender identity, including among other attributes those of selfless cooperation, nurturance and empathy (see, e.g., interview with R.M., 21 August 1991, p. 26, lines 401–435). In identifying the special qualities in mother–daughter relationships which follow from the presumed sharing of a feminine identity and gender roles, the women interviewed in this study may be pointing to a view of mother–daughter relationships as uniquely, and perhaps even universally, close. This has been a key element in social science thinking for many years (Young and Wilmott, 1957).

However, the emergence of the other side of the coin – over-closeness – suggests that such closeness may be an idealized view of mother–daughter relationships which is complicit with cultural definitions of femininity; tentatively therefore we could say that it is part of a wider 'femininity discourse'. My reasoning here is derived from research on cultural representations of motherhood, which suggest that dichotomous images of the 'good and bad' mother simultaneously idealize and devalue women. This was first brought to mind by the use in some of the interviews (with C.N. and D.P.) of powerful metaphors of demon-like mothers who clutch on to their children or keep them on an apron string. These are coded on both 'overcloseness' and the 'good/bad mother' cards.

Following the lines of such reasoning, the source of at least one interviewee's (V.V.) sadness and hurt in her relationship with her daughter could only be understood by inferring that the daughter has contravened some extra-locally organized standard of conduct for adult daughters, which obliges them to be closely involved with their mothers over matters such as the care of the daughter's children.

Source: Henwood (1993).

---

much more mixed view of the emotional intensity of the relationship, ranging from a welcome but painful sense of gratitude and debt to a state of hypersensitivity (in which, for example, a mother's remarks could 'pierce into' her daughter) and a desire to flee from a relationship that involved confinement or smothering. However, the inextricable link between the two concepts resulting from this subdivision was retained and was coded through their respective labels

'Closeness' and 'Overcloseness'. This link then became a key stimulus and focus for conceptual integration and theoretical development and reflection, in turn mediated by the writing of subsequent analytical memos.

Writing definitions

Operations such as splitting categories, converting two categories into one or relabelling categories are likely to occur repeatedly at an early stage of analysis (and a record of the previous labels used for a category can be useful for keeping track of the analytical process). However, there comes a time when the collection and coding of additional data no longer contribute further insights. At this point, a category may become 'saturated', to use Glaser and Strauss's (1967) term. The researcher's task is then to try to make the analysis more explicit by summarizing why all the entries have been included under the same label. One way of doing this is to write a definition for the concept that explicitly states the qualities that were already recognized in an implicit manner when a new entry was classified under the relevant category (Turner, 1981). This is a demanding task, but one that can nevertheless be crucial to the analysis. It can lead to the development of a deeper and more precise understanding of the nature of the category and the analyst's interpretations of it.

Borrill and Iljon Foreman (in press) carried out an evaluation of a brief cognitive–behavioural programme for alleviating the fear of flying. This was based on interview data obtained from ten clients who were judged to have been treated successfully at the end of the therapeutic programme. Borrill and Iljon Foreman used the clients' understandings of the therapy to inform the clinicians about how change had occurred. These were coded in terms of six core categories: 'Establishing the therapeutic relationship'; 'Tolerance of anxiety'; 'Rational thinking'; 'Facing up to fear'; 'Trusting and being trusted'; and 'Joining the club'.

To illustrate the process of definition writing, we will use Borrill and Iljon Foreman's work in defining the category 'Tolerance of anxiety', which in addition reflects the researchers' wider interest in control over debilitating psychological and behavioural states. The member concept in question was indicated by various comments, including the following:

> You don't have to like it but you want to tolerate it – and that's what I draw on today.

> . . . and now I think it's perfectly O.K. to feel anxious and just to let it happen, but I can control it.

> I think: Oh, it's there again. . . . It's like having a pain in a foot or something; just wait for it to go, and carry on with your business.

> I can say: Sabre-toothed tiger, come and get me. Because I know it's not a real tiger, I won't actually be killed by it.

Box 7.4 Example definition from the fear-of-flying study

'Tolerance of anxiety'

This category is concerned with allowing the physiological symptoms of anxiety to be experienced in order to change cognitions about the consequences of anxiety. The first stage of this process is for the client to be able to access knowledge of the underlying physiological mechanisms of anxiety, which provides a rational explanation for the symptoms. The client is then encouraged to experience emotional arousal; when this is not followed by adverse consequences, a process of cognitive invalidation begins. The final stage is when the threat is seen as unreal, and the symptoms become cognitively relabelled, either as discomfort or as excitement. The therapeutic power of this process lies in its potential for generalization: i.e., clients who perceive that through tolerating anxiety symptoms they can exert control over them, can use this in other situations of emotional arousal.

Source: Borrill and Iljon Foreman (in press).

Incidentally, it is interesting that this member category (defined as such because it appeared verbatim in at least one of the interview transcripts) at the same time expresses the language and perspective of the therapist. One aim of this study was to inquire into how much of the cognitive–behavioural therapy, designed to produce tolerance, was assimilated by the clients.

By writing a definition of this category, the researcher is able to show how the respondents' understandings of their experiences of anxiety had become decoupled from the feared consequences (for example, crashing or panic attacks); it was this decoupling that seemed to make tolerance possible. The researchers also identified a number of stages in the process of attaining tolerance, which again were referred back to the respondents' remarks: 'Accessing knowledge about symptoms', 'Emotional arousal without adverse consequences' and 'Cognitive relabelling'. Their final definition, shown in Box 7.4, also formed part of the written report of the work, and linked these elements more directly with the theoretical frameworks used in cognitive–behavioural therapy.

Category integration

Later stages of analysis are also likely to involve attempts to integrate the emerging categories by creating links between them. In addition to exploring the links suggested in the course of coding and memo writing, it is often useful to sort and group sets of related concepts. This might involve drawing up various forms of diagrammatic representation, such as matrices or flow charts, to illustrate salient links between the concepts (see, for instance, Miles and Huberman, 1994). Borrill and Iljon Foreman (in press) provided one demonstration of this technique by using their categories to inspire an overall diagram that modelled the workings of cognitive–behavioural therapy. At this stage of analysis, their aim was not mere representation, but to recount the interrelationships between the categories in the light of their wider theoretical relevance. This is the crucial final stage in the way out of the maze to a grounded *theory*.

One example where this stage is achieved is in Currie's (1988) study of reproductive decision making. She began her study from a position of dissatisfaction and scepticism towards existing theoretical accounts of both pregnancy and reproductive decision making. In her search for a new approach that could encompass both the participants' lived experiences and their socio-structural circumstances, she analysed data from unstructured interviews carried out with 76 London women concerning their postponement or their rejection of motherhood. Initially, Currie developed a variety of member categories (namely 'Deliberations on motherhood', 'Right time' and 'Feelings of conflict and guilt'). She then went on to establish a dense, fine-grained and multifaceted theoretical account of the interconnections between them, which can be summarized as follows.

Currie documented a mixture of positive and negative themes in her participants' 'Deliberations on motherhood', and she inferred from this that her participants were exhibiting an ambivalence towards this issue. Motherhood, she suggested, offered an 'impossible' choice of relational rewards at the expense of material disadvantage. In other words, the lack of any conclusive reasons either for or against motherhood was connected to the way in which her participants' decisions often rested ultimately on the notion of a 'Right time', which was a core category in her analysis. This was interpreted by Currie as a personal resolution by her respondents of the material constraints upon motherhood (for example, attaining financial and career security, and the ability to employ child care).

In addition, the rhetoric of 'reproductive freedom' was identified as a further ideological barrier to the women's realization that they had internalized structural antagonisms as personal ones. Currie maintained that 'by discussing their experiences in a biographical context of "time" rather than a social one of "process", women's own decision making often remained inexplicable even to themselves' (p. 248). In short, her global analysis was that the 'Feelings of conflict and guilt' that marked these women's decision making were the inevitable outcome of a personalization of problems that were generated by material structural processes, and that these feelings occurred irrespective of any final decision the women may have made either to have children or not to have children.

We have argued elsewhere that Currie's application of grounded theory enabled her to interweave details of her participants' discourse with her own readings as a feminist researcher and trained social scientist, rather than providing a strict redescription (see Henwood and Pidgeon, 1995b). Her exploration of similarities and differences between and within both categories and her participants' accounts illustrates the use of constant comparison. Currie also made it clear where she had raised descriptive categories to an analytical level. The most obvious example is the way that Currie identified 'Right time' as a euphemism, since it referred not to chronological time at all but rather to a configuration of socio-material circumstances. Taken together, these practical and textual devices render explicit the constructed nature of the analysis and account, in which a range of interconnections were being made between the member categories and the researcher categories. In this sense, Currie was also *reflexively* incorporating into her account the process and origin of her emerging theoretical interpretation.

Conclusions

By discussing the implementation of the grounded theory approach, we have seen some of the ways in which it is being used by psychologists, as well as by others working on psychologically relevant problems. There are a number of reasons to believe that this approach will increasingly be used, as psychologists seek to answer questions that cannot be addressed through traditional experimental methods. Another significant trend is the advent of computer software packages developed for category generation and, in some cases, theory-building applications in empirical qualitative social science (Fielding and Lee, 1991; Kelle, 1995; Weitzman and Miles, 1995). There are many improvements that still need to be made to these packages, and they will not remove the need for hard interpretative work, upon which good qualitative analysis depends. Their development does, however, bring the benefit of being able to carry out such operations as indexing and searching on large and complex data sets. This latter consideration is particularly important, given that grounded theorists are typically interested in substantive problems and multiple contextual domains in the move towards formal theorizing.

Of course, not all psychologists who carry out qualitative research require large samples. For example, research questions asked by discourse analysts are usually concerned continually to interrogate the assumptions and diverse and contradictory meanings that are to be found in texts (see Chapters 10 and 11, by Jonathan Potter and Rosalind Gill). We can all learn a good deal from this close attention to the signifying properties of qualitative data when construed as language. Certainly, in our own work, it helps us to understand the complexities, multiplicities and shifts of meanings that cannot be avoided when doing qualitative work. There is a palpable difference between the approaches of grounded theory and discourse analysis: the former aims for coherence in its final account (even if it does not always achieve it), whereas the latter sets its stall in undermining coherence by promoting distrust and constant deconstruction of accounts. However, it is possible to look beyond this difference to argue that good grounded theory must constantly address diversity en route to its goal. The other side of the coin is that discourse analysis theory cannot entirely free itself from organizing principles (such as values and judgements) if it is to provide a communicable narrative account (see, for instance, Gill, 1995). In our view, these may well be productive tensions for qualitative psychology in the immediate future.

To return to grounded theory: as originally conceived, its goal was to build comprehensive theoretical systems from purposively sampled sets of relevant cases. However, it may not be possible to realize such an ambitious goal in all projects. We have found this to be a particularly important issue for researchers starting out upon their own qualitative studies, who may have to accept more achievable goals for preliminary or small-scale investigations. Indeed, one can specify a range of research activities that can be achieved using grounded theory, but that do not require the building of a total conceptual system. These would include: basic taxonomy development; focused conceptual development; and cycles of interpretation.

A final and particularly important issue for all forms of qualitative psychology is the evaluation of the research outcomes. Elsewhere, we have documented a number of principles that might be used to assess qualitative research projects based on grounded theory (see Henwood and Pidgeon, 1992; see also Chapter 8, by Nick Pidgeon). The various projects considered as examples in the present chapter would all lend themselves to assessment in terms of such criteria. For example:

(1)   Was respondent validation attempted?
(2)   How well documented was the process of analysis?
(3)   Were concepts linked together in justified ways?
(4)   Was the problem of reflexivity (the role played by personal, ideological and cultural assumptions in knowledge) addressed?

Equally, as we have also argued elsewhere (Henwood and Pidgeon, 1994; see also Chapter 3, by Karen Henwood), the issue of criteria cannot be subsumed within one unifying framework. Depending in particular upon the aims of each project and the researcher's epistemological position, quite different evaluative criteria may need to be applied.

Chapter 8

Ethnography: theoretical background

Christina Toren

Ethnography is the comparative, descriptive analysis of the everyday, of what is taken for granted. However, I should be leading the reader astray if I suggested that ethnography was easy to do, that its methods were 'obvious', or that in this chapter and the next Janet Rachel and I could deliver a neat package of recipes for the reader to go out and apply. So what I aim to do instead is to suggest how very enlightening ethnography can be, even though, from the point of view of the psychologist or of other social scientists, it may appear to be unwieldy, to take too long, to encompass too much or, worst of all, to be simply 'subjective'.

'Ethnography' is the term applied to the analytical descriptions produced by anthropologists. Traditionally, these have been descriptions of the lives of people who live, for example, in New Guinea, the Amazon, Africa, India and South-East Asia, of European peasants or of the native peoples of North America and of the Pacific. Ethnographic analysis has undergone significant change since its earliest manifestations in the writings of Bronislaw Malinowski, who held the first chair in social anthropology at the London School of Economics, and Franz Boas, the founder of American cultural anthropology. However, its primary method of data gathering is still that of participant observation.

Participant observation is the most radical of all the qualitative methods, and properly used it can produce data that are enlightening precisely to the extent that they are unlooked for. It is a method that can be applied to any people, anywhere. Indeed, ethnographic studies, especially in fields such as health and illness, are increasingly being carried out 'at home'. But the use of the ethnographic method 'at home' is crucially dependent upon the insights gained from the existing corpus of 'exotic' studies. An understanding of the validity of other people's descriptions of the world and of how these descriptions are historically constituted throws into question your own taken-for-granted assumptions and thus prompts their ethnographic analysis. For example, ethnographic studies make it clear not only that our own ideas of kinship are no more valid that anyone else's, but also that domains of relationship such as kinship or political economy always have implications for one another. Thus, the idea of the nuclear family is congruent with a capitalist economy, while the idea that your kin at their widest extent take in all of the members of some named group is congruent with a subsistence economy in which land tenure and production, circulation and exchange are all articulated in terms of relations among kin.

In this chapter, I shall try to give a brief account of what constitutes, in my view, the ideal contemporary approach to ethnography 'at home': one that is open, phenomenologically oriented, reflexive and free of predetermined hypotheses. This is not to say that ethnography is ever 'theory free' or that it is ever possible to carry out 'theory free' research. Indeed, perhaps the most useful insight to be gained from contemporary anthropology is that everyone, everywhere, is always and inevitably enmeshed in historical processes. From the analysts' point of view, this means that their first obligation is to interrogate the history of their own explicit and implicit theories, and, having done so, to make these theories play reflexively against the data which they gather through participant observation and other methods.

To begin with, I want to make five basic points. Practical examples of each point can be found in Chapter 9, by Janet Rachel. The first is that ethnography is directed towards the analysis of contemporary collective processes as these are manifest in the day-to-day relations between particular persons. Ethnography is self-consciously historical and comparative. Analysts begin with the awareness that they are at once a product and a producer of history, and hence that their analysis is itself historically constituted and cannot be otherwise. The comparative thrust of ethnography resides in the way that both data and analysis are inevitably (if only implicitly) made to play reflexively against the analyst's own under-standings. And, while any particular ethnographer may glory in the theory that emerges from the analysis, it is obvious that what is most important from the point of view of those who come after is the quality of the field data. These should be so rich and detailed as potentially to allow for reanalysis in the light of new field data or a different theoretical position.

My second point is that participant observation is not so much a method as a particularly intense way of living, a day-to-day experience in which you are simultaneously caught up and distant: at once a participant and a questioning observer of your own and others' participation in ordinary events. Anthropologists tend to complain that they were poorly trained, unprepared for the field. This is true even nowadays because, while we all go into the field armed with a battery of methods and having previously read a good portion of the existing ethnography on our area, nothing can prepare field workers for the intensity of the field work experience, during which they come to understand what participant observation means. In other words, you end up teaching yourself.

The third point is that, in the course of the day-to-day experience of participant observation, nothing that is said or done by yourself or the people with whom you are working is irrelevant. You have to be constantly on the *qui vive*, to ask yourself not only what people are doing, but how they come to be doing it, and most important to question too your own ideas about the 'what' and the 'how'. The discipline of writing up field notes is vital here because the obsessional and detailed description of the most ordinary and everyday details feeds back, as it were, into your capacity for noticing, so that you become better and better at participating, better and better at observing, and better and better at writing down your observations.

The fourth point is that participation is just as important as observation, and this is as true for your field notes as it is for everyday activities. In other words, you should be there in your field notes, because this is *you* seeing and *you* conversing, and what *you* say is just as important as what your informants say. If you're amused, you write it down; if you're angry, you write it down; if you're bored, you write it down. You always include your own responses to what is happening or what is said. When the time comes to analyse the data gathered, this practice forces analysts at once to recognize and to incorporate into their analysis the awareness that it is informed not only by the data that have been gathered, but by the ideas that the analyst brings to the collection of those data and to the analysis, ideas which themselves have a history, one that implicates particular forms of relations among the people with whom the analyst lives.

My final point is that the method of participant observation is directed in large part towards what is taken for granted. For ethnographers at home, it can be immensely difficult to get at what this might encompass, precisely because they are themselves at once a product and a producer of the very historically constituted processes which they are trying to describe and analyse. In other words, the ethnographer at home is almost bound to take for granted ideas and practices that should themselves be a focus for analysis.

In short, ethnography is the analysis of the way in which collective relations between people at large inform what particular persons, considered as historically located subjects, do and say. The idea is that everyone, everywhere, including ourselves, is the locus of the relations in which we engage with others and in which others engage with us. So, however small and circumscribed the situation upon which the ethnographer initially focuses, it will inevitably prove to have ramifying implications in respect of collective processes that go well beyond that initial focus. To show why this is so, I am going to try to demonstrate here why it would be extraordinarily interesting to set about doing an ethnographic study of a situation in which we, as social scientists, might find ourselves: for example, the situation of a workshop on the use of qualitative methods in psychology, such as one of the workshops to which John Richardson referred in Chapter 1 and from which all the chapters in this volume have been derived. Such a study would, I suggest, throw into question certain of our existing analytical categories and suggest a perspective from which they might be reworked to achieve greater validity.

Rendering strange what we take as given

I begin my proposed study of a hypothetical workshop on qualitative methods in psychology with a deliberate attempt to render strange what we as students of psychology or as social scientists take to be perfectly ordinary. To do this, I make those attending the workshop (including myself) objects of analysis to produce a crude, partial, and necessarily brief, account of our historical position. (My readers will no doubt recognize that they too are implicated here.) I use the present tense as a rhetorical device in order to make my account more vivid. What follows may be taken as the 'starting point' for a study of certain of the ideas that underpin the human and social sciences.

Account of a hypothetical workshop on qualitative methods in psychology

Qualitative methods having become of increasing interest to a broad range of human scientists, a number of them meet together to hold a workshop on the subject. Strictly speaking, a workshop is a room or building in which manufacture is carried out; however, as used here the term refers to the manufacture not of material objects but of abstractions, of abstract ideas that might be used to study what humans do and say. This meeting takes place outside term time: that is to say, at a time when the participants are not obliged to be teaching in their respective institutions, mostly universities devoted to the pursuit of knowledge in manifold forms. The primary tasks of persons employed as human scientists in universities are said to be those, first, of teaching others who themselves wish either to become human scientists or to understand something of the human sciences, and, second, of researching areas of interest to other human scientists in order to increase knowledge in this domain. While human scientists (like other academics) say that much of their working time is given over to administration (that is to say, to the maintenance and reproduction of the institutional structure of the university itself), they tend to consider this aspect of their practice to be irrelevant to the nature of the knowledge that they produce.

Human scientists are a particular kind of specialist in the pursuit of knowledge. The very notion of 'knowledge' is crucial to people with a generically European history and informs relations between them wherever they are found. While other peoples also have a concept of knowledge and are likely too to have ideas of specialist or expert knowledge in particular domains, it is not always the case that value is placed on knowledge in the abstract, and neither is it the case that everywhere, among all peoples, forms of knowledge are hierarchically ranked.

However, in the case of peoples with a generically European history, the abstract notion of knowledge constitutes in itself a value of massive cultural weight. This is because, while knowledge for these people may pertain to any domain, it takes its most highly valued form in the invention and elaboration of concrete technologies of control over universal physical processes and over physiological processes in the people themselves. These technologies of control inform politico-economic relations across collectivities and between people within them. Historically, the elaboration of knowledge into concrete technologies of control both allowed for and justified the colonial expansion of Europe into the rest of the world. It has underwritten and continues to underwrite a distinction between civilization and barbarism, today transformed into one between developed and under-developed or between the complex and the simple. It has informed, and still informs, notions of evolution as progress so that many (perhaps most) Europeans still hold to the idea that they are a 'race' (that is to say, different in kind from other peoples) and that, as such, they are more intelligent, more knowledgeable, than those others.

Considered as specialists within the hierarchy of knowledge, human scientists are one of the lesser-valued forms in that they have been unable (at least so far) to produce reliable technologies with reliable material effects. It is this perceived failure, rather than the supposed greater objectivity of other sciences, that underwrites the distinction between the 'hard' sciences of physics, chemistry, biology, and so on, and the 'soft' human sciences. However, given the value that is placed on pushing out the boundaries of knowledge in any domain that *might* have technological implications, given the high salience of knowledge in relations of power within and across collectivities, and given that the politico-economic processes in the collectivities within which human scientists work can be broadly characterized as capitalist and democratic, they are allowed and enabled to pursue their particular specialty.

Human scientists are interested in understanding what makes humans what they are, how they come to do the things they do. To deserve the name, they have to have had a university training and, in the case of those who take part in the workshop on qualitative methods, most of them are psychologists. Psychology is a particular branch of inquiry in the human sciences. The broad aims of psychology, since its appearance in the 19th century as a distinct domain of inquiry, have been to discover everything possible about the 'mind'. The history of psychology has traditionally rested on the Cartesian distinction between matter and spirit, or body and mind, and even today the subdisciplinary branches of psychology still implicate that distinction. For example, psychologists make distinctions between cognitive, developmental, social, clinical and other domains of the discipline. In contemporary psychology, these domain distinctions are beginning to break down. The workshop itself is a partial manifestation of that breakdown, in that when the ethnographer studied psychology as an undergraduate at University College London in the late 1970s, the notion that qualitative methods might be applicable to psychological investigations was virtually non-existent; at that time, any aspect of behaviour that came under the rubric of the 'social' or the 'cultural' could only be a source of 'error', something that got in the way of what might otherwise have been a good experimental design. All the partipants in the workshop would probably argue that psychology is in the process of undergoing radical change.

However, from the ethnographer's point of view, psychology considered as the product of what psychologists do, and what they write about what they do, is inevitably rooted in its own history, and it is this history that the ethnographer wants to render sufficiently transparent to suggest how it informs current practice such as the workshop on qualitative methods.

All those present at the workshop (including the ethnographer) are interested in what makes humans what they are, in how humans come to know the things they know and do the things they do. However, from the ethnographer's point of view, and bearing too on her own practice, this in itself is a peculiar endeavour. The participants may feel inclined to protest about this view on the grounds that, everywhere in the world, people have notions about the physical and spiritual substance of themselves and others; everywhere people have ideas about what informs the behaviour of the people they know, about how children become adults, about what leads people to do this or that, about how they come to know what they know. But in human scientists these everyday interests take on a particular, historically specific form, for these people are engaged in an institutionalized endeavour to explain systematically the nature of the human mind and human behaviour.

They take it to be self-evident that this is an important and worthwhile endeavour, but how did they come to assume this was so? Here, it is important to realize that the history of generically European science and, in this case, the history of psychology, is closely bound up with the history of other ideas and practices that, for the most part, human scientists take for granted. Perhaps the most important of these ideas is that of 'the individual in society', for it implicates all those other binary distinctions that human scientists are used to making between culture and biology, mind and body, subject and object, structure and process, rationality and emotion, and so on.

From the ethnographer's point of view, this idea of 'the individual in society' cannot be taken to be self-evident. Rather, it has to be viewed as just one, historically specific, idea of the person, and as such it can be compared with all those other, equally valid, but very different, ideas of the person held by other peoples. Ideas of the person are always crucial to any ethnographic analysis because inevitably they inform people's day-to-day relationships and their collective life as this may be described in terms of political economy, religion, kinship, and so on. The human science notion of the person as 'an individual in society' has its historical roots in the Protestant Reformation, in 18th and 19th century theories of classical economics, in the Industrial Revolution and the development of worldwide markets, in the further elaboration of the dissenting churches' notion that all persons were equal in the eyes of God, in the rise of democracy based on universal suffrage as a form of government, in the legal axiom that all persons have equal rights before the law and, importantly, in Spencerian ideas of 'social evolution' as 'progress', which preceded and which, at least in popular understanding, were grafted on to Darwinian ideas of biological evolution.

Human scientists in general, and psychologists in particular, tend (at least in respect of what they write) to take the idea of 'the individual in society' to be axiomatic. As such, it remains at once unexamined and fundamental to their theories about humans. It goes along with a distinction between 'biology' and 'culture' that implicitly renders biology an ahistorical given, such that 'history' can refer only to a subset of what is human: that is, to 'culture'. But, from the ethnographer's point of view, biology is a domain of human knowledge, and as such it cannot provide a transparent, objective description of the material substance of humans. Biology too has a history, and, while human scientists may acknowledge that this is so, paradoxically this awareness does not usually inform their theories of human psychologies or of human politico-economic processes.

So, for instance, to take but one example, human scientists who are concerned with gender tend to argue that the biology of sexual distinctions is given, immutable, outside history and that it can axiomatically be distinguished from gender, which is in history and thus 'culturally constructed'. From the ethnographer's point of view this idea is paradoxical, one might even say bizarre. For it cannot be the case that any aspect of ideas is immune from history. This means that the human scientists' idea that one can make a distinction between 'sex as biologically given' and 'gender as culturally constructed' is not so much a theory of gender as a contemporary transformation of an earlier distinction between 'sex' and 'sex role', between 'nature' and 'nurture'. From the ethnographer's point of view, the making of this distinction itself constitutes the historically specific concept of gender that is held by human scientists.

This becomes plain when we look at how the domain of gender is constituted by human scientists and compare it with how gender is constituted, by, for example, various New Guinea peoples. Human scientists make the whole person identical with their biological sex; from this point of view, each human is through and through either a biologically female individual or a biologically male individual. Indeed, this thoroughgoing distinction is, in English, enshrined in the pronouns 'he' and 'she'. However, for the Bimin Kuskusmin of Papua New Guinea, 'male' and 'female' are biological attributes of all persons; this is because all persons have flesh, which is female, and bone, which is male; moreover, all persons have fertile fluids, which are male, and all contain blood, which is essentially menstrual and female. From the ethnographic point of view, ideas of gender are always linked with ideas of the person, and, for the Bimin Kuskusmin, the person is ideally male, a manifestation of ancestral agnatic spirit. Thus, for them, gender is a process in which, over the course of life and finally in death, all persons become male in that their enduring human substance – that is, bone – is male. So Bimin Kuskusmin men say, 'We must be kind to our sisters, because, after all, they might have been our brothers'. The profound significance of these ideas can be gauged by the extent to which they inform those other domains of Bimin Kuskusmin daily life that we might describe in terms of kinship, political economy, and religion.

In like fashion, the human scientists' idea that sex is biologically given and gender culturally constructed is bound up with their idea of the person as 'an individual in society'. Here it is interesting to note that historically, and still today, women considered as 'individuals in society' are viewed in large part as prisoners of their biology in a way that men are not. So, it is hardly surprising that the individual in classical economics theory and its contemporary transformations is prototypically male: that is, a freely choosing subject of his own actions, making rational choices so as to make the best use of his finite means in pursuit of his own self-interest. This individual can only be male, precisely because biology is not a consideration with respect to the individual as an ideal type. Further, the notion of the male individual as the subject of his own actions can be contrasted with the notion of the female individual as an object of the actions of other people (in other words, of men).

We human scientists who take part in the workshop are concerned to know more about qualitative methods. This very concern suggests that we are more aware of ourselves as implicated in our own research than were our teachers. Ethnography as a qualitative method challenges us to render transparent our own involvement and to understand the difference it makes to the theories that emerge from the data we derive from participant observation.

Ethnography as research, ethnography of research

This brings to an end my attempt to make explicit at least some aspects of the ideas that the participants might be said to have brought to this hypothetical workshop on the use of qualitative methods in psychology. If I were, in fact, going to carry out an ethnography of such a workshop, my historical survey would have to be less crude and more questioning. However, this would be only the starting point for my proposed ethnography of the nature of research in the human sciences as understood by myself and those others involved in the workshop. In other words, as yet I have no field data. To gather these data, I should do a number of things:

(1) I should write obsessionally detailed descriptions of as much of the action as I could remember, including accounts of the participants' institutional positions and the style of their interaction, outside the formal sessions as well as inside them, in the bar as well as in workshop sessions. I should try to take note of what was spoken about, by whom and under what circumstances.

(2) If possible, I should record the formal sessions in which I took part myself and ask those running other sessions to record them for me.

(3) Ethnographic analysis does not pretend to rest on any 'representative samples'. Rather, the challenge is to know as much as possible about the people whose ideas and behaviour are the object of analysis. So, I should find out as much as I could about everyone at the workshop. Since I could not achieve this during the workshop itself, I should ask if I might interview the participants at a later date at their places of work. I should wish, if possible, to record these interviews, which would be largely unstructured and open ended. I might start by asking why a participant had attended the workshop and then encourage him or her to talk in general about psychology and in particular about his or her own interests. It seems likely that these interviews would include references to 'the individual', to 'human psychology', to 'social construction' and so forth, and if necessary I should ask the participants to expand on these and other ideas that emerged in the course of the interview.

(4) Since there is little existing ethnography concerning the idea of 'the individual in society', I should also be interested to find out whether the workshop participants, as my informants, actually saw themselves as 'individuals' in the theoretical sense of that term. To this end, I should arrange a second interview, if possible to take place in the participants' own homes; in this interview, I should

encourage each person to tell me about their own history and family life and what they consider to have been formative experiences.

(5) These two sets of interviews would be transcribed, so that I could carry out a content analysis to reveal the ideas of each informant and any inconsistencies and contradictions within and across the interviews with each person. I should also, of course, be using this content analysis to compare interviews across persons.

(6) However, since people do not and cannot have transparent access to their own history, to the processes in and through which they become who they are, I should also wish to do a broader-based ethnographic study of how the idea of 'the individual in society' is constituted over time by particular persons. To this end, I should carry out participant observation in an urban state primary school and in an urban private primary school for, say, around three months in each case. This would entail the writing up of those obsessional descriptions that I have already referred to with respect to day-to-day life in the classroom, playground, and staffroom. I should also use some kind of projective technique to obtain systematic data from children of different ages as to their ideas of the person, as well as a relatively unstructured interview technique to elicit from teachers their ideas of the child as person. Having completed this work, I should carry out a similar participant observer study with selected children in two contrasting secondary schools. This part of the research would take about six months. I should then use my institutional position as a university lecturer to obtain data on ideas of the person among university students.

(7) I should analyse the cross-sectional data that I had obtained to find out which ideas of the person were held by people at different ages; whether and how these ideas varied as a function of age, class, and gender; and, assuming that the idea of the person as 'an individual' was there to be found in the data, how it varied as a function of age and other characteristics.

(8) Finally, I should look at how the results of all these separate analyses played against one another in the light of the data derived from participant observation and my own understanding of historical data concerning the idea of the 'individual in society' and its emerging salience at different points in European history. Given my previous experience as an anthropologist, I might expect to find that the analysis would reveal a constellation of ideas and practices that I could not have predicted at the outset. On the other hand, given that I am myself at once a product and producer of these same ideas and practices, I might not be especially surprised by what I find. However, since I already know that the constitution of cognitive processes over time is inherently transformative, it seems likely that the analysis would throw into relief aspects of this process that I had not previously considered.

All in all, this in-depth investigation and analysis of the idea of 'the individual in society' would take about three years or so to complete. However, this dedication of time and effort would be almost bound to have fruitful results, and it could lead to a radical reappraisal of psychological and sociological notions of the person. In other words, it would bear not only upon an idea that is crucial to the human sciences, but upon one that informs politico-economic relations in the collectivity of which we are all members. More generally, participant observation as a method can give rise to rich and systematic data that allow the analyst to build theories that are new, enlightening and historically valid.

Conclusions: the ethnographic process

I would argue that ethnographic analysis should be oriented towards an understanding of the *processual* nature of life. Humans are biologically social beings and therefore their every act is historically constituted by virtue of an inevitable engagement in their relations with others, who are themselves at once constituting and being constituted by their own history. On this account, cognitive development is the micro-history of persons who come to be who they are in and through their relations with others. This further suggests that, with respect to our key epistemological assumptions, it would be enormously useful to try to understand how collective processes (as evinced in, for example, the workings of the market economy, the politics of democracy, or relations within the nuclear family) inform the cognitive constitution of these same epistemological assumptions in particular persons.

I pointed out at the beginning of this chapter that ethnographic analysis is self-consciously historical and comparative. It follows that it should be able to recognize that continuity and change are aspects of a single phenomenon and to show how ideas are transformed in the very process of their constitution. To understand what people are doing you have to analyse how they come to be doing it, and to understand the 'how' you have also to analyse the 'what'. What any person does is always embodied, and so any cognitive act implicates the whole person as physiologically constituted; and what people do is also affective, symbolic and material or, in other words, intentional. Moreover, the acting person and the historically constituted environment in which any act takes place are always mutually constituting; consequently, particular forms of intentionality are informed by the politico-economic processes that describe collective social relations. This is as true of walking or eating as it is of devising a research study, of writing or reading a book, or of crowning the Queen.

So ethnographic analysis is bound to address first the very concepts that we take for granted as being given in the nature of things, as being self-evident. The idea of 'the individual in society' is beginning to be challenged within social psychology, but there is little sign that the categorical distinction between 'the individual' and 'society' is about to be abandoned (and the concomitant distinction between 'biology' and 'culture' still appears to remain unquestioned). Ideas are historically constituted, and so what 'the individual in society' means to people in Britain in the late 20th century is not going to be the same as what it means to people in the United States or Australia in the late 20th century, to say nothing of the transformations in meaning that have occurred over time within, as well as across, populations. All of this suggests that the idea of 'the individual in society' as an analytical category in psychology should itself be self-consciously questioned by the psychologists who make use of it, rather than taken for granted as being in the nature of things and as such universally applicable.

One does need analytical categories, of course, but one does not need to claim more for them than is proper. The idea of the person as an individual in society is not universal, nor is it clear what the concept means, even to those people who routinely make use of it. Together with other, more focused methods, the ethnographic analysis of data gathered by means of participant observation is an excellent means of arriving at an understanding of the processes whereby people come to be enchanted by ideas that they have themselves brought into being. It allows the analyst to arrive at an appreciation of the historically specific nature of their explanation and hence to an appreciation of the necessity for generating data that are as rich and varied, as detailed and circumstantial, and as systematic as the analyst can produce.

Some suggestions for further reading

As one of the oldest examples of qualitative research methods to be used in the social sciences, there is a large amount of published literature in ethnography. Some useful introductions are that by Ellen (1984) from an anthropological perspective and that by Burgess (1982) from a sociological perspective. Interesting discussions of anthropological field work can be found in the book edited by Sanjek (1990), especially the chapter by Wolf (1990), in which the author showed how her particular perspective led to a rethinking of the classical model of the Chinese family. Lewis (1980, ch. 3) provided transcripts of taped conversations about ritual conducted with informants from the Gnau of New Guinea; it can be noted that what they had to say about ritual depended upon the point and the setting of the overall conversation. Similar examples can be found in the books by Willis (1977) and McDonald (1989).

Geertz's 'Thick description' (in Geertz, 1973) is a classic paper in 'cultural anthropology', and has important implications for field work methodology (cf. Toren, 1994). Obeyesekere (1981) discussed the relation between cultural symbolism and the psychology of particular persons, and also examined how the personal symbolism of the researcher informs analysis. For more information about gender among the Bimin Kuskusmin and how it implicates other domains of relationship such as kinship, political economy, religion and so on, see Porter Poole (1981). My own book (Toren, 1990) combined anthropological and psychological research methods with an historical perspective in order to analyse collective processes and their (re)production. It provides a generally applicable method for analysing the way in which politico-economic and kinship relations between people in the collectivity at large are manifested in everyday ritualized behaviour and thus mediate the (trans)formation over time of cognitive processes in particular persons (cf. Johnson and Johnson, 1990).

Finally, Csordas (1990) shows that the phenomenology of Merleau-Ponty is becoming increasingly important for anthropological analyses and has some important implications for research methods (see also Haraway, 1989a; Ots, 1990); while Haraway (1989b) provided a witty, readable and scholarly work in the history and philosophy of science that analysed the way in which politico-economic processes in the collectivity at large inform scientific research and practice.

Chapter 9

Ethnography: practical implementation

Janet Rachel

In this chapter, I am going to write about some of my experiences of doing an ethnographic study of a computer systems design office. The main theme of the chapter will be the implications the *craft* of ethnography has for the subject as a whole. I shall focus on the problem of 'dividing the subject', that of bringing the experience of the world together with the writing about it. The 'subject' here refers to two things: first, *me* as a subject of the practices and discourses of the various communities that constituted my study (including my academic discipline); and, second, my writing, the disciplinary output that will constitute 'the subject' in more conventional terms. Dividing the subject like this draws attention to the way in which one is connected to the world through a number of different regimes. We are simultaneously connected to and separated from the world through the various practices of our minds and bodies.

Like the word 'subject', the word 'ethnography' also splits into these two different but related subjects. On the one hand, there is the long drawn out, lived experience of '*being* in the field'; while, on the other hand, there is the written account that comes to stand for that experience. Part of the character of the ethnographic study is to give the researcher a chance to reflect the experience of 'being there' in the writing. There is thus no need to conceal the connection between the researcher and the results: on the contrary, the ethnographic method provides an opportunity to celebrate this connection. However, it is not simply a matter of 'writing what happens', as so much happens. There are many different styles of writing (see, for example, Clifford and Marcus, 1986; Van Maanen, 1988), but I shall not be using this chapter to discuss a variety of literary techniques. I have instead decided to use the idea of experience to focus attention upon the phenomenology of ethnography, to question 'where' the data are and to look at the implications this has for understanding and representing them.

The purposes of the chapter are therefore to focus upon the practice of ethnographic work, to give a sense of what it might be like, and to show how even the bad experiences can be used to contribute to the written results. By the end of the chapter, I hope that I will have given you more than 'a picture' of the office life I studied: I hope that you will have an idea of my experience as a novice ethnographer as well as an insight into the way in which I used this experience to address the disciplinary questions that gave structure to my craft.

The craft: techniques and technology

The idea of ethnography as a craft is a particularly interesting one. It implies a mode of working that is utterly implicated in the product: for example, a craftsman merges with his tools to work directly on the raw material and produce a thing of beauty and utility. It is a process that is generally acknowledged to take time, to cost a little more, and to require extensive training (that is, an apprenticeship). It implies an embodied subject. The traditional image of ethnographer as craftsman or craftswoman invokes a lone figure, entwined with pencil and notebook, or tape recorder and camera. Today, one might include a video-camera and a laptop computer in the picture, but the emphasis is always very much on the individual *person* venturing out into the unknown, engaging with and talking to the people of the community to be studied.

The underlying assumption of the ethnographic method is that the world is essentially a social business, produced through the interactions of people as they go about their life in an everyday, mundane way. In order to find out how a particular community operates, one must invest an extensive period of time (traditionally measured in years, rather than in hours, days or weeks) living with them: being physically, verbally and emotionally present, moving among their interactions, joining in their discourses, using their objects and technologies and becoming part of the economy of things, values, morals and money. This is the character of ethnographic work.

The idea of ethnography as a craft can also invoke the image of the researcher setting off in a small boat: the research project can then be thought of as a journey, a quest for knowledge. This interpretation draws our attention to the nature of the craft. It is not a luxury liner, which takes the familiar world with it; it is not a home from home. It is more like a small sailing boat, requiring one to engage more directly with the elements, and making it easier to get out of it, to mix with the locals at the next port of call.

My ethnographic experience involved me in venturing into a computer systems design office in a large town in south-east England. I took with me notebooks, a camera, and a small tape recorder to help to 'capture the culture'. I brought back reams of paper, miles of tape and stacks of photographs. But the more I snapped, taped and photocopied, the more I realized that this was separating me from the world I was trying to understand. In other words, it is one's *relationship* to the various recordings that is important: not only will these come to be taken as data, but, more important, they are a vital part of the *process* of understanding. (See also the advice offered by Christina Toren in Chapter 8.) The frenzy to 'get it all' resulted in piles of paper and plenty of proof that I had in fact been doing an ethnographic study, but it was not getting me much of a story to *write* for the result.

Although much of the rhetoric around the ethnographic method depends upon the idea of finding out 'what actually goes on' (Woolgar, 1983), the job is much more than going out and collecting the data. Every method has links to the disciplinary questions that begin the inquiry, and without a firm grip on these questions ethnographers might well find themselves shipwrecked. The skill then becomes that of finding a way in which to apply the research questions through the distinctive characteristics of ethnography: to maintain oneself as a member of an academic community while opening oneself up to the possibilities that would follow from belonging to the community that one wants to study.

My study was carried out in response to questions from two academic communities, those of computer science and sociology. The computer scientists wanted to know what kind of human factors were at play in the process of technical work. Behind this question lies a disciplinary tradition of treating technical work as a fundamentally asocial activity. However, the sociologists wanted to see how technical work had come to be seen as 'asocial': behind this question lies a disciplinary tradition of believing that all human activity can be understood in the terms of the social sciences and in particular that 'asocial' activity is in fact a thoroughly social accomplishment. These two orientations mark different systems of community beliefs that are potentially at odds. My position as ethnographer, then, began on a point of conflict, and could be expected to produce moments of discomfort throughout the study. The only thing to do with a situation like this, it seemed to me, was to try to turn these discomforts into moments of data for my project.

The subject(s) of the study

For the most part, my ethnography was carried out in a small, open-plan office in which 25–30 people came to work on 'The Customer Project'. Most of these people were part of the 'Systems Team', which was the technical team responsible for designing and making a new computerized system that would change the way in which the company related both to its customers and within its own internal operations. The system was part of a radical organizational change for this company. A second, smaller team was the 'Change Management Team'. Unlike the Systems Team, who knew little about the company (they were mostly consultants, contractors or new recruits), the Change Management Team was made up of company employees who knew about the history and practices of much of the work in the business. Their involvement in the computer project was a special feature of the strategy, and it represented a commitment by the company's management to address the organizational aspect of the new computer system.

Although these two teams were working together in the same small office, their identities were nevertheless subject to different sets of organizing principles that were quite effective at keeping the two teams separate. This boundary between the teams was one that I kept 'tripping over' throughout the study. This tripping, however, was not simply a mark of my own cultural incompetence leading to personal embarrassment, but it became a signal of the various dimensions of the office structure. They were a sign for me that I should reach for my notebook and write down what was happening. I shall use these awkward feelings to structure

115

the rest of my chapter and begin an inquiry into 'The Body as an Ethnographic Tool'.

As I have said, the organization of the research project itself was based upon a split (and a union) between my university's Computer Science and Human Science Departments. Each discipline was hoping to produce new knowledge from the partnership. This reflected the division and union in the Customer Project between the Change Management Team (who monitored the organizational aspects of change) and the Systems Team (who concentrated on the technical details). As I progressed through the project, I noticed that these splits were becoming manifested in me, too. When I joined the office to commence the study, I was assigned to the Change Management Team and introduced as an ethnographer, as a social scientist. However, I made a point of establishing myself as a transitional object between the two teams in order to ensure that I incorporated the technical work as well. A more detailed account of how I pursued the 'technical' aspects of this project is contained in Rachel and Woolgar (1995).

A simple and yet difficult part of this transitional work was to walk the five steps that it took me to get from one side of the office to the other. The office was a long oblong shape, the bottom third of which was divided off by filing cabinets and a wall and was generally reserved for the managerial kinds of work in the project. The first time that I ever walked down this office was to attend a meeting with the project manager in the latter part of the room. Here is my 'field notebook' entry of this first encounter with the space:

> Drive to Booking. 30 miles. Easy to find. Phoned earlier to get a parking space: 'It would be easier for you to get a train from London!', so parked in station lot. 30 mins to spare. Headed off for 'shops'. Bloody miles away! And pretty uninspiring at that. I've heard so many stories about how awful Booking is. Am I mad?
>
> Back to Nugget House. This time in through the revolving doors, slowly. Noticed the paper notice stuck onto a metal one telling me to wear a security tag. Walked to the desk, gave my name, received a tag in exchange and fixed it to my skirt waistband, under my jacket. Made a visit to the Ladies. Through a door from the sleek reception into the chaos of cardboard boxes and chipped paint work. Back to reception. Wait. Watch the courtesy video: sludge, tunnels, water, birds, frogs, computers, company logo.
>
> The receptionist called out my name and a direction. What? Where? The old man walked out from behind the desk towards me, past me, through the door, pointing my direction for me. A small, half-hidden building next to the bridge. No doorman waiting for my entrance. In easily, and up the stairs. On the first floor, more bits of paper stuck over metal plaques announcing changes. The doors I have to get through are locked. There is an entry phone. There is a paper notice about using entry passes to get in. There's all sorts going on here – can't take it all in. Next thing, the entry phone is addressing me abruptly. I bend my body towards it, give my name. 'The door's open', it says. Look through the glass door, down a long stretch of carpet flanked by desks, I can see a young woman sitting at a desk looking straight up at the door, at me. Unimpeded view.
>
> Through this door, into a small lobby lined with clocking-in cards, more paper stuck to the walls. Through another door (like an air-lock, antechamber) and into

the gauntlet. Desks to the left of me. Desks to the right. Screens (both solid and computer) all over, young, quiet people bent over keyboards, gazing into screens. The secretary's eyes lock onto mine and seem to pull me straight through the office, avoiding any other contact. Faint smile on my lips, reflected on hers. 'Albert's just, just hovering, he won't be long, please wait in here a moment'.

'The gauntlet' was the long straight space that divided the office into two. Although I did not realize it at the time, on my left as I glided towards the secretary was the Change Management Team, and on my right was the Systems Team. Many months later, after I had achieved my somewhat ambiguous status and established my routine of crossing the boundary, I found myself part of a small episode that re-established the split, and I discovered that not only was it represented in the office space, but that it also ran straight through the middle of *me*.

It was a fairly relaxed afternoon for me that day, tension was low, and the office was not so full of people as it had been recently. I had been out to visit someone in another part of the company, and, when I came back in through the two sets of doors, I was greeted by a shout, 'Janet!' This in itself was a remarkable occurrence. That first day I had entered the room, I had been aware of a quiet hum of hard work, where low voices barely rose above the murmur of machines. This call now, today, was a glorious flaunting of a human voice, cutting across the barriers and entering everyone's ears, whether they liked it or not. I hesitated slightly and looked to my left, towards where the voice had erupted. Nick had pushed his chair away from his desk and was leaning back in it, expansively. His smile was broad and warm. I felt myself tense up a little, as one part of me responded to his call, while the other wanted to turn to the right and signal a greeting to my colleagues (friends?) in the Systems Team.

Nick stood up, smiling and looking directly at me. I followed my cue and walked towards him, reflecting his smile and copying his open gesture, taking up more space with my arms. I tried to forget the Systems Team, even though I knew this was a display intended especially for them. By the time that I had reached Nick and concluded the act by embracing in a top-to-toe hug, the rest of the Change Management Team were flung back in their chairs, beaming huge grins around at each other, at us, and flicking their eyes and smiles swiftly across the room at the Systems Team. We (for I was certainly implicated in this) were marking ourselves as a separate group, characterizing ourselves as 'human' – smiling, embracing, laughing and looking, and disconnecting from the computer terminals, the pens and the paper on the desks.

This brief encounter was marked in me by several sensations. The first was the tension at being called into an act without precedent in the office. We were deliberately breaking an implicit rule. This rule had never been spoken, and it was difficult to imagine how it would ever have been articulated. I felt a little scared, and I began to realize how the social practices of the office ran through my body, governing actions from inside my skin. It also drew my attention to the hierarchy in the office. Change Management had grabbed an opportunity to reaffirm their preferred way of being, a way that was normally not available for them. As a rule, a different mode of interaction was the favoured practice in the office. The second sensation was pleasure: a top-to-toe hug surrounded by wide smiles and laughing voices was sufficient to release a good warm flush and a flood of goodwill all round this small corner of the room.

The third sensation was an unease, a sense of guilt and petty betrayal, which came from my certain knowledge that this act on the part of Change Management was precisely pitched against the acts of the Systems Team. A little later that afternoon, I slipped across to the other side of the room to see what damage had been done. As far they were concerned, it didn't even register as a conversation topic. Did something happen? They seemed uninterested. They were reluctant even to pull themselves away from their computer screens, hardly taking their eyes off the display to meet mine in our conversation. I felt that I was making a fuss about nothing; a cold stone sank in my abdomen.

The skin, you see, is not the only boundary

The mistake that I was making was to think of people as that which can be found within the boundaries of the skin. This was despite the fact that, as an ethnographer, I was interested in the *relationships* between people and things: in the social fabric. I was still presuming that I needed face-to-face, eyeball-to-eyeball contact to get at 'the data'. But one of the features that distinguished the Systems Team from their colleagues was the ease with which they moved beyond the skin to form relationships.

When I first joined the office and had been assigned to the Change Management Team, I was given a desk that was one of a block of four, all butted up against each other. The Change Management Team was much smaller than the Systems Team, and this meant that they did not fill the whole of the left-hand side of the office: some of the Systems Team also sat this side of the gauntlet, and my new desk was directly facing one of these. It took some time before I could catch the eye of the man sitting opposite me, but, when I did, I smiled to invite an introduction. He folded his arms across his body, leant forward a little towards me, and with his head bowed slightly he looked at me from under his eyebrows and said, quietly, '*Hi*'. I was still very new at this point, and so I answered, 'Hi', in a regular kind of voice. '*Who are you?*' he whispered. 'PARDON?' I replied. '*Who are you?*' 'OH, I'M JANET, I'M. . . '. But before I could continue I saw that he had pulled his arms in tighter to his body, had turned his head away to the side and was looking at the keyboard of his computer. 'Who are you?' I ventured, a little confused. Silence. He resumed his working position in front of his computer screen and began tapping the keyboard. I looked around me, wondering whether there were any witnesses to my embarrassment or, indeed, whether anything had happened at all. It took me a little while to realize that, if I wanted to become part of a conversation with this man, I would have to speak much more quietly, to be much more discreet, and that it would be especially good to learn to speak without moving my lips at all.

As it turned out, the man sitting opposite, the man who taught me to speak quietly, was called 'Biff'. A couple of weeks later, I was roused from my work by Biff, as he laughed out loud and flung himself back in his chair. His actions pushed him away from the desk, and he leant back to look over to the other side of the office. He beamed a smile over to Richard, the technical architect, who also sat back in his chair, smiling mischievously. Their eyes met for several seconds in a warm embrace before they resumed their scowling stance in front of their machines. The office continued as if its quietness had not been at all interrupted. No one asked Biff what was happening; no one remarked upon it to anyone in my earshot. It increased my sense of outsiderness: as far as I could see, no one else had been puzzled by the display, and yet it was so unusual that it must have been noticed. Either everyone else knew what was going on and took it for granted (which I thought extremely unlikely), or else they were pretending to be nonchalant. I decided to opt for the latter myself: by this time, I was tired of being a 'cultural dope', and, anyway, I had my own work to be getting on with.

It was three months before I found out what had happened there. By this time, I had managed to establish a relationship with one of the Systems guys; he had started working at the company at roughly the same time as I had joined the office, so we had found something in common, which helped me cross the office space. I was sitting next to him at his desk, and he was showing me something of the work he was doing. I was watching his screen and listening to him talk. As he described to me some of the features of the new system, I heard his machine utter a very faint beep. The screen changed, but I couldn't see exactly how at first. I just registered some kind of flash. He continued talking to me about the routine of his work, but he moved forwards in his seat and seemed to be more intensely typing. 'What happened, William?' I asked. He resisted my question and continued to talk about the system. I had waited days for him to have time to tell me about the system, and so part of me wanted to let him continue his dull speech (his voice low, and to my ears flat, without modulation) about the organization of the structure. On the other hand, I was attracted by the possibility of pursuing something elusive. I persisted in my questioning and ignored his monotonous recitation of the logic of the system. Finally he paused, looked at me conspiratorially and began to reveal the secret of talking through the machine.

It turned out that there was a facility on all of the machines in the office whereby anyone (anyone, that is, who *knew*) could send a single line of text through the machine to anyone else who was using the network. (In practice, everyone was using the network, both in Change Management and in Systems.) Via what I thought to be a tortuous navigation through a number of screens (which to William was a simple procedure consisting of ten key strokes), William could write a single line of text and send it instantly to his colleagues. It would arrive on the very bottom line of the screen. It could be sent anonymously. And it was the practice, it seemed, to send it in a kind of code, such as 'Have you grounded the penguin?' or 'Don't stretch the putty'. Short, quiet, cryptic, anonymous talk. At that time, however, none of my colleagues in the Change Management Team knew about this, and it became my pleasure to teach some of them the process. In this way, I came to learn about the tight economy of information in the office and about the importance of secrecy in that economy.

The overt display among the Change Management Team that I described earlier was part of a display that linked them to other parts of the company. In particular, it was these parts of the company that were the subject of change by the new computer system that was being designed in the Customer Project. The project manager had described the role of the new system as one that would capture the customer's voice and control it in order to make sure that inquiries and complaints were dealt with efficiently. The new project was itself part of an overall corporate strategy that was intended to display to the national regulators that the organization was moving away from its public utility image, to a more businesslike one. Overt talk and expansive gestures had come to be seen as a threat to this new image. The Systems Team, then, were designing a machine that was to change the company's behaviour. The character of the machine was reflected in the character of the team, who became a community skilled in capturing and quieting voices, channelling them carefully around the office in ways that could be seen only by those who were invited to see: an image of quiet, controlled efficiency.

Glossing over the tedium

To return to the problem of transferring experience into writing, you may have noticed how the time and tedium of months of life have been condensed into a few pages. Between my first encounter with Biff and my eventual discovery of talking through the machine, weeks had slid by. My notebooks from this time are filled with the detailed duties of a temporary worker within a large and difficult project. Telephone calls, frustrations, memos, minutes, photocopying, clock-watching, lunch dates and coffee rituals occupy these pages. And these are just the things that I wrote down.

You spend a lot of time when you do ethnographic work. You collect a great deal of paper and tape. You get old. Your relationships back home loosen and break up. Your identity becomes fragmented. But, in return (if you keep the faith), you might get the most unexpected and fascinating stories. That is the mark of ethnography.

Contrasting research styles

Doing an ethnographic study of this computer-systems design process emphasized a sharp distinction between different research methods and their results.

Part of the work of the Customer Project was to find out what went on in the company: systems analysts are also business analysts. As a result of their research into organizational life, a computer system was being developed that was part of a large-scale change in work relationships and practices. I accompanied William while he was undertaking this analysis, and I volunteered to write up the minutes of one of the more complex of his meetings. This consisted of an interview with a woman who knew all about one of the existing practices that would be subject to change. She described how people in the communications room shouted information across to each other when they received it over the telephone. Their colleagues would themselves be busy speaking into telephones or radio equipment, but the calling voice could carry without intruding into these conversations. The woman was highly animated, and she conjured up an image of excitement that gave her work an air of importance: crisis handling. I tried to report this in the minutes, but I found the short 'bullet-point' format quite difficult to master. In the end, I managed to write that 'people shout information out across the room'.

I passed my minutes to William to read before I circulated them. He sent them back to me with a handwritten note in the margin next to this item: 'Are you taking the piss?' He asked me to rewrite this minute without any reference to people shouting. In the end, the minutes were approved without this comment at all and circulated for information to the other members of the project. For him, this reference to a loud, overt practice was completely inappropriate. For me, it was a remark about a vital part of the work of that office. Minutes were one of the important means of moving voices around in their office. No one came through those double doors and shouted out what they had just found: instead, they came in quietly, sat at their computers and typed a note into a preformulated document against a numbered point. Information from other parts of the business was transferred around by these documents. It was not uncommon to be told to refer to the minutes or to be handed a large wad of paper if I asked directly for information. Part of the System Team's work was to dissuade face-to-face talk and to persuade interactions between people and things. The process was a way of subduing the voice and breaking it away from the lungs and the lips: this was a mark of its order and rationality.

The value of subduing voices

Staying with the subject of voices, their style of representation and the economy of information, I want to conclude this chapter with one further story. This example is where I learned the value of tight-lipped speaking and the virtue of pushing my voice through a well contained technology. Part of the deal that bought my research team access to study the Customer Project was that I myself would be a 'spare pair of hands' in the work of the office. As a participant, as well as an observer, I was given the job of 'training' during the first half of my study. This was part of the work of the Change Management Team, and it involved visiting all of the operational sites to tell the people there what the new computer system would mean to their work.

The very first job that I had been given was the task of writing the booklet that went with this training activity and designing the overhead transparencies that would accompany our presentations. There were about 60 transparencies in all for a presentation that would last about an hour. In thinking about these from an 'observational' point of view, I had been amazed at the effort required and investment made for these events. The illustrations were all in colour and all showed the project logo. A special machine had been procured (through personal relationships, not through bureaucracy – this was the Change Management Team, remember!) for the purpose of producing these illustrations, and many attempts had had to be made before a perfect set of overhead transparencies was finally assembled.

In the spirit of an ethnographer, I had been treating this process as 'strange'. I had been looking for ways of turning the 'familiar' into the 'unfamiliar', in order to get a different purchase upon what was going on. Consequently, I possessed a whole repertoire of different versions of the transparencies. I also had a long list of reasons why the computer system would *not* improve the working practice in the operational sites. I could think of many reasons why decentralized operations should *not* be separated from the customers. I felt that I had a well rounded view of the process, that I knew the pros and cons, and that I would be able to discuss it easily with or without the slides. By the time we drove off to deliver the word in the local depots, I was saturated with ethnographic versions of these events.

It was raining when Ewan and I drove up to the Cricklewood Depot, a miserable, grey Monday. We had left the head office in Booking in our head-office suits and shiny shoes. When we got to Cricklewood we sloshed across the muddy access road and found the works canteen. This is where we were to present our news, as it was the only room that was big enough to collect everyone together for the presentation. We did have a little difficulty finding a place to set up the overhead projector, because the tables and chairs in the canteen were all screwed to the floor, but we eventually found a corner and began to build our island of head office.

I had already begun to feel rather uneasy (stomach in turmoil, sticky armpits). I could see that Ewan was in a similar state, his neck flushing a little red. For a brief minute I wondered whether I could get away with just being an ethnographer for this meeting and introducing myself just as a researcher interested in the human aspects of computer system design. I asked Ewan whether he thought it would be all right if I tape-recorded the meeting. I thought it was a wonderful idea, a safe place to be, quietly taking notes on the side and thinking of some distant audience to whom I would later relate them, but another look at Ewan's rising blood pressure banished the thought from my mind. In any case, I would probably be safer in the tight ship of the Customer Project than in my small ethnographic craft for this occasion. But it was not so easy to swap: I had embodied my craft, it was running though me, and it was no longer simply a matter of stepping from one craft into another.

Ewan started the seminar, and I watched him carefully, picking up tips for my own performance, trying to match my head-office clothes with a head-office frame of mind. He stood close to the projector and switched it on. As he began his talk, an image of the first overhead transparency, announcing 'The Customer Project', shone out behind him. He never spoke unless there was an image behind him, and he never said anything that was not connected to that image. The words, the images, and his voice were working together to keep him within the frame of his reference. Questions from the floor were absorbed, translated and deflected with quiet ease and controlled coolness. Ewan stayed close, both physically and verbally, to the prepared text. Then it was my turn.

Clicking across the canteen floor in my head-office shoes did nothing for my composure. On the contrary, the sound simply reinforced the split that I felt. However, when I reached the overhead projector, arranged my transparencies on the machine and found my place in the script, I began to rally to the cause. When I switched the lamp on and the image sprang to life, I began to speak words that I had helped to write, and I found that I was as good a vessel for this message as Ewan had been. However, as I grew in confidence, I began to leave the close quarters of the machine and walked a little way into the room. I improvised a little on the script, and I met the gaze of one of my audience. That was the thing that Ewan had avoided, which I had not remarked well enough.

A man in blue overalls caught my eye. I lingered a moment too long in his gaze, and this gave him the opening he was looking for. He began a tirade against the system, against the project, against head office, and against 'me'. (Who was I?) His mate joined in. The script was lost now – they had successfully blown me off course, and I had to improvise. Before I knew where I was or *who* I was, I found my mouth repeating some of the worst clichés about computers that my ears had ever heard. I was talking about progress, efficiency, utility, as if I believed that this was what computers were all about. Later, Ewan told me that my fists were clenched and my face was glowing a furious red. He liked what I had said; he just didn't agree with the way I had said it.

I, however, was surprised that I had not exploded. I had loosened my attachment to my disciplinary craft in order to get into the head-office craft. But I had not embodied enough of this to be able to venture away very far at all. I felt that I had stepped outside the technology at that point, but my mouth had still been engaged with it. The questions from the floor had pushed words out of my mouth that my ears were surprised to hear. Yet, for the purposes of the presentation at that moment, they were 'my' words. My interlocutor used them to launch a more personal attack on the stupidity of head-office staff and my complete inability to understand anything that was going on at local level. I knew that Ewan would never have forgiven me if I had agreed with him out loud. So, I tightened my lips, moved back to the projector, picked up the script and carried on.

At the end of the presentation, the man in blue overalls took me by surprise once again. He came up to me with a friendly smile and told me that he didn't think I *personally* was an idiot, just 'head-office people in general'. The five-o'clock boundary had been safely crossed, and the meeting was over. Out-of-work hours meant out-of-work relationships. No offence, he said.

Conclusions: where are the data?

Since completing this ethnographic experience, I have been asked to speak to a number of postgraduate students who were considering using the method for their own research. There is one question that I am asked most often and most urgently: 'How did you gain access to the organization?' I hope that my account has begun to show that 'access' is not just a matter of walking through the door. It is an ever-present, ongoing concern, which includes inventing yourself as an ethnographer and deciding what counts as data (although, as you will have seen, you are not always in control of these processes). It is not just a matter of 'being there' and snapping it up, writing it down or photocopying it. You still have to work out how to 'be' and where 'there' is (see, for example, Hine, 1994, on conducting 'virtual ethnography' with computer networkers).

This orientation towards 'data' (that is, appreciating that they are constituted in the research yet simultaneously constitute the researcher) raises important questions about disciplinary affiliation. I began this chapter by talking about a divided subject. As in the study that I have described in this chapter, you are likely to be using anthropological methods to pursue questions from other disciplines. My study was designed in part to identify the 'human factors in information systems design'. Clearly, this is not an 'ethnographic' question, since ethnography takes as its starting point the social organization of people and things. The differences that exist between particular disciplines, as I hope I have shown, are not merely interesting to remark upon for this study. They constitute the world we move in, and they bring us to life as subjects as much as we bring them to life in our subject. Indeed, the conflicts and tensions between the differences can be quite a sensation to contend with.

I chose to focus upon the craft of ethnography to get at the embodied nature of the work. This enabled me to talk about the experience of the research and at the same time to show how this constitutes the results of the work. If you want to read about the experiences of other researchers, I can recommend the books by Bowen (1964), Powdermaker (1966), Latour and Woolgar (1986), Traweek (1988), Wolf (1992), and Bell and Caplan (1993). However, my hope is that I have forewarned you of some of the perils of ethnographic research, while persuading you that these are at the same time its pleasures and that an apparent failure in ethnographic research can turn out to generate one's best data.

Chapter 10

Discourse analysis and constructionist approaches: theoretical background

Jonathan Potter

This chapter is structured in terms of questions and answers. There are several reasons for adopting this format. First, people often consult a handbook to find the answers to questions, and so the format may simplify this task. Second, most constructionist approaches emphasize dialogue, and question–answer sequences are dialogue in one of its most prototypical forms. Third, constructionist researchers have been at the forefront of moves to rethink the literary forms in which the social sciences are presented.

I shall start with some general questions about constructionism and its place in psychology, and then I shall move on to focus upon issues of method and analysis. I shall concentrate upon general principles and arguments, however: this is not intended to be a how-to-do-it chapter. Chapter 11, by Rosalind Gill, provides a more fleshed out example of one particular style of constructionist research.

What is constructionism?

On the face of it, this seems to be a very sensible question with which to start. What could be wrong with giving a broad characterization, offering a compact definition and going on to describe constructionism in detail? The problem is that it would be a profoundly anti-constructionist approach to the question. It would imply that there was a simple thing that could be neutrally and objectively described and defined as constructionism, and this would be a *realist* account of constructionism. It would do precisely the thing that constructionism rejects. Instead of seeing constructionism as one simple describable thing, another approach would be to consider the way in which constructionism was itself constructed: how it was described differently in handbooks on research methods and theoretical overviews, say, by psychologists and sociologists; how these different perspectives were treated as constructionist; and what was taken to hang on this ascription. However, I do not intend to attempt such an ambitious enterprise here.

Having cautioned against treating definitions realistically, I think that they can nevertheless be a useful ladder to a better understanding of the concept in question. Here is a definition of social constructionism from the important series of books with a constructionist theme edited by John Shotter and Kenneth Gergen (1994):

> [Social constructionism] has given voice to a range of new topics, such as the social construction of personal identities; the role of power in the social making of meanings; rhetoric and narrative in establishing sciences; the centrality of everyday activities; remembering and forgetting as socially constituted activities; reflexivity in method and theorizing. The common thread underlying all these topics is a concern with the processes by which human abilities, experiences, commonsense and scientific knowledge are both produced in, and reproduce, human communities.
>
> (p. i)

This quotation implies an underlying unity, but the listing also shows a mix and match of different theoretical perspectives.

Gergen (1994a) identified five basic assumptions for a social constructionist science:

(1)   'The terms by which we account for the world and ourselves are not dictated by the stipulated objects of such accounts' (p. 49).
(2)   'The terms and forms by which we achieve an understanding of the world and ourselves are social artefacts, products of historically and culturally situated interchanges among people' (p. 49).
(3)   'The degree to which a given account of the world or self is sustained across time is not dependent on the objective validity of the account but on the vicissitudes of social process' (p. 51).
(4)   'Language derives its significance in human affairs from the way in which it functions within patterns of relationship' (p. 52).
(5)   'To appraise existing forms of discourse is to evaluate patterns of cultural life, and such evaluations give voice to other cultural enclaves' (p. 53; italics removed from all these quotations).

Another way to come at the same question is not to attempt any definition, but to consider the different approaches that have been commonly called 'constructionist' (with the warning, however, that 'commonly called' hides a range of complications).

What approaches have been called 'constructionist'?

One of the features of the different approaches that have been called 'constructionist' is that they have often been developed at the margins of disciplines, in the spaces where psychology blurs into sociology, where literary studies border on political science, where feminism and rhetoric intersect. Even a rather cursory survey of constructionist approaches can easily gather together a dozen such perspectives (see Table 10.1). One should note, however, that there

TABLE 10.1 *Varied constructionist approaches*

Approach	Example
Conversation analysis	Atkinson and Heritage (1984b)
Discourse analysis	Potter and Wetherell (1987)
Ethnomethodology	Button (1991)
Ethogenics	Harré (1992b)
Feminist studies	Radke and Stam (1994)
Post-structuralism	Culler (1983), Hollway (1989)
Post-modern political science	Der Derian and Shapiro (1989)
Rhetoric	Billig (1987)
Reflexive ethnography	Clifford and Marcus (1986)
Sociology of scientific knowledge	Latour and Woolgar (1986)
Sociocultural psychology	Wertsch (1991)
Symbolic interactionism	Hewitt (1994)

are all sorts of potentially contentious features of this list and its absences. Reviewing the research literature is itself a constructive and sometimes highly contentious business (see Ashmore *et al.*, 1995). What should count as an 'approach'? And what is its defining reference?

Some of these approaches, such as ethogenics, are developments that have specifically occurred from within or directed at psychology. Others, such as post-modern political science, have been carried on almost in complete isolation from the problematics of psychology. Several of these perspectives have some psychological adherents but have their main site of development outside the disciplinary boundaries of psychology.

Is there an underlying unity to these approaches?

Having identified these different approaches as constructionist, it might seem straightforward to identify features that they have in common. Yet, it is hard to find any single characteristic that is central to them all. The idea of family resemblance gives something of a sense of the pattern. First, they all tend to be oppositional movements of one kind or another to traditional social science positions and, in particular, their realist assumptions. Second, they all tend to stress the way in which mind and action are contingent on specific cultural forms. They see minds not as having fixed essences but as being built from the symbolic resources of a culture. Indeed, in some constructionisms, 'mind' is not a mental entity at all, but a discursive move: a set of stories that people tell or a set of different discursive practices for dealing with one another as moral and accountable (cf. Coulter, 1989; Harré, 1992b). Third, they all tend to treat discourse, variously theorized, as the central organizing principle of construction.

What does this mean for traditional institutional boundaries?

Clearly, constructionism cuts across traditional disciplinary boundaries. In many cases, current boundaries are a product of particular views of the social sciences and human sciences that were established during university expansion after World War II, particularly in the United Kingdom and the United States. The proliferation of constructionist approaches during the late 1970s and the 1980s coincided with a period of lack of expansion, and this means that there is often a disparity between the intellectual and the bureaucratic structure of departments. Constructionist researchers in psychology often have more in common with colleagues in the disciplines of linguistics or the sociology of science than they do with their colleagues who study ganglion sprouting or the ergonomics of car dashboards.

One of the challenges for constructionists is therefore to be able to thrive within these traditional structures, while operating in a genuinely interdisciplinary manner. This can cut both ways. At times, it can be a struggle to establish the legitimacy of constructionist research with more mainstream psychological colleagues; yet, at other times, this can become a context that promotes superficial theorizing and loose analysis.

Is constructionism the same as social constructionism and constructivism?

In psychology, this kind of work has normally proceeded under the title of '*social* construc*tion*ism', with concern being expressed that social construc*tiv*ism could be confused with the artistic movement known as 'constructivism' (Gergen, 1985). In contrast, in the sociology of scientific knowledge, construc*tiv*ism is a well established perspective (with no concern about the artistic movement), and 'constructivism' is increasingly favoured over '*social* construc*tion*ism' (cf. Latour and Woolgar, 1979, 1986). One reason for this is that 'social construction' in the context of the sociology of scientific knowledge is associated with rather limited perspectives that seek to relate knowledge to scientists' social background and group allegiances. Sociological constructionists often see such accounts as reductionist (see Mulkay, 1979; Woolgar, 1988c). Moreover, they may want to make recourse to explanations involving processes in texts and rhetoric that are not 'social' in this more traditional way (Knorr Cetina, 1995). More radically, they have also started to question the coherence of the very distinction between the 'social' and the 'non-social' (Latour, 1987).

Is there something that could be called a constructionist method?

The short answer to this question is no. If anything, there is even more variation of method than there is of theory in constructionism. For many of these approaches, indeed, it is not clear that there is anything that would correspond to what psychologists traditionally think of as a 'method'. Perhaps the most appropriate consideration in many cases would be what Billig (1988a) called 'scholarship'. In other words, the lack of a 'method', in the sense of some formally specified set of procedures and calculations, does not imply any lack of argument or rigour; nor does it imply that the theoretical system is not guiding analysis in various ways.

One constructionist approach where it makes more sense to talk about a research 'method' is that of discourse analysis, and I shall concentrate upon this approach for the rest of this chapter. Nevertheless, even here the term 'method' is understood in a very different way from that which is accepted elsewhere in psychology. For example, one point of contrast is in the justification of results. In much traditional psychological work, this justification is provided by carrying out the procedures of analysis in a correct and complete manner. A sample is collected, some 'variables' are operationalized, conventional statistical tests are carried out and so on. In contrast to this, in discourse analysis the analytical procedure is largely separate from how claims are justified.

What is discourse analysis?

Discourse analysis focuses on talk and texts as social practices and on the resources that are drawn on to enable those practices. For example, discourse analysis of racism has been concerned with the way in which descriptions are marshalled in particular contexts to legitimate the blaming of a minority group (Potter and Wetherell, 1988) and with the resources (or 'interpretative repertoires') that are available in a particular cultural setting for legitimating racist practices (Nairn and McCreanor, 1991; Wetherell and Potter, 1992).

Discourse analysts have focused upon issues concerning stake and accountability, looking at the way in which people manage pervasive issues of blame and responsibility (Edwards and Potter, 1993; Gill, 1993b; Antaki, 1994). They have also studied the way that descriptions are put together to perform actions and manage accountability (Potter, 1996). For example, Edwards (1994) studied 'script formulations' in conversations, and he showed how events could be variously described to present them as regular and routine, to treat them as being a characteristic consequence of personal dispositions or to make them out to be an unusual result of outside pressures. Such descriptions manage questions of fault and thus provide legitimation for courses of action.

Discourse analysts have rejected the more traditional, cognitive explanations of social interaction that are provided within psychology. Rather than trying to explain actions as a consequence of mental processes or mental entities, their interest has been in how mentalist notions are constructed and used in interaction. For instance, instead of attempting to explain sexism in terms of the attitudes of individuals, the concern is with how evaluations are managed in particular interactions and either linked up with or separated from particular individuals (Wetherell *et al.*, 1987; Gill, 1993b).

These are some of the characteristic strands of discourse work, but they do not define it. New studies are being carried out that push back the limits of discourse work, and the problematics of discourse analysis are providing a new 'take' on a range of psychological issues.

Does that mean there is a discourse analysis answer to any psychological question?

No. One of the mistakes that people sometimes make when they are starting to carry out discourse work is to treat discourse analysis as a method that can simply be plugged into a predefined question: for example, 'I am interested in the factors that cause people to smoke: should I use an observational study, an experimental simulation, or discourse analysis?' What this misses is, first, that discourse analysis is not just a method but a whole perspective on social life and research into it, and, second, that all research methods involve a range of theoretical assumptions.

Traditional psychology has often been concerned with factors and with outcomes, and these ideas are thoroughly enmeshed in thinking about both experimentation and questionnaire design. The logic of discourse analysis is however a rhetorical and normative one. Any rhetorical move can have a rhetorical counter-move: categorization, for example, can be countered by particularization (Billig, 1985). Effectiveness is not guaranteed as it should be with a causal process, for a norm is not a mechanical template. People orient towards norms, but they also regularly deviate from them (although such deviations may themselves be marked by a range of accounts or sanctions). One of the skills involved in discourse analysis lies in formulating questions that are theoretically coherent and analytically manageable. Simply importing a research question 'cold', as it were, from a traditional psychological framework is asking for trouble.

Another important difference in the formulation of questions is that traditional psychologists have become devoted to hypothetico-deductivism, in which quality research is seen to hang on a well formed question or a precisely specified hypothesis. Without wishing to endorse some naïve, assumption-free inductivism, discourse researchers have often found it productive to collect and explore a set of materials (perhaps interview transcripts or natural records of some kind) without being hampered by a need to start from any specific hypothesis. Indeed, their devotion to a fully formulated prior hypothesis has probably been one of the reasons why psychologists have been so reluctant to study records of natural forms of social interaction, such as everyday conversations between familiars or interactions in the workplace.

What are interpretative repertoires?

I pointed out earlier that discourse analysis is concerned both with the organization of texts and other talk in various practices and with the discursive resources that those practices draw upon. The notion of 'interpretative repertoires' is intended primarily to help to specify the features of one class of interpretative resources. Interpretative repertoires are systematically related sets of terms that are often used with stylistic and grammatical coherence and often organized around one or more central metaphors. They develop historically and make up an important part of the 'common sense' of a culture, although some are specific to certain institutional domains.

The idea of an interpretative repertoire is intended to accommodate two considerations: first, that there are resources available that have an 'off-the-shelf' character and that can be used in a range of different settings to carry out particular tasks; and, second, that these resources also have a more 'bespoke' flexibility, which allows them to be selectively drawn upon and reworked, according to the setting. It is the attempt to accommodate this flexible, local use that differentiates interpretative repertoires from the more Foucaultian notion of 'discourses' (Potter *et al.*, 1990; Parker, 1992). Participants will often draw on a number of different repertoires, flitting between them as they construct the sense of a particular phenomenon or as they perform different actions.

The classic research using this notion is Gilbert and Mulkay's (1984) study of scientists' discourse, which recorded the way in which scientists used one interpretative repertoire in their formal writing for justifying facts and another interpretative repertoire in their informal talk when accounting for why competing scientists were in error. More recently, the same notion has been developed in a number of studies that have a more social psychological focus (see, for instance, Potter and Reicher, 1987; Wetherell *et al.*, 1987; Wetherell and Potter, 1992; Marshall and Raabe, 1993). The overall analytical goal in these studies was the identification of repertoires and the explication of the practices that they are part of. Methodological discussions relating to repertoire analysis were provided by Potter and Wetherell (1987, ch. 7; 1995), Wetherell and Potter (1992, ch. 4), Wooffitt (1992a) and Coyle (1995).

Although the notion of interpretative repertoires has proved to be analytically fruitful, it does have certain limitations. For example, it is much more difficult to make clear and consistent judgements concerning the boundaries of particular repertoires outside constrained institutional settings such as science discourse; another problem is that the generality of the notion of a repertoire may obscure local interactional 'business' that is being achieved by particular forms of discourse (see Wooffitt, 1992b; Potter, 1996).

Is repertoire analysis the main task of discourse analysis?

No. Although it has been one important development, it is increasingly being supplemented or replaced by studies of the way that specific actions are accomplished or of the devices and procedures through which factual versions are constructed. These are studies that ask the following sorts of questions: How is a particular type of blaming achieved? How is a particular version of the world made to seem solid and unproblematic? How are social categories constructed and managed in practice? Questions of this sort require an understanding of what Billig (1987) calls the 'witcraft' of rhetoric: that is, the detailed, contextually sensitive manner in which versions are constructed and arguments deployed, as well as an appreciation of the conversational organizations within which these procedures are embedded. Indeed, it is here that the study of discourse shades into both the study of rhetoric and work on conversation analysis.

Less has been written on the methodological aspects of this style of discourse research. However, Wooffitt (1992a, 1992b) provided a clear and helpful introduction to this sort of analysis, while Potter and Wetherell (1994) described the methodological decisions and analytical practices in one study of this kind, trying to show how specific conclusions had been arrived at.

In what ways are discourse analysis and conversation analysis similar and different?

Conversation analysis (CA) has developed from the pioneering work carried out by Sacks, Schegloff and Jefferson, which aimed to provide an elaborate and systematic account of talk-in-interaction. This is sometimes crudely stereotyped by psychologists as the study of the rules of turn taking in fairly trivial conversations. However, the point of CA is to explicate the fundamental sense that interactions have for their participants. It is a fast-growing and notably cumulative field, which has highlighted major deficiencies in the 'speech act' approaches to which psychologists often look for accounts of linguistic practices (see Levinson, 1983; Schegloff, 1988), and which has provided striking analyses of topics as diverse as intersubjectivity (Schegloff, 1992), public speaking (Atkinson, 1984) and courtroom interaction (Drew, 1992).

Conversation analysis is relevant to discourse analysis in two ways. First, it provides a powerful and general understanding of interaction that has the potential to illuminate a wide range of research questions. After all, much human interaction is performed through conversation, and in order to understand many of the more psychological and social phenomena in which discourse analysts are interested, it is necessary to understand how they emerge out of the general pragmatics of conversation. This involves being mindful of such basic features as turn organization, pairing of actions and normative ranking of alternative turns, as well as considering the findings of many studies that illustrate the delicate way in which actions can be embedded within sequences of discourse. A basic practical understanding of CA is a prerequisite for producing high-class discourse analysis. Currently, the most accessible and detailed introduction to CA is undoubtedly the book by Nofsinger (1991), but the book by Heritage (1984) has an excellent chapter situating CA in its ethnomethodological context (see also Heritage, 1988).

There are specific areas in which discourse analysis and CA come together. Like discourse analysts, conversation analysts have paid much attention to the way that versions are constructed and actions performed. One of the points argued by Sacks (1992) is that interaction is not merely organized in its general forms but is also organized in its particulars. Any level of detail in talk (for example, word choices, hesitations or repairs) can be crucial for a piece of interaction; indeed, much of the business of interaction may be happening in the details. Workers in this tradition have also developed a sophisticated critique of cognitivist approaches to interaction (see Coulter, 1989; see also Chapter 2, by Steve Woolgar). CA and discourse analysis are starting to develop complementary alternatives to cognitivist theory (Edwards, 1996).

Making conversational interaction a topic of study is also important for methodological reasons. CA highlights a certain symmetry between the position of the participant and that of the analyst in a conversation. In conversations, speakers provide their own ongoing interpretation of what is going on. In most cases, a turn of talk is based on and displays some sort of analysis of the sense of the previous turn of talk. A turn may be responded to as a question, a criticism, an invitation and so on – and in responding to it in this way speakers display their own understanding. Then, if the displayed understanding is faulty, various repair mechanisms can be brought into play during the next turn in order to sort things out. What this provides is a way for the analyst to use the participants' own, situated analyses to help to check the adequacy of the analyst's claims. Note, however, that the analyst is not forced to take such displayed understanding at its face value; nor are interactions always well oiled and explicit. Nevertheless, this is one important resource for understanding interactions.

This capacity for using the participants' understandings to help to build up the analyst's account distinguishes this kind of work from other types of constructionist research that have focused on texts or documents or have considered talk that is abstracted from its conversational context. While discourse analysts have often worked with interview material, conversation analysts have worked almost exclusively with naturally occurring records of interaction, collected using audio or video recorders and transcribed to a high degree of detail.

There are a number of discussions focused on CA methods. A range of practical issues are covered by Atkinson and Heritage (1984a), Heritage (1995), Wooffitt (1990) and Wootton (1989). Psathas (1990, 1995) has attempted to characterize the analytical mentality involved in this work, and Drew (1995) provided an introduction to CA designed specifically for psychologists.

In what ways are discourse analysis and rhetorical analysis similar and different?

The study of rhetoric was revived in the 1970s, with a particular focus on the argumentative organization of texts and the different rhetorical forms used to make them persuasive (Perelman and Olbrechts-Tyteca, 1971). Billig (1987) highlighted the ways in which rhetorical ideas can be exploited to reformulate thinking within psychology. For instance, the metaphor of an argument can be used in order to make sense of thought processes: instead of viewing thought as the operation of a computing mechanism that operates upon internally consistent systems of belief, thought can be seen as being riven with argumentative dilemmas whose structure comes from the available interpretative repertoires of a culture (Billig *et al.*, 1988). So, while a more orthodox social psychologist might be concerned with an evaluative expression as an index of a person's attitude, a rhetorical analyst might be concerned to reveal the way in which that evaluation is put together to counter an established alternative (Billig, 1992b; 1992).

Conversation analysis and rhetorical analysis emphasize two different orders of relationship: CA stresses sequential organization across turns; rhetorical analysis stresses the relationship between opposing argumentative positions. The latter may themselves be sequentially organized, but this is not necessarily so. Sometimes, different positions may be expressed as direct and explicit argumentative claims using the speech act vocabulary of argument (for instance, 'I don't agree with that'). At other times, rhetorical contrasts may be built implicitly, often through competing descriptions of the same action or event, for instance, at a rape trial (see Drew, 1992; Edwards and Potter, 1992):

> *Counsel*: And during the evening, didn't Mr. O [the defendant] come over to sit with you?
> *Witness*: Sat at our table.

Discourse analysts sometimes collect a wide range of different materials (newspaper reports, interactional materials, interviews, parliamentary records) in order to facilitate the rhetorical analysis of some domain. In this way, it becomes possible to identify the rhetorical targets and oppositions of particular arguments and descriptions.

What is the role of interviews in discourse analysis?

Interviews have been used extensively in discourse analysis, but they are construed in a novel manner. Traditionally, the goal of an interview was to produce a piece of colourless, neutral interaction. However, in practice, interviews are as complex and vivid as any other type of social interaction, and responses to answers that in the abstract seem neutral and non-committal may have an important effect upon the trajectory of the interaction.

In discourse analysis, interviews have been extensively used because they allow a relatively standard range of themes to be addressed with different participants, something that is hard to achieve when simply collecting naturalistic materials. Interviews also allow a high degree of control over sampling. They are conceptualized as an arena in which one can identify and explore the participants' interpretative practices, and not as an instrument for accessing a veridical account of something that happened elsewhere or a set of attitudes and beliefs (Potter and Mulkay, 1985; Mishler, 1986). An interview can be a particularly effective way of getting at the range of interpretative repertoires that a participant has available, as well as at some of the uses to which these repertoires are put. Billig (1992) and Wetherell and Potter (1992) reported extended discourse-based studies that worked principally from interview material and that illustrate some of the analytical possibilities that they provide. Widdicombe and Wooffitt (1995) drew extensively on CA in order to show how an interview could be dealt with as an interaction rather than a research instrument, and they explored the way in which different social categories were worked up, used and avoided in the course of interview talk.

Despite the virtues of this use of interviews, there are problems in relating the practices that happen in interviews to what goes on elsewhere and in avoiding the interaction being swamped by the interviewer's own categories and constructions. Even the most open ended of interviews is guided by a schedule that specifies topics and themes as being important. Moreover, even when an interview is understood as a social interaction in its own right, the dominant question-and-answer format is not ideal for getting at the sorts of turn-by-turn display of action and understanding that conversation analysts have utilized so effectively. Partly for these reasons, discourse analysts have been increasingly turning to the study of records of natural interaction.

What is the role of records of natural interaction?

Arguably, one of the most astonishing omissions in psychology for most of the 20th century has been the study of what people do: their interactions in the home and workplace. The few attempts made in this direction were marred by a simplistic behaviourism that ignored interaction or reduced it to brute movements. Inspired in part by the success of conversation analysts in working with records of natural interaction, discourse analysts started to work with transcripts of conversations, newspaper articles, recordings of counselling sessions and similar materials.

The term 'natural' should be understood contrastively here. These settings are made up of 'natural' interaction in the sense that it has not been got up by the researcher. The test is whether the interaction would have taken place, and would have taken place in the form that it did, had the researcher not been born. Of course, the use of recording technology can itself affect participants' understandings of a situation and of their actions. However, in practice there is a range of techniques for minimizing the intrusive effects of recording (such as using a period of acclimatization). Experience would suggest that such effects are often surprisingly small or irrelevant to the research question.

In most cases, records of this sort cannot be used directly. A tape (particularly a video-tape) is a very clumsy way to deal with materials. What is required is a type of transcription which turns the record into a form that can be read through quickly, which allows different sections to be compared and which can easily be reproduced in research papers. The transcript does not replace the tape, however; indeed, it is often most helpful to work in parallel with both.

What kind of transcript is most useful?

A transcript is not a neutral, simple rendition of the words on a tape (see Ochs, 1979). Different transcription systems emphasize different features of interaction. For example, a researcher with an interest in speech therapy will need a system that records phonetics; a sociolinguist concerned with language variety will need some way of indicating accent. What system would a discourse analyst need? One common approach claims that a discourse analysis concerned with broad content themes such as interpretative repertoires needs only a relatively basic scheme that represents words and relatively gross features such as corrections and hesitations, whereas a discourse analysis more concerned with interactional specifics needs to represent pause length, emphasis, various intonational features, overlap and so on. Although there is some sense to this, it obscures certain tensions that need careful consideration.

In the first place, it is neither easy nor analytically satisfactory to make a strong distinction between content and interaction in this way. Indeed, one of the consequences of using only a basic transcription scheme is that it will often fail to capture exactly those features that show how the content is occasioned by the interaction that is taking place. In the case of a research interview, for instance, it may obscure just how much the participants' 'responses' are a product of various activities (some of which are very subtle) on the part of the interviewer. Moreover, one of the virtues of discourse analysis is that readers should be able to assess the interpretations that are made because at least a selection of the original materials have been reproduced. It might be argued that, even if the analyst is not making use of interactional specifics, readers should have them available so they can make their own judgements.

Given this strong argument for a fuller approach to transcription, it is important to stress that generating a good transcript is very demanding and time consuming. It is hard to give a standard figure for how long it takes, because much depends on the quality of the recording (fuzzy, quiet tapes can double the time that is needed) and the type of interaction (a couple talking on the telephone presents much less of a challenge than a multi-party conversation with much overlapping talk and extraneous noise). Nonetheless, a ratio of one hour of tape to 20 hours of transcription time is not unreasonable. This should not however be thought of as 'dead' time before the analysis proper. Often, some of the most revealing analytical insights come during the transcription because a profound engagement with the material is needed to produce a good transcript, and so it is always useful to make analytical notes in parallel to the actual transcription.

The system that is used most commonly in CA (and increasingly, too, in discourse analysis) was developed by Jefferson. This was developed to be used easily with the characters on a standard QWERTY keyboard, and it records features of interaction that have been found to be important for talk in interaction. For fuller accounts of this system see Atkinson and Heritage (1984b), Jefferson (1985), Button and Lee (1987) and Psathas and Anderson (1990).

Can you illustrate the value of a good transcript?

There are numerous CA studies that show how features of interaction that are often missed out in more basic transcripts can be analytically useful and interactionally consequential. For example, most of the research on 'preference organization' (the differential marking of responses such as acceptances and refusals, agreements and disagreements) is inconceivable without the availability of high-quality transcription (Levinson, 1983).

Here is a fragment of talk from a relationship counselling interview. A counsellor is asking a woman about the sequence of events that had led to her request for counselling. In the transcript, a dash marks a sharp cut-off of the preceding word; a colon marks an extension to the preceding sound; a dot in brackets indicates a noticeable pause that is too short to measure; an underline marks emphasized delivery; a downward-pointing arrow marks falling intonation in the following word; a full stop indicates a 'completing' intonation; a comma indicates a continuing intonation; and a code at the end shows the initials of the transcribers, the number of the couple, the number of their session, and the page number in the transcript from which the fragment is taken.

> *Counsellor*: Wha– (.) what happened at that point.
> *Woman*: At that poi:nt, (0.6) Jimmy ha– (.)
> my– Jimmy is extremely jealous.
> Ex– extremely jealous per:son.
> Has a:lways ↓been, from the da:y we met.
> Y'know?
>
> (DE-JF/C2/S1 – p. 4)

Two things will be immediately striking about this extract. First, the transcription symbols make it hard to read very easily. Second, there seems to be a lot of 'mess' in it: that is, repairs and changes of gear. On the first point, reading a transcript is itself something of a skill that develops with familiarity. After a period getting used to materials of this kind, in fact, it is the transcript without the symbols that looks odd – idealized, cleansed and shorn of its specificity – whereas the fuller transcript becomes evocative of the interaction captured on the tape. It starts to be possible to hear, in a sense, the delivery.

On the second point, what seems on first reading to be simply a mess is quickly understandable as something much more organized. The woman breaks off from her direct answer in order to provide a description of her partner. This description is reformulated and emphasized until it has a precise sense that is suitable for the business in hand. Put briefly and over-simply, it starts to display how the problem with their relationship is his fault (for more on this, see Edwards, 1995; Potter, 1996). The careful transcript here allows one to see this final version being actively shaped, and it gives one a feel for the versions that are being rejected as unsatisfactory.

What about reliability and validity?

Increasingly, the notions of reliability and validity have taken on a mix of everyday and technical senses within traditional forms of psychology. Reliability is taken to be established in a quantitative fashion by such techniques as test–retest correlations or interrater reliability, whereas validity is often taken to be established by a congruence among different instruments or perhaps by a triangulation from different research methods. Because of the different theoretical assumptions in discourse work, along with its largely non-quantitative nature, these approaches to reliability and validity are largely unworkable in this context. Nevertheless, these are important concepts that can be and have been addressed in this work. For a start, reliability and validity are not so clearly separated from each other in discourse analysis. Four important considerations relevant to this are deviant-case analysis, participants' understanding, coherence and readers' evaluation.

Deviant-case analysis. A discourse analysis study will often work with a collection of instances of some putative phenomenon with the aim of showing some pattern or regularity. For example, a researcher might claim that, when politicians or others are interviewed on news broadcasts, they generally avoid treating the interviewer as responsible for views expressed in questions (Heritage and Greatbatch, 1991). Some of the most useful analytical phenomena are cases that seem to go against the pattern or are deviant in some way. In this type of work, deviant cases are not necessarily disconfirmations of the pattern (although they could be). Instead, their special features may help to confirm the genuineness of the pattern (see Heritage, 1988). For example, when a news interviewee does treat the interviewer as accountable for a view posed in a question, it can create serious trouble for the interaction (see Potter, 1996). The deviant case can highlight exactly the kind of problem that shows why the standard pattern should take the form that it does.

Participants' understanding. As I noted in my discussion of CA, one of its important elements is its use of participants' own understandings. Thus, instead of the conversation analyst saying that a turn of talk is a compliment (say), the focus is upon how the participants treat it. At its simplest, is it responded to with an acknowledgement, perhaps, or with an expression of self-depreciation ('Oh that's very sweet of you, it's just an old top I picked up cheap')? A common criticism of discourse analysis is that there is no check upon its interpretations. However, a close attention to participants' understandings provides one kind of check.

Coherence. One of the features of CA and increasingly of discourse work is its cumulative nature. A set of studies can be combined together and can build upon the insights of earlier work. For example, research on fact construction builds upon insights about accountability from earlier studies, and its success provides further confirmation of the validity of those studies (Edwards and Potter, 1993). There is thus a sense in which each new study provides a check upon the adequacy of the previous studies that are drawn on. Those studies that capture something about interaction can be built on, whereas those that do not are likely to be ignored.

Readers' evaluation. Perhaps the most important and distinctive feature in the validation of discourse analysis is the presentation of rich and extended materials in a way that allows the readers of discourse studies to evaluate their adequacy. This has two facets. On the one hand, it allows the readers to assess the particular interpretation that is made, since it is presented in parallel with the original materials. This is not the case in much ethnographic work, where the interpretations have to be taken largely on trust, and where any data that are presented are largely pre-theorized. Nor is this the case with much traditional experimental and content analysis work, where it is rare for 'raw' data to be included or for more than one or two illustrative codings to be presented. On the other hand, readers are themselves skilled interactants, with a wide range of cultural competencies as viewers of news interviews, members of close relationships, recipients of compliments and so on. Thus, they can make judgements not merely about the abstract relations between materials and interpretations but also about the adequacy of more general claims.

I have one final comment to make about validity. These features are not all present in all discourse analysis studies, nor do they singly or in combination guarantee the validity of an analysis. However, as sociologists of science have repeatedly shown, there are no such guarantees in science.

Is constructionist research necessarily qualitative?

Some researchers have treated the issue of quantification as definitional: they have assumed that it is part of the meaning of constructionist work in general and of discourse analysis in particular that it is qualitative. However, I believe this gives too much importance to the quantity–quality divide and risks an uncritical support of qualitative work and rejection of quantitative work, thereby simply replacing one set of prejudices with another. I would prefer to see quantification as being quite appropriate in certain situations, depending upon a range of analytical and theoretical considerations. Nevertheless, arguments for quantification in discourse work can easily miss the point that the research goal is often to explicate instances of a specific category: what is a compliment, or blaming, or an error account? That is not something that can be decided by counting but is itself a prerequisite for counting.

The issue of how far quantification is appropriate in conversation analysis and discourse analysis has recently received detailed attention. A useful source is a discussion among various researchers on conversation, communication and discourse that explores different perspectives on the role of counting (Wieder, 1993). Schegloff (1993) and Heritage (1995) both provided clear arguments for being cautious when seeking to quantify, because of a range of difficulties that arise when transforming discursive materials into a numerical form. However, the issue of quantification is undoubtedly going to become more important with the future growth of this research area.

In parallel with these discussions of the role of quantification in research on discourse, there is an increasing interest in quantification practices as a research topic in their own right. This research has looked at quantification in both technical and everyday situations. Some of the classic work in this area was carried out by Sacks (1992) on participants' measurement systems. He was particularly concerned to show that mundane practices of quantification were not a poor imitation of the apparently more precise and more accurate technical practices of statisticians and scientists but had a subtle and sophisticated logic of their own. For example, a request for an appointment at 'half past four' is not simply a less precise way of requesting an appointment at 4:28. Rather, different sets of expectations about punctuality, the type of meeting it is, and what delay would count as 'late' are called into play in each case.

Other work in 'ethnostatistics', as Gephart (1988) dubbed the study of statistics as a cultural practice, has looked at the way in which health economists have performed cost–benefit analyses (Ashmore *et al.*, 1989), the construction of accounts of the success of charity-funded cancer treatment (Potter *et al.*, 1991) and the textual practices for representing the 'subjects' in social psychology experiments (Billig, 1994). This work eats away at the idea that there is a straightforward choice between doing quantitative and qualitative research and shows that entirely different considerations are involved in each.

Conclusions: is that it?

There are many other considerations about the nature of discourse research and of constructionist work more generally that could be addressed here. However, coming to see these abstract considerations is quite different from learning to do discourse analysis, which is very much a craft skill like riding a bicycle or sexing a chicken. Rosalind Gill will give her own account of what is involved in the practical implementation of discourse analysis in Chapter 11, but there is no substitute for learning by doing. Moreover, such learning is almost always better carried out collaboratively, so that interpretations and ideas can be explored with co-workers. Such learning is time consuming, it is hard work, and it is often frustrating. However, the ultimate goal is to develop an analytical mentality that is sensitive to the action orientation of talk and texts.

Chapter 11

Discourse analysis: practical implementation

Rosalind Gill

One of the most exciting developments within the social sciences in recent years has been the development of interest in the analysis of discourse. Distinctive approaches have emerged from different disciplinary locations and different theoretical traditions, and there is now a huge variety of perspectives that lay claim to the name 'discourse analysis'. What these perspectives share is a rejection of the idea that language is simply a neutral means of reflecting or describing the world and a conviction of the central importance of discourse in constructing social life. In this chapter, I am going to discuss just one of these different approaches, that elaborated by Jonathan Potter and Margaret Wetherell (1987) in their ground-breaking book *Discourse and Social Psychology*. The chapter is divided into three sections and a Conclusion. In the first, I shall set out the basic themes of the approach. Next, I will discuss the issues raised by the practice of discourse analysis. Finally, I shall give a brief example based on a magazine article in order to give an indication of the type of analysis that is generated by this approach.

Themes of discourse analysis

It is useful to think of discourse analysis as having four main themes. First, discourse analysis takes discourse itself as its topic. The term 'discourse' is used to refer to all forms of talk and texts, whether they be naturally occurring conversations, interview material or written texts. Discourse analysts are interested in texts in their own right, rather than seeing them as a means of getting at some reality that is assumed to lie behind the discourse, whether social or psychological. This focus clearly differentiates discourse analysts from most other social scientists, whose concern with language is generally restricted to finding out what 'really' happened in some situation or what some individual's attitude to X, Y or Z 'really' is. Instead of seeing discourse as a pathway to some other reality, discourse analysts are interested in the content and organization of talk and texts.

Another theme of discourse analysis is that language is constructive. Potter and Wetherell (1987) argued that the metaphor of construction highlights three facets of this approach. First, it draws attention to the fact that discourse is manufactured out of pre-existing linguistic resources. As Potter *et al.* (1990) remarked, 'language and linguistic practices offer a sediment of systems of terms, narrative forms, metaphors and commonplaces from which a particular account can be assembled' (p. 207). Second, the metaphor illuminates the fact that the assembly of an account involves a choice or selection from a number of different possibilities. Even the most simple of phenomena can be described in a multiplicity of different ways, and any particular description that is chosen will depend upon the orientation of the speaker or writer (see Potter *et al.*, 1990). Finally, the notion of construction emphasizes the fact that we deal with the world in terms of constructions, not in a way that is somehow 'direct' or unmediated; in a very real sense, texts of various kinds *construct* our world. The constructive use of language is an aspect of social life that is taken for granted. The notion of construction, then, clearly marks a break with traditional, realist accounts of language, in which it is taken to be a transparent medium, a relatively straightforward path to 'real' beliefs or events, or a reflection of the way things really are.

The third feature of discourse analysis that I want to stress here is its concern with the 'action orientation' or 'function orientation' of discourse. Discourse analysts regard all discourse as a social practice. Language is viewed not merely as an epiphenomenon but as a practice in its own right. People use discourse in order to *do* things: to offer blame, to make excuses, to present themselves in a positive light and so on. This underlines the fact that discourse does not occur in a social vacuum. As social actors, we are continuously orienting to the interpretative context in which we find ourselves and constructing our discourse in order to fit that context. This is obvious in relatively formal contexts such as hospitals or courtrooms, but it is equally true of all other contexts. To take a crude example, you might give a different account of what you did last night depending upon whether the person inquiring was your mother, your boss or your best friend. It is not (or, at least, not necessarily) that you would be being deliberately duplicitous in any of these cases but just that you would be saying what seemed 'right' or what 'came naturally' for that particular interpretative context. All discourse is occasioned.

It is important to note that the notion of 'interpretative context' is not a narrow or mechanistic one. It is used not simply to refer to the gross parameters of an interaction, such as where and when it takes place and to whom the person is speaking or writing, but also to pick up on more subtle aspects of the interaction, including the kinds of actions that are being performed and the participants' orientations. Discourse analysts are involved *simultaneously* in analysing discourse and in analysing the interpretative context.

Even the most apparently straightforward, neutral-sounding utterance can be involved in a whole range of different activities, depending on the interpretative context. Take the sentence, 'The printer on my computer has broken'. Its meaning can change radically in different interpretative contexts:

(1)   when said to a flatmate after you have lent it to her for a weekend, it may be part of an accusation, an implicit blaming;

(2)   when said to a tutor or a colleague who is waiting for a paper from you that is late, it becomes perhaps part of the process of offering an excuse;

(3)   when said to a friend who has a printer that is compatible with your computer, it may be the beginning of a request to borrow her printer.

And so on. As Jonathan Potter argued in Chapter 10, drawing on the insights of conversation analysis, one way of checking your analysis of the discourse is to look at how the participants involved responded, as this can offer valuable analytical clues. For example, perhaps the tutor or the colleague being addressed replied, 'Oh, I see. Well, can you get the paper to me by Friday, do you think?' This indicates that your story of the broken printer was heard as an excuse, even though no mention of the late paper was in fact made. More generally, the important point is that there is nothing 'mere' or insubstantial about language: talk and texts are social practices, and even the most seemingly insignificant statements are involved various kinds of activities. One of the aims of discourse analysis is to identify the functions or activities of talk and texts and to explore how they are performed.

This brings me to the fourth theme: discourse analysis treats talk and texts as being organized rhetorically (Billig, 1987, 1991). Unlike conversation analysis, discourse analysis regards social life as being characterized by conflicts of various kinds. As such, much discourse is involved in establishing one version of the world in the face of competing versions. In some cases, this is quite obvious: for example, politicians are clearly attempting to win people around to their view of the world, and advertisers are clearly attempting to sell us products, lifestyles and dreams. However, it is also true of other discourse. The emphasis on the rhetorical nature of texts directs our attention to the ways in which all discourse is organized to make itself persuasive.

Doing discourse analysis

It is much easier to explicate the central tenets of discourse analysis than it is to explain how actually to go about analysing discourse. In attempting to specify the practice of discourse analysis, one walks a tightrope between, on the one hand, what one might call the 'recipe book' approach to doing research, which involves laying out procedures step by step, and, on the other hand, the complete mystification of the process. Neither of these is satisfactory. While the attraction of the methodical recipe is easy to understand, somewhere between 'transcription' and 'writing up', the essence of doing discourse analysis seems to slip away; ever elusive, it is never quite captured by descriptions of coding schemes, hypotheses and analytical schemas.

This does not mean that you should abandon all hope of learning how to analyse discourse. As Widdicombe (1993) argued, although the skills of discourse analysis do not lend themselves to procedural description, 'they are not mysterious and can be developed through practice and example' (p. 97). In this respect, learning to do discourse analysis is like learning many other professional tasks: journalists, for example, are not given a formal set of rules for identifying what makes an event 'news', and yet after a short time in the profession their sense of 'news values' is hard to shake. Equally, in the case of discourse analysis, there is really no substitute for learning by doing, as Jonathan Potter pointed out in Chapter 10.

The most useful starting point is a suspension of belief in what is normally taken for granted in language use (Potter and Wetherell, 1987). This is analogous to the process that anthropologists often describe as 'rendering the familiar strange' (see Chapter 8, by Christina Toren). It involves changing the way in which linguistic material tends to be seen, so that instead of seeing discourse as reflecting underlying social or psychological realities, the focus of interest shifts to the ways in which accounts are constructed and to the functions that they perform. It is difficult to exaggerate the significance of this shift in emphasis. From my own experience, doing discourse analysis fundamentally changes the way in which you see and hear language and social relations: it involves the development of an 'analytic mentality' (Schenkein, 1978), which does not readily fall away when you are not sitting in front of a transcript.

Because discourse analysis is not simply a method that can be used off the shelf but entails a radical epistemological shift, it is not surprising that it has rather different ways of proceeding from those to be found in traditional social science research. As Billig (1988a) noted, the analysis of discourse and rhetoric requires the careful reading and interpretation of texts, rigorous scholarship rather than an adherence to formal procedures. It also involves asking different questions from other researchers. The kinds of question you should ask are not self-evident: the same text can be interrogated in a whole range of different ways by discourse analysts. For example, consider the transcript of a discussion among teenagers concerning safer sex. One researcher might be interested in looking at how the speakers warranted their decisions about whether or not to use condoms. Another might be concerned with examining the functions of different kinds of presentations of the self during the discourse. Yet another might be interested in looking at the ideological significance of constructions of what it means to practise safer sex. And this does not exhaust the range of possible questions. How you analyse discourse, then, depends upon the questions that you are asking.

Nevertheless, there are some commonalities to most forms of discourse analysis. Once the data collection is complete and the material has been painstakingly transcribed (see Chapter 10, by Jonathan Potter), the time has come for the analysis to begin. This is the moment that you have been waiting for and simultaneously dreading. A good place to start is by simply reading and re-reading your texts and your transcripts and getting to know them. By the time that you have got to writing up, they will be echoing around your head verbatim as you try to get to sleep! Joking apart, there is really no way of getting away from this, and many discourse analysts talk about the process of analysis as one of 'immersion'. It takes time really to immerse yourself in the material, and, like ethnography, it is not the kind of research activity that can be practised in a spare couple of hours between a seminar and a lecture. It can take days or weeks to become familiar with the material, during which time it will be with you while you are driving, cooking or involved in a variety of other activities.

The process of becoming familiar with your material is a necessary preliminary to coding. The categories used for coding will obviously be determined by the questions of interest. Sometimes they will seem relatively straightforward: for example, one part of my analysis of interviews with broadcasters involved examining the accounts that they gave for the lack of women working in radio (see Gill, 1993b). The initial coding process involved going through the transcripts and highlighting or selecting out all the occasions when the broadcasters referred to female broadcasters. On other occasions, coding can be much more difficult, and the phenomena of interest may not be clear until some initial analysis has been completed. Potter and Wetherell (1987) described how, in their study of New Zealanders' accounts of racial inequality, their own understanding of what should be coded changed repeatedly as their analysis became more sophisticated. Indeed, in my own study of accounts given for the lack of female disc jockeys, it became clear that many other aspects of the interview material were relevant to the analysis in addition to direct references to female broadcasters. For example, references to the 'qualities' that 'all good DJs should possess' turned out to contain a number of hidden assumptions about gender.

This highlights an important point about coding: that it should be done as inclusively as possible (see Potter and Wetherell, 1987). At the preliminary stage, all instances that seem only vaguely relevant and all borderline cases should be included. What 'inclusion' or selecting out for coding actually means depends upon one's style of working: it may mean files full of photocopies, it may mean long lists with relevant transcript page numbers or it may mean file cards in index boxes. For me, the end of the coding process means that I have come to the stage where my household is subjected to colonization by a plethora of small piles of paper, each representing the data in one particular category of interest.

Once the initial coding is complete, it is time to move to the most difficult stage, that of analysis. In their useful summary of 'how to analyse discourse', Potter and Wetherell (1987, p. 168) pointed out that academic training teaches people to read for gist, but that this is precisely the wrong spirit in which to approach analysis:

> If you read an article or book the usual goal is to produce a simple, unitary summary, and to ignore the nuance, contradictions and areas of vagueness. However, the discourse analyst is concerned with the detail of passages of discourse, however fragmented and contradictory, and with what is actually said or written, not some general idea that seems to be intended.

Thus, doing discourse analysis involves you in the interrogation of your own assumptions and the ways in which you make sense of things: 'The analyst constantly asks: Why am I reading this passage in this way? What features produce this reading?' (Potter and Wetherell, 1987, p. 168).

It can be helpful to think of the analysis as being made up of two related phases. First, there is the search for pattern in the data. This will take the form of both variability (in other words, differences within and between accounts) and consistency, and it may also involve the attempt to identify interpretative repertoires. For a discussion of this notion, see Wetherell and Potter (1988) and Chapter 10, by Jonathan Potter; and see also Parker (1992) and Burman and Parker (1993) for discussion of an alternative formulation in terms of 'discourses'. Second, there is the concern with function, with formulating tentative hypotheses regarding the functions of particular features of the discourse and checking these against the data (Potter and Wetherell, 1987). Of course, presenting it in this way makes it sound easy and glosses over hours of frustration and apparent dead ends. In practice, identifying the patterning and functions of discourse is often difficult and time consuming.

One useful analytical strategy, suggested by Widdicombe (1993), is that of regarding the ways in which things are said as being 'a solution to a problem' (p. 97). The analyst's task, therefore, is to try to identify the problem and how what is said constitutes a solution. In my study of how broadcasters accounted for the small number of women in radio, one of the discursive problems to which the broadcasters whom I interviewed had to orient was that of being heard as sexist while still wanting to offer 'legitimate' reasons for the lack of women. The transcripts are full of disclaimers (cf. Hewitt and Stokes, 1975), such as 'I'm not being sexist but . . .', which preceded the expression of something that could easily be heard as sexist. Widdicombe's suggestion would have been useful in drawing attention to the fact that the broadcasters were attempting to solve a discursive problem. This focus has also been useful in work on ideological dilemmas (Billig *et al.*, 1988).

Discussing the analysis of interactions, Wooffitt (1990) proposed a number of further questions that could help in examining the material. For example: What interactional business is being attended to during the discourse? How do speakers display their orientation to this business? And what strategies do they use to accomplish this? Such questions can offer helpful pointers in analysing discourse.

Nevertheless, there is no way of avoiding the fact that discourse analysis is a 'craft skill' that can be difficult and is always labour intensive. As Wetherell and Potter (1988) noted, it is common to work with one analytical schema for several days, only to have to revise it or discard it because the linguistic evidence does not fit precisely. It is important that the discourse analyst remains open to alternative readings of the text and does not fall prey to the suppression of variation that characterizes much mainstream psychology. Doing discourse analysis means finding a way of making analytical sense of texts in all their fragmented, contradictory messiness.

Discourse analysis requires a sensitivity to the way that language is used. However, as Billig (1991) pointed out, it requires a sensitivity to what is *not* said, as well. As analysts, we are concerned with talk and texts, but we are also concerned with silences. Moreover, our membership of particular social groups and cultures does not debar us from producing valuable analyses. On the contrary, it is necessary for analysis that we use our knowledge of those groups and cultures. Without an awareness of the social, political and cultural trends and contexts to which our texts refer, we would be unable to carry out any analysis. We would be unable to see the alternative versions of events or phenomena that the discourse we were analysing had been designed to counter; we would fail to notice the (sometimes systematic) absence of particular kinds of account in the texts that we were studying; and we would not be able to recognize the significance of silences. Nevertheless, to say that an awareness of the context of discourse is vital is not to imply that this can be neutrally and unproblematically described. When one talks of relevant contextual features, one is also producing a version, *constructing* the context as an object. To put it bluntly, our own discourse as discourse analysts is no less constructed, occasioned and action oriented than the discourse that we are studying. For this reason, many discourse analysts have become interested in what it means to be reflexive as analysts (see Edwards and Potter, 1992; Edwards *et al.*, 1995; Gill, 1995).

What discourse analysts do is to produce *readings* of talk, texts and contexts. We do not claim to 'discover' the 'truth' or even to produce a 'definitive' reading, for we are aware that the same text can be read and interrogated in many different ways. However, what analysts can do is to produce readings that are warranted by attention to the detail of texts and that lend coherence to the discourse being studied. In Chapter 10, Jonathan Potter discussed the ways that discourse analysts have of checking the reliability and validity of their analyses. Therefore, I will turn now to giving a brief illustrative example of the practical implementation of the discourse analysis approach.

A discourse analysis case study: accounting for vegetarianism

To demonstrate some of the insights produced by discourse analysis, I am going to present a preliminary analysis of a short (one-page) article on vegetarianism (Box 11.1). The piece is taken from the BBC magazine *Vegetarian Good Food*, and it is one of a number of regular features concerning well known personalities who are vegetarian, in this case the actress Hayley Mills. These features appear on the back page of the magazine, and they take the same form every month, the individuals explaining why they became a vegetarian and discussing the impact this has had on their life. Although the article purports to be an interview, with the text enclosed between quotation marks throughout, the interviewer's questions are not reproduced and the article omits many of the features that a discourse analyst's transcript would have highlighted, such as pauses, 'ums' and 'ahs', false starts and corrections (see Chapter 10, by Jonathan Potter). The speech is not presented in its 'raw' form, then, but has already been 'processed' (to use an appropriate food analogy). This means that many significant aspects of the interview are not available for analysis. Nevertheless, as a magazine article that purports to offer a genuine account of issues relating to vegetarianism, it is still of considerable interest.

Box 11.1 Text extract

01   To be honest, although I'd always been attracted to the idea of
02   becoming vegetarian, I'd also thought it would be both unpopular
03   with my family and impractical on a day-to-day basis. But then,
04   in 1983, I watched a TV documentary narrated by Julie Christie
05   which catalogued – in a totally unsensational way – man's
06   inhumanity to animals.
07   From abattoirs through the fur trade to testing cosmetics on
08   defenceless animals, the horrors unfolded. It presented such an
09   appalling and unflinching picture of cruelty that I couldn't sleep;
10   indeed, I was so upset, so deeply moved, I wept and wept all that
11   night. I'd been shown a picture of hell on earth and I couldn't
12   easily remove it from my mind.
13   Up until that point, I have to admit my dietary intake had been
14   pretty traditional. It was roast beef on Sunday, steak tartare as a
15   treat in a restaurant, and bacon, eggs and sausages for breakfast —
16   I'd never known any different. But once you accept the inevitable
17   truth of what you're doing, you can't pretend any more; you can't
18   pretend it doesn't matter, or that it has no effect on the planet or
19   your consciousness. There's no denying your actions.
20   Very soon after I made my decision, I was working with Martin
21   Shaw, who'd been a vegetarian for years. We had to rehearse some
22   scenes at a remand home and the boys were intrigued to have
23   Martin in their midst because he was something of a hero to them
24   through his television role in *The Professionals* – they saw him as
25   a bit of a tough guy.
26   One day, one of them suddenly said, 'I hear you're a vegetarian,
27   Martin', amongst much nudging of ribs, 'Why's that then?' Martin

— Continued —————————————————————

Before proceeding, it is worth acknowledging one final issue. Some readers may think that, in analysing an account concerning why somebody became vegetarian, I am implicitly criticizing it. This is not so. As it happens, I am myself a long-standing vegetarian, and my own account of the reasons for giving up animal products would not differ markedly from that given by Hayley Mills. However, there are more important issues at stake behind this objection. A significant body of work within the discursive tradition has been concerned with what one might broadly characterize as ideological critique (Wetherell *et al.*, 1987; Potter and Wetherell, 1988; Billig, 1991; Parker, 1992; Wetherell and Potter, 1992; Gill, 1993a, 1993b). This work has explored the means by which racism and sexism are reproduced, and it has drawn attention to the ways in which everyday talk often serves to justify inequities or injustice. This tradition has been so powerful that discourse analysis is nowadays often regarded as if it were

—— *Continued* — — — — — — — — — — — — — — — — — — —

28   didn't bat an eyelid. 'Simple', he said. 'It's because I can't think
29   of one good reason to eat meat other than that I like the taste'.
30   That struck me as so true, so right. We do not need to tear into
31   flesh with our teeth any more than we need to tear food with our
32   hands. . . . [A few lines omitted here]
33   It's not difficult to serve any number of delicious dishes that
34   don't use meat. But then it's becoming increasingly easy to find
35   vegetarian dishes in restaurants – and even at functions, as long
36   as you tell them in advance. Invariably the people at the same
37   table who are eating beef Wellington for the ninth time that
38   month look rather wistfully at your delicious lasagne dish.
39   Too many people still assume that your energy levels are
40   somehow depleted when you become vegetarian, but it just isn't
41   true. The body needs protein, but meat is not the only source; you
42   can also get it from milk and cheese and yoghurt and wheat and
43   corn and nuts and beans and vegetables — the list goes on.
44   What you don't get if you give up meat are all the drugs and
45   chemicals and fear poisons that the animal releases just before
46   it's killed. I would say my energy levels are better now than they
47   ever used to be. My weight is also constant, which it never was
48   when I used to eat meat. . . . [A few lines omitted here]
49   I could never go back to eating meat, nor am I spurred on by
50   sentimentality towards animals. It's just common sense allied, I
51   hope, to a more compassionate way of living. I believe totally
52   that if we countenance the kind of cruelty that is perpetrated to
53   animals, we're more likely to countenance cruelty to each other.
54   And vegetarianism is part and parcel of a kinder, gentler world.

Hayley Mills, from *BBC Vegetarian Good Food*, April 1995, p. 82.

synonymous with critique, especially within psychology. One problem with this equation is that it ignores types of discursive work that do not take as their primary focus questions about power or ideology (see Chapter 10, by Jonathan Potter, for a discussion of different strands of discourse analysis research).

More fundamentally, though, this idea is implicitly circular, because it suggests that what needs to be criticized is always already known (see Edwards *et al.*, 1995). This contradicts the spirit of discourse analysis, which has shown the subtlety and situated nature of ideological practice. Rather, discourse analysts have argued that the relation between discourse and power should be an analytical question, and they stress that showing how a text is constructed is not the same as attacking it or undermining it. Nevertheless, the practice of analysing texts does raise ethical dilemmas, as it breaks with a more humanist tradition of critical research in which respondents' talk is treated as 'authentic' and is accorded respect.

It also raises political questions for feminists and others who are concerned with radical social transformation, in the way that it seems to objectify and distance participants, rather than seeking to empower them.

There are a number of different ways in which the text that follows could be analysed, but I am interested in two broad orientations. First, there is a group of questions about how the speech is organized to warrant the decision to become vegetarian and about how it is made persuasive. In Widdicombe's (1993) terms, the implicit 'problem' for the speaker in this case is to account convincingly for a radical change in the way in which she lives her everyday life. Second, I am concerned with how the speech is designed to defend the speaker from criticism; how it is organized to offer rhetorical protection. Here the 'problem' is to defend the decision to be vegetarian in a climate where there is still much hostility towards vegetarianism. It will become clear that these two orientations are not separate but are inextricably meshed together within the discourse, and I have separated them merely for analytical purposes.

Generating rhetorical effectiveness: constructing vegetarianism

The aim of this part of the analysis is to examine how vegetarianism is constructed in the text. My preliminary analysis of the interview would suggest that at least five different strategies are employed to achieve this. These construct:

(1) the moral nature of vegetarianism, and its role in bringing about a more just society for people *and* animals;
(2) the benefits of vegetarianism to health and wellbeing;
(3) the horror of people's cruelty to animals;
(4) the delicious variety of food available for vegetarians (which make them the envy of carnivores); and
(5) an appeal to other well known and well liked vegetarians to warrant the decision.

There is not space to discuss all of these constructions here. Instead, I will focus my attention on examining how the decision to become vegetarian is warranted and made persuasive.

The account offered takes the form of a classic tale of *revelation*, in which a new insight about the world is constructed as the origin of a fundamental *transformation*. Mills's narrative constructs for us an image of someone who had thought about becoming vegetarian but who had rejected it because of the sacrifices or inconvenience that it might entail. But then one day she gained an insight which transformed her way of seeing the world. So powerful were the feelings she experienced in response to this revelation, that they over-rode all her misgivings and anxieties about vegetarianism, and since that day she has never eaten meat. Part of what makes the story so rhetorically effective (aside from its sheer drama, the depiction of one thing that changed her life) is our familiarity with it as a cultural narrative. It has resonances with religious and political discourse, and it also the organizing theme of many films. In many ways, the story represents one of the classic narratives of realist discourse, depicting as it does the transformative effects of the 'discovery' of some 'truth'. Indeed, so widespread and deeply embedded is it that I was very tempted to use the same narrative earlier in this chapter to describe the effect on my life of encountering discourse analysis. Like Mills on her vegetarianism, I would have constructed a contrast between two periods in my life, one 'before' becoming a discourse analyst, the other 'after', and in doing so I would have stressed the revelations that discourse analysis produced and its transformative effect upon the way that I see the world.

One of the basic points made by discourse analysts is that in talking about events and phenomena people are involved not in neutral description but in constructing versions to serve specific discursive purposes. It is thus worth looking in some detail at the way in which Mills constructs the nature of the experience that she had in order to make her decision to give up meat seem to flow naturally or straightforwardly from it. Mills's transformative experience took the form of a revelation about the way in which animals were treated that was brought about by a television documentary. She constructs an image of someone realizing, for the first time, the 'truth' about 'man's inhumanity to animals'. This is contrasted with a time before the documentary when 'I'd never known any different'.

A common feature of accounts of revelation and transformation seems to be the level of detail that they involve. Speakers frequently go to considerable lengths to supply (often apparently irrelevant) contextual information, such as the date or the location or the weather at the time. In this case, the information that Mills supplies concerns the year and the name of the programme's narrator. One function of this detail seems to be to underscore the authenticity and veracity of the account. But what of the manner in which the programme is described? 'From abattoirs through the fur trade to testing cosmetics on defenceless animals, the horrors unfolded. It presented such an appalling and unflinching picture of cruelty that I couldn't sleep'. What this extract illustrates quite clearly is that description and evaluation are not separate activities (Potter and Wetherell, 1988). The constructions are already evaluated: 'defenceless animals', the unfolding 'horrors' and the 'appalling and unflinching picture of cruelty'. Compare these formulations with the language that might be used by farmers or by scientists who carry out experiments on animals. The point is not that either is true but simply that in *all* cases discourse constructs versions of the world.

The picture presented here is an apocalyptic one, a vision of 'hell on earth' (line 11). The use of extreme case formulations is striking: 'I couldn't sleep; indeed, I was so upset, so deeply moved, I wept and wept all that night. I'd been shown a picture of hell on earth and I couldn't remove it easily from my mind'. Taken together, they generate a powerful rhetorical effect that suggests it was a realization about *the nature of the world* that caused Mills to become vegetarian, rather than anything to do with her interests or disposition. The emotional reaction that she experienced is warranted by her account of the programme, which was itself simply showing in an 'unflinching' and, she stresses, 'totally unsensational' manner the way we treat animals. Her deeply felt grief in turn becomes a warrant for the decision to become vegetarian; indeed, it accomplishes the decision to give up meat as the only proper course of action. In this way, vegetarianism is presented as the only appropriate way to deal with the knowledge of humans' cruelty to animals and is seen to flow straightforwardly from possession of this knowledge.

Another interesting feature of Mills's construction of what made her become vegetarian is the contrast between the level of detail given about her emotional reaction to the documentary and the vagueness with which she describes what it was that she came to 'know' through that programme. She talks about accepting 'the inevitable truth of what you're doing' and of no longer being able to 'pretend it doesn't matter' without specifying the referent of either formulation. She goes on to conjure global concerns about 'the planet' or 'consciousness' and concludes her argument with the rather platitudinous claim, 'There's no denying your actions'.

What characterizes this passage, then, is its vague and inexplicit nature. Research has shown that systematic vagueness like this can be a powerful way of defending one's argument from attack (Drew and Holt, 1989; Edwards and Potter, 1992). Vague, epigrammatic or global formulations can provide a barrier to an easy undermining precisely because they do not allow the argumentative leverage for the initiation of criticism. Moreover, if they fail and criticisms are made, the speakers can deny the particular meaning being attributed to them. One function of Mills's vagueness, then, is to provide a defence against potential criticisms. In the next section, I shall explore further ways in which her decision to become vegetarian is rhetorically defended.

Rhetorical protection: defending vegetarianism

One of the basic insights of discourse analysis, as I argued earlier, is that speech and writing are not simply designed to offer convincing or persuasive accounts of events or phenomena, but they are also involved in various activities. I want to explore next the way in which the discourse is designed to protect itself from potential criticisms. In a rhetorical context in which there is still hostility towards vegetarianism, including specific campaigns against it from the meat industry, one of the problems for vegetarians is that of how to defend the decision to stop eating meat. Before concluding this chapter, I will explore how Mills's discourse is organized in order to rebut several common objections to vegetarianism: namely, that it is impractical, that it will make you unpopular, that it is unhealthy and that vegetarians are motivated by sentimentality.

One way that Mills orients to potential objections to vegetarianism is to imply that she herself once agreed with these objections. In the opening lines of the interview, she claims that despite her long-standing attraction towards vegetarianism, she had always thought that it would be 'unpopular' and 'impractical'. This is framed as an admission, something about which she has owned up to the interviewer ('To be honest'). Having raised these objections herself, Mills then counters them. Her first way of countering them is by deeming them to have been mistaken. Although her sons were 'a bit cheesed off at first not to be served meat any more', they 'quickly lost their appetite for meat and became fully vegetarian' (lines omitted from extract). Her fears about unpopularity within her household are thus presented as having been ground-less. In the same way, vegetarianism is constructed as causing no practical problems: 'It's not difficult to serve any number of delicious dishes that don't use meat. But then it's becoming increasingly easy to find vegetarian dishes in restaurants – and even at functions' (lines 33–35). Both these objections, then, are presented as having been entirely without foundation, and she has effectively 'inoculated' her argument against criticism on these grounds. Indeed, she goes further, arguing not only that it causes her no problems, but that her vegetarian food is a source of envy from meat eaters, who look 'wistfully' at her 'delicious' food while they are consigned to eating the same old meat dish 'for the ninth time that month'.

The second way in which she counters potential criticisms is by making them seem trivial and of little consequence when compared with the force of the moral realization that she had about human beings' cruelty to animals. This new knowledge meant that she could not 'pretend it doesn't matter' or 'that it has no effect'. The implication here is that she was 'pretending' or engaged in self-deception before she took the decision to stop eating meat, and that critics using the same argument are guilty of the same offence. She implicitly contrasts the problems of unpopularity or impracticality with 'man's inhumanity to animals', with the 'horrors' of the abattoir and with the 'appalling . . . picture of cruelty' in such a way as to render them insignificant as objections to vegetarianism. The implication, then, is that only people devoid of moral sense would use such trivial excuses not to become vegetarian, once they had become aware of the 'horrors' of our 'inhumanity to animals'.

A different strategy for rhetorically defending her argument is used in lines 39–45. Here, Mills orients directly to a potential criticism of vegetarianism on health grounds, and she argues that 'it just isn't true'. It is interesting to look at how these critical views are formulated. The views of 'Too many people' are cast as assumptions that mistakenly are 'still' held, against all the evidence. Their assumptions are constructed as vague and lacking in rigour: 'your energy levels are somehow depleted'. This is contrasted with the factual-sounding account constructed by Mills herself. This asserts, 'The body needs protein, but meat is not the only source', and goes on to list some other sources. The list, which contains no fewer than eight items ('milk and cheese and yoghurt and wheat and corn and nuts and beans and vegetables') plays an important part in undermining the criticism of vegetarians and suggests that this is borne of ignorance of all non-meat protein sources. This is reinforced by Mills's statement, 'the list goes on', which gives the impression that there were many more eligible foods that she could have mentioned had she had the time or the inclination to do so.

A common way of defending arguments from criticism is through attack, and this is another strategy that Mills uses in order to counter potential criticisms of the effects of vegetarianism upon health. Continuing in an impersonal and descriptive style of discourse, she argues: 'What you don't get if you give up meat are all the drugs and chemicals and fear poisons that the animal releases just before it is killed' (lines 44–46). The implication is clear: namely, that it is meat eaters, who are routinely ingesting chemicals and toxins, who should really be the focus of health concerns, not vegetarians. Mills concludes the paragraph by saying that not only are her energy levels better now than when she ate meat, but also her weight has stayed a healthy constant.

The final potential criticism to which Mills's account is oriented is the charge that vegetarians are motivated solely by sentimentality in their feelings towards animals. Given the extent to which Mills uses discourse about emotions as a resource to account for her vegetarianism (see the previous section), it is not surprising that accusations of sentimentality are salient for her. She is clearly sensitive to the possibility of being heard as overly sentimental. One way in which she orients to this at various points in the interview (as already noted) is through the use of a seemingly factual, impersonal, descriptive discourse. Several discourse analysts have pointed out that this kind of discourse is more likely to be persuasive than discourse that seems to be motivated by particular interests or psychological dispositions (e.g., Smith, 1978; Potter and Wetherell, 1988). More importantly in this context, it serves to offer a cool, apparently rational defence of vegetarianism alongside an emotional response towards cruelty to animals and thus to play down the accusation of 'sentimentality' in her talk, or some related criticism.

This charge is also refuted directly in lines 49–51: 'I could never go back to eating meat, nor am I spurred on by sentimentality towards animals. It's just common sense allied, I hope, to a more compassionate way of living'. The assertion that one's views are 'just common sense' is, of course, a common rhetorical strategy, one that is used frequently by politicians. As well as operating to rebut claims of sentimentality, Mills's claim can be seen as part of an hegemonic struggle, an attempt to rearticulate the meaning of vegetarianism. More specifically, it can be seen as a strategy to contest depictions of vegetarians as being eccentric or extreme. It serves to distance Mills from contemporary cultural images of vegetarians as 'political', as 'fanatical' about animal rights and as advocating (sometimes violent) direct action. It re-presents the decision to become vegetarian as part of an ethics of kindness, gentleness and compassion, and it locates that decision inside rather than outside the domain of common sense.

Conclusions

In this short analysis, I have been able to discuss only a small number of the features in which discourse analysts are interested. Nevertheless, I hope to have given some indication of the potential of discourse analysis for offering new insights. In analysing that most ubiquitous of cultural texts, the short, chatty magazine interview, my aim has been to demonstrate that even apparently commonplace, trivial texts are complex rhetorical accomplishments. My analysis discussed some of the means by which the interviewee warranted her decision to become vegetarian (and pointed to several others, which there was no space to explore); and it also explored some of the ways in which she defended her decision from attack or criticism. These two orientations are not separate, but they were treated independently for the purposes of analysis. I could have looked at a number of other, inextricably linked features of the text, such as the way in which it was designed to produce particular positive identities or subject positions for the interviewee or how it was organized to attack people who still eat meat. The simple point is that even in a short text such as this one, there is a huge amount going on that is of interest to psychologists and other social scientists.

One potential objection to discourse analysis is that it does not produce broad empirical generalizations of the sort that much traditional research sees as its goal. For instance, readers may point out that this kind of analysis does not help one to theorize the causes of vegetarianism or get one any closer to explaining why some people become vegetarians but others do not. The simple answer to this sort of criticism is that it is misplaced. Discourse analysis does not set out to identify any universal processes. Indeed, discourse analysts are critical of the idea that such generalizations are possible, arguing that discourse is always constructed from particular interpretative resources and always designed for specific interpretative contexts. Thus, we might have expected Mills to construct a rather different account of her vegetarianism, had she been interviewed for the magazine of the Meat and Livestock Commission rather than for a vegetarian publication. In short, all discourse is occasioned: there are no trans-historical, transcultural, universal accounts, except those that might be 'produced' by the artificiality of the research context.

Another, related objection concerns the issue of representativeness. It might be argued that the interview I selected for analysis is not representative of accounts of why people become vegetarian. Again, this criticism somewhat misses the point. My interest was in the way that the account was constructed, the kinds of rhetorical resources that were used and the functions that they served. The aim was not to say anything about how commonly these kinds of warrants for vegetarianism may be used. This does not mean, however, that discourse analysts do not sometimes wish to make claims of representativeness for their analyses. For example, if I were to interview 100 vegetarians in Britain concerning their reasons for changing their diet, it is likely that after about ten interviews I would not be generating any new material in terms of the broad explanations that were offered, but simply finding again and again that people were citing cruelty to animals, health reasons, the depletion of global resources and so on as their reasons. Having completed the interviews, then, I might claim to have obtained a representative sample of the discursive resources available for justifying vegetarianism in Britain in the 1990s. However, simply making this claim would be to miss a whole range of other crucial features of the interviews, such as those highlighted in my analysis. As Jonathan Potter argued in Chapter 10, while discourse analysts do not reject quantification altogether and indeed question the idea of a straightforward quality–quantity distinction, a prerequisite for counting the instances of a particular category is a detailed explication of how to decide whether something is an instance of the relevant phenomenon. This will undoubtedly prove much more interesting and complex than apparently straightforward attempts at quantification.

A third disadvantage for people thinking about carrying out discourse analysis is the sheer effort that is involved. As I pointed out earlier, discourse analysis is extremely labour intensive. In addition to the data collection and the long process of transcribing interview material, there is the amount of time that it takes to develop the skill of analysis, and this in itself can be considerable. Even when one has some experience of doing analyses, there is no way of avoiding the lengthy process of coding and interpretation or of heading off the many false starts and dead ends that are an integral – and inevitable – part of the process.

Against this, though, are the many strengths and opportunities that discourse analysis has to offer. It represents both a practical way and a theoretically coherent way of analysing a whole variety of talk and texts, taking them seriously in their own right and treating them in their full specificity. In the few years since it was fashioned as an approach, it has made enormous achievements within psychology and moved from attempts to reformulate traditional psychological questions to a far more radical critique of cognitivism that raises the possibility of a thoroughly 'discursive psychology' (Edwards and Potter, 1992).

In addition to disciplinary critique, discourse analysis has produced a range of fresh questions concerned, for example, with the construction of facts and the social organization of texts more generally. Moreover, discursive work has made important contributions to ideological critique, examining the ways in which relations of domination and subordination are reproduced and justified, and highlighting the flexibility of ideological practice.

Finally, discourse analysis together with feminist research has been significant in opening up questions about the practice of research in psychology and about the way that it is written. Analysts have not sought to exempt their own texts from the claim that all discourse is constructed and constructive, and have begun to explore ways of practising reflexivity within their own research. In particular, they have used a variety of new literary forms to challenge authorial authority and to draw attention to the status of their own texts as constructions. However, these moves are only just beginning, and a serious exploration of questions about ethics, reflexivity and empowerment promises many urgent and exciting directions for the discourse analysts of the future.

Part III
Evaluating qualitative
research methods

The relationship between qualitative and quantitative research: paradigm loyalty versus methodological eclecticism

Martyn Hammersley

During the past 30 years or so, the distinction between qualitative and quantitative research has become a key axis in methodological discussions within psychology and the social sciences. And there is no doubt that it captures something of importance. However, it is a distinction that is by no means straightforward, either in its meaning or in its significance. Indeed, it often acts as a lightning conductor for numerous other disagreements about the principles and practice of research. In this chapter, I will examine the main attitudes taken towards this distinction and consider their cogency.

One of the most influential forms of quantitative research, experimental method, has long been central to the identity of psychology as a discipline, and it still shapes the thinking of the majority of its practitioners. Indeed, for many, experimental work is the *sine qua non* of scientific inquiry. (Symptomatic of this is that, in a book which is otherwise highly critical of scientific psychology, Kline (1988, p. 13) treats scientific method as identical with experimentation.) At the same time, there have always been competing definitions of research within the discipline of psychology. These have been particularly strong in the clinical and developmental areas. While the experimental paradigm has had powerful sway even there, psychoanalysis (for example, Kvale, 1986), observational studies of children (for example, Wright, 1960) and other approaches have from very early on offered rather different conceptions of psychological research, many of these being closer to what would today be regarded as qualitative method. More recently, especially within social psychology, there has been a strong reaction against experimentalism, and it has been subjected to a series of challenges, listed by one commentator as the 'artifacts crisis', the 'ethics crisis' and the 'relevance crisis' (Rosnow, 1981).

This has led to so-called 'new paradigm' research, itself internally diverse, and more recently still to the development of contextualist and constructionist approaches (Harré and Secord, 1972; Armistead, 1974; Reason and Rowan, 1981; Gergen, 1985, 1994b; Rosnow and Georgoudi, 1986). There have also been applications within psychology of various qualitative methods, developed in sociology and other disciplines, notably discourse analysis and grounded theory

(Potter and Wetherell, 1987; Henwood and Pidgeon, 1992). In addition, the influence of feminism upon psychology has been important in methodological as well as theoretical terms, and one effect of this has been to promote qualitative research yet further (see Wilkinson, 1986; Hollway, 1989).

These various 'alternative' approaches have adopted rather different attitudes to experimentalist orthodoxy. As in research in the human sciences more generally, these can be ranged along a spectrum. At one end is the idea that 'qualitative' and 'quantitative' refer to internally coherent and comprehensive research paradigms, which are founded on incommensurable philosophical or political presuppositions. At the other end of the spectrum is the belief that quantitative and qualitative methods are complementary and should be used as and when appropriate, depending upon the focus, purposes and circumstances of the research. I will examine each of these contrasting views in turn.

Competing paradigms

The most common position held by *qualitative* researchers concerning the relationship between 'qualitative' and 'quantitative' approaches is that these represent fundamentally different paradigms. This view can take at least two forms. Some see these approaches as in conflict, with one as the true way, the other as the way of error or even of sin! For example, in his introduction to an influential early collection of articles about qualitative methods, Filstead (1970) comes close to this position, though he seems to back off from it towards the end of his discussion. Others regard quantitative and qualitative approaches as alternatives, where each is true in its own terms, and where the choice between them is a matter of taste or personal preference. Smith (1989) takes this view, although he makes it clear which paradigm *he* regards as superior (see Hammersley, 1992a). Whichever form of this view is adopted, however, it implies a sharp distinction between quantitative and qualitative approaches in terms of their fundamental assumptions about the world and how it can and should be studied. Bryman (1988, p. 94) provides a useful summary of the contrasting features that are often ascribed to these two paradigms, and this is shown in Table 12.1.

There are, however, some serious problems with this 'paradigm' view of the relationship between quantitative and qualitative research. For one thing, if we look at research today in the human sciences, we find that much of it does not fall neatly into one or other of these two categories. There are multiple method-ological dimensions on which research varies: these do not lie in parallel, and each involves a range of positions, not just two.

At the level of method, for example, quantitative and qualitative research are sometimes defined as involving the use of different sorts of data. As Bryman (1988) indicates, the contrast is frequently formulated as being between 'hard data', on one side, and 'rich data', on the other. These terms are not very illumin-ating, but some writers have been more specific. For instance, Miles and Huberman

TABLE 12.1 *Some differences between quantitative and qualitative research*

	Quantitative	*Qualitative*
Role of qualitative research	Preparatory	Means to exploration of actor's interpretations
Relationship between researcher and subject	Distant	Close
Researcher's stance in relation to subject	Outsider	Insider
Relationship between theory/concepts and research	Confirmation	Emergent
Research strategy	Structured	Unstructured
Scope of findings	Nomothetic	Ideographic
Image of social reality	Static and external to actor	Processual and socially constructed by actor
Nature of data	Hard, reliable	Rich, deep

Source: A. Bryman (1988) *Quantity and Quality in Social Research*. London: Unwin Hyman, p. 94.

(1994) begin their discussion of qualitative data analysis by defining qualitative data as 'usually consisting of words rather than numbers' (p. 1). As their qualification allows, however, this difference is a matter of degree. It is certainly not the case that there are just two kinds of researcher, one who uses only numbers and another who uses only words. It *is* true that there are research reports that provide only numerical data and others that provide only verbal data, but there is also a large proportion of studies that use both. Thus, many research reports (including some that are regarded as examples of qualitative research) combine tables and statistical analysis with the use of quoted extracts from documents, interviews or field notes.

More than this, though, the distinction between numerical and verbal data is itself of questionable value. In most cases quantitative data are ultimately based on accounts in words, whether those of the researcher or of the participants, so that there is one sense in which all psychological and social data are fundamentally verbal. Conversely, it has frequently been pointed out that qualitative researchers regularly make quantitative claims in verbal form, using formulations like 'regularly', 'frequently', 'sometimes', 'generally', 'typically', 'not atypically' and so on; and the fact that they use words instead of numbers does not alter the character of their claims.

Several distinct issues are involved in the contrast between numerical and verbal data. One is the question of the *precision* of description. However, this does not involve a clear-cut choice between two options. The levels of precision adopted by quantitative researchers vary according to the nature of the data available and the purposes for which their measurements have been carried out. It is widely recognized that one should not express one's results in terms that imply a greater degree of precision than their likely accuracy warrants; and it is also true that adequate precision may not always require the use of numbers. Sometimes it may not be legitimate to use terms that are more precise than 'sometimes', 'often', 'generally' and so on (even where what is being measured is scalable in principle), given the nature of the data and the purposes for which they are being used. (Indeed, my own use of imprecise formulations might not have been lost on the reader!) And, where we are concerned with the presence or absence of a particular type of feature in a situation, this can often be described quite precisely in verbal terms (although, needless to say, there are times when qualitative researchers use verbal formulations that are insufficiently precise for their purposes: see Hammersley, 1991, pp. 65–66).

Precision is not the only issue involved in the contrast between quantitative and qualitative data, of course. References by qualitative researchers to the 'richness' of their data relate to at least two other features. One is the fact that such data are framed in terms of the broad and flexible resources of natural language, rather than using the finite descriptive repertoire provided by a measurement scale. The other is that these data are not narrowly restricted to the information that is directly relevant to the research question being investigated, so that information about the wider context is also provided (see Delamont and Hamilton, 1984). Here again, though, how valuable these features are is a matter of degree and of judgement, as also are how wide a range of descriptive resources is used and how much contextual information is to be collected and provided. We are not faced with a choice between finite or infinite resources and between no contextual or full contextual information, but rather with a choice between varying amounts of both resources and information.

There is no stark contrast to be found, then, between verbal and numerical data, or even between precise and imprecise, structured and unstructured, and contextualized and uncontextualized data. Rather, there is a range from more to less precise, more to less structured, and more to less contextualized types of data from which to choose. Furthermore, our decisions about what levels of precision, structure, and context are appropriate in relation to any particular study should depend upon the nature of what we are trying to describe, upon the likely accuracy of our descriptions, upon our purposes, and upon the resources available to us, not on ideological commitment to one methodological paradigm or another.

Much the same is true of another much-cited putative difference between qualitative and quantitative methods. It is sometimes argued that quantitative researchers collect data in 'artificial' settings, but that qualitative researchers use 'natural' settings. Thus, experiments are artificial in the sense that they involve the study of a situation that has been specifically established and controlled by the researcher. By contrast, ethnographic research, in particular, is usually concerned with the investigation of situations that would have occurred without the researcher's presence, and generally involves the adoption of a role in that situation that is designed to minimize the impact of the researcher upon what occurs.

Once again, this is not a simple dichotomy. Quasi-experiments and field experiments are specifically intended to reduce the 'artificiality' of the experimental situation while maintaining some control of variables. Moreover, some quantitative researchers carry out their research in natural settings, notably in the form of 'systematic observation' (see Croll, 1986). Conversely, qualitative researchers, even ethnographers, use interviews as well as observation, sometimes adopting quite directive interviewing strategies and thereby creating what may be relatively 'artificial' contexts for data collection (see Hammersley and Atkinson, 1995, ch. 5). There is, then, a complex array of potential data-collection settings that are more or less 'artificial' and 'natural'.

Over and above this, though, the distinction between artificial and natural settings is potentially misleading. What happens in a school classroom or in a court of law, for example, is no more natural than what goes on in a psychological laboratory. To treat classrooms or courtrooms as natural and experiments as artificial is to forget that research is itself part of the social world, something that should never be forgotten. Of course, there is an important issue implicit in this distinction, which relates to variation in the extent to which the researcher is able to control variables and the degree to which reactivity is introduced; but these too are matters of degree. While experiments provide us with a much stronger basis for drawing conclusions about causal relationships than do either surveys or case studies (other things being equal), they never give us total and guaranteed control of variables. Conversely, we can sometimes draw reasonable conclusions about the validity of theoretical claims on the basis of evidence from the naturally occurring comparative cases that are studied by survey and case study researchers (Hammersley, 1985).

In much the same way, qualifications must also be applied to the criticism that the findings from experiments do not generalize to the 'real world', that is, to non-experimental situations (see Rosnow, 1981, ch. 3; Greenwood, 1982). While it is true that the participants' behaviour is often influenced by the experimental situation and by the personal characteristics of the researchers, this by no means renders the results of experimental research of no value. Much depends upon whether the reactivity involved affects the results in ways that are relevant to the research topic and in a manner that cannot be allowed for. Moreover, even ethnographic research in 'natural' settings is not immune to reactivity. While ethnographers may strive to minimize their effects on the situations being studied, this cannot be guaranteed; and sometimes these effects can be significant, despite the researcher's best efforts. We must also remember what the significance of reactivity is: it makes the setting being investigated unrepresentative of those others about which the researcher wishes to generalize (what is sometimes referred to as the issue of 'ecological validity'). But reactivity is not the only source of ecological invalidity. A natural setting can also be unrepresentative because it differs in important ways from most other cases in the same category. Simply choosing to investigate 'natural' settings and seeking to adopt a low profile within them, or analysing 'naturally occurring data' such as recorded talk or published texts, does not ensure ecological validity (see Dipboye and Flanagan, 1979).

In summary, then, the difference between quantitative and qualitative approaches is not clear cut as regards the use of particular kinds and sources of data. Rather, what we find is a range of methods being used by researchers in psychology and the social sciences, a diversity that cannot be reduced to a bare dichotomy without serious distortion. Furthermore, selection among these methods requires judgement according to situation and purpose, rather than judgement based on a commitment to one or another competing philosophical view of the world and of the nature of inquiry.

Some of those who take 'quantitative' and 'qualitative' to refer to incommensurable paradigms recognize that there is diversity at the level of the methods used, but they insist nevertheless that there are just two (or, at least, a very small number of) coherent philosophical perspectives underlying research in psychology and the social sciences, often tracing the history of these competing paradigms back to the 19th century (see, for example, Smith, 1989). However, while it is certainly true that much of the debate in that century about the scientific status of the discipline of history foreshadowed arguments made about quantitative and qualitative methods in psychology and the social sciences in the 20th century, these earlier discussions did not take place between representatives of just two contrasting positions, nor is there direct continuity between positions adopted in the 19th century and those adopted today (see Hammersley, 1989). Moreover, the appeals made by psychologists and social scientists to philosophical rationales for their work are as diverse as the methods that they use.

Let us look briefly at three respects in which quantitative and qualitative paradigms are often taken to be philosophically opposed: in terms of realism versus idealism, naturalism versus anti-naturalism, and deductivism versus inductivism. Smith (1984), among others, has argued that quantitative research is wedded to a 'realist' epistemology, in the sense of assuming that true accounts correspond to how things really are, and that competing accounts must be judged in terms of whether the procedures that are adopted ensure accurate representation of reality. By contrast, he claims that qualitative research is 'idealist', in that it rejects any possibility of representing reality: it recognizes that there may be 'as many realities as there are persons' (p. 386).

I think that it can be shown with little difficulty that this is inaccurate as a characterization of the distribution of philosophical perspectives among researchers. First, not all quantitative researchers are realists. Take the following example:

> In any valid epistemological or scientific sense we must say that the substitution of a Copernican for the Ptolemaic theory of the universe represented a major change in the universe. To say that it was not the universe but our conception of it which changed is merely a verbal trick designed to lead the unwary into the philosophical quagmires of Platonic realism, for obviously the only universe with which science can deal is 'our conception' of it.

What we have here is an idealist account of knowledge in natural science, in which there is a denial that it can represent some independent reality. But it does not come from a qualitative researcher. It comes from George Lundberg (1933, p. 309), a positivist champion of quantitative method in sociology during the 1930s who was strongly influenced by contemporary developments in psychology. There was a strong element of phenomenalism in the late 19th century and early 20th century positivism (see Kolakowski, 1972), by which I mean the view that we can have knowledge only of how things appear to us (in Kant's terms, we can only know *phenomena*, not *noumena*). This was reflected in psychology in the form of operationism, a position whose advocates insisted that it made no sense to see measurement operations as representing some reality existing beyond them, since there could be no knowable reality beyond experience (see Benjamin, 1955).

By contrast, as Karen Henwood pointed out in Chapter 3, qualitative researchers have often adopted a realist position, by which I mean the idea that the task of research is to document features of objects that exist independently of the researcher's interpretation of them. Thus, Blumer (1969a) wrote in a characteristically realist fashion of naturalistic, or qualitative, research as being concerned with 'lifting the veil' that covers reality and 'unearthing' what is going on (p. 39). More recently, Harré (1979; Harré and Secord, 1972) has based his advocacy and practice of ethogenic research in social psychology on an explicit realism. Many other contemporary exponents of qualitative method have also declared their allegiance to realism (see, for example, Porter, 1993; Miles and Huberman, 1994, p. 4). Indeed, it is precisely the reliance of ethnography upon realism that has come under increasing criticism from constructionists (for example, Woolgar, 1988a) and from qualitative researchers influenced by post-structuralism (Clifford and Marcus, 1986; Denzin, 1990). What this suggests is that there is no simple match between the realist/idealist and quantitative/qualitative distinctions.

Again, quantitative method is often regarded as taking natural science as its model, while qualitative researchers are seen as rejecting that model. In other words, quantitative research is believed to be founded on 'naturalistic', and qualitative work on 'anti-naturalistic', assumptions. (I am using the original meaning of 'naturalism' here. It is necessary to note that some qualitative researchers have radically redefined it and applied it to their own approach: see Lofland, 1967; Blumer, 1969a; Matza, 1969.) Yet many qualitative researchers have treated the natural sciences as exemplary. Early advocates of qualitative method (for instance, Thomas and Znaniecki, 1927) saw their work as modelled upon the successful approach of natural science. And, while today most qualitative researchers are more guarded about the parallels between their work and that of natural scientists (some even rejecting the natural science model outright), there are still advocates of qualitative method who justify their approach in naturalistic terms. (Once again, the work of Harré and those influenced by him provides an obvious example.) It is also worth noting that some of the techniques that are employed by qualitative researchers assume much the same law-like conception of the world as natural science (see Hammersley, 1989, ch. 8).

In fact, the issue of whether natural science is an appropriate model for research in the human sciences is by no means a simple one. There are at least three complications:

(1)   Which natural science is being taken as the model and which period of its development is being considered? There are significant differences in method between physics and biology, for example, and there has been variation within each of these disciplines over time.

(2)   Which interpretation of the methods of natural science is being adopted? Keat and Urry (1975) identified positivist, conventionalist and realist interpretations of these methods, and even these distinctions do not exhaust the variety of views that are to be found among philosophers of science.

(3)   What aspects of natural science method are being treated as generic? Not even the most extreme positivist would argue that the methods of physics should be applied *in toto* to the study of human beings. And there are few who would insist that there is no aspect of natural scientific inquiry that is relevant to research in the human sciences. Once again, what is at issue is a matter of degree.

In terms of naturalism also, then, we do not find a contrast between just two incommensurable philosophical positions, and neither quantitative nor qualitative research is wedded exclusively to one position. Much the same is true of deductivism versus inductivism. Qualitative researchers sometimes characterize their approach as inductive, contrasting it with the deductive or hypothetico-deductive method of quantitative research. But this too is an oversimplification. Not all quantitative research is concerned with hypothesis testing. Many psychological and social surveys are straightforwardly descriptive, and some quantitative research is explicitly concerned with theory generation. (Baldamus (1979) provides an example of inductive quantitative analysis, and Erickson and Nosanchuk (1979) describe techniques specifically designed to explore quantitative data sets.)

At the same time, by no means all qualitative researchers reject the hypothetico-deductive method. For example, grounded theory was originally characterized by Glaser and Strauss (1967) as opposed to deductivism, but Strauss (1987, pp. 11–12) has subsequently insisted that it involves not only induction but also deduction and verification. In fact, of course, all research involves both deduction and induction in the broad senses of those terms: in all research, we move from ideas to data as well as from data to ideas. One *can* distinguish between studies that are primarily exploratory, concerned with description and with generating theoretical ideas, and those that are more concerned with testing hypotheses. But these types of research are not alternatives: we need both. Nor is the former necessarily quantitative and the latter qualitative.

It seems clear, then, that the paradigm view of the relationship between quantitative and qualitative approaches is empirically inaccurate, not just at the level of method but also at that of the philosophical assumptions guiding research.

It is also misleading in its portrayal of the options available to researchers: it implies that we are faced with two homogeneous traditions that are internally coherent and based upon opposed philosophical views. In fact, there is a considerable range and variety of techniques for data collection and analysis in psychology and the social sciences; and there is no fixed relationship between particular philosophical views and the use of particular methods. Furthermore, even the most superficial perusal of the philosophical literature shows that there are not simply two epistemological positions from which to choose. We do not have to be either naïve realists and empiricists, on the one hand, or idealists and relativists, on the other. In epistemology, as in methodology, such dichotomies obscure the range of possibilities that is open to us.

Rather than reducing the methodology of psychology and the social sciences to just two (or even three or four) approaches, we need instead to recognize the diversity of methodological options available and to note that these arise not just from differences in philosophical views but also from variations in substantive theoretical ideas and in practical goals.

Methodological eclecticism

My discussion of the paradigm view of the relationship between qualitative and quantitative approaches implies that there might be a good deal to be said for the opposing view, for the notion that these are simply different methods that are appropriate according to purpose and circumstance. What is being implied here is a form of methodological eclecticism; indeed, the *combination* of quantitative and qualitative methods is often proposed, on the ground that this promises to cancel out the respective weaknesses of each method.

Such eclecticism has a long history in the research literature (see, for example, Zelditch, 1962; Sieber, 1973). It has the advantage of recognizing the diversity of methodological approach that is to be found in psychology and the social sciences, in particular the way in which quantitative and qualitative techniques are often used side by side in the same research (see Bryman, 1988, 1992). This can take at least three forms:

(1) *Triangulation*. Here, the findings obtained from quantitative and qualitative techniques are used to check each other on the basis that they are likely to involve different sorts of threat to validity. For example, children's responses to a questionnaire about with whom they are friends can be compared with ethnographic observation of whom they talk to and play with in the classroom and playground (for example, Denscombe *et al.*, 1986).

(2) *Facilitation*. Here, one approach acts as a source of hypotheses, or as the basis for the development of research strategies, in the other. For example, qualitative interviewing can be used as a preliminary to survey research, both to generate hypotheses and to develop questionnaire items that are intelligible to the intended audience. It may also be used as a means of debriefing participants who have taken part in experiments, in order to understand why they behaved in

the way that they did (Crowle, 1976). Alternatively, the findings of experiments or survey research may serve as a basis for the initial framing of research problems in qualitative work and even as a source of hypotheses to test. A famous example is the testing of cognitive dissonance theory by Festinger *et al.* (1964) through a participant observation study of an apocalyptic religious group.

(3) *Complementarity*. Here, the two approaches provide different sorts of information that complement one another. Qualitative research is sometimes regarded as being better able to produce information about interactional processes and about participants' perspectives, whereas quantitative research is presumed to be better at documenting frequencies and causal patterns. Thus, experiments may be regarded as providing a strong basis for revealing causal relationships among variables, but one which is usefully complemented by qualitative research that can show how these relationships operate in 'natural' situations. Equally, qualitative research is sometimes regarded as more capable of providing detailed and accurate information about a small number of cases, while some kinds of quantitative research establish the basis for wider generalization.

This methodologically eclectic view of the relationship between quantitative and qualitative method also has the advantage of emphasizing the *practical* character of research. One of the weaknesses of the paradigm view is that it seems to imply a form of linear rationality, whereby researchers first decide on their philosophical commitments and then base their selection of research topics and strategies on those commitments. Little needs to be said to establish that this is not true empirically. In large part, as researchers, we acquire the resources that make up our methodological orientations from others working in the field, and in this way we inherit practical methods and philosophical assumptions simultaneously. Indeed, there are probably presuppositions built into our chosen approaches of which we are not even aware. Thus, the way in which research is carried out is not in any simple sense derived from, or built upon, a set of fundamental philosophical presuppositions. The decisions that have to be taken in research necessarily rely heavily upon a variety of practical considerations regarding the particular goals of the research, the resources available, the obstacles faced, and so on.

Despite all this, however, methodological eclecticism is not entirely satisfactory as a way of thinking about the relationship between quantitative and qualitative approaches. For one thing, it may encourage us to forget the many unresolved methodological and theoretical problems concerning research in psychology and the social sciences. For example, where quantitative research necessarily tends to assume the existence of reproducible causal patterns, qualitative researchers have often stressed the contingent and diverse character of human perceptions and actions, and the role in these of cultural interpretation. Thus, some qualitative researchers fear that a *rapprochement* with quantitative research would lead to the distinctive methodological features that are associated with their approach being forgotten (see Smith and Heshusius, 1986). There is certainly a danger of this, and it would result in us losing sight of something important about human behaviour: that it does not seem to be a causal product in the same sense, or to be generated by the same sort of mechanisms, as the behaviour of physical or even of biological phenomena.

The reverse danger also applies. Experimental psychologists have often insisted that research in the human sciences cannot avoid assuming some sort of causality or law-like relationship, analogous to what is characteristically assumed by natural scientists. And they have also emphasized the weak capacity of non-experimental research for identifying causal relationships. These are important points which could also be lost in the adoption of a methodologically eclectic approach. It is not uncommon to find qualitative researchers apparently believing that they are able to 'see precisely which events led to which consequences' (Miles and Huberman, 1994, p. 1). There is a fundamental disagreement here about the nature of the 'orderliness' of phenomena that is assumed and about how it can be identified; this is a disagreement that has not as yet been satisfactorily resolved.

It is tempting for the methodologically eclectic to dismiss such matters as merely 'theoretical', yet they have important implications for how we do research and for what conclusions we can draw on the basis of our data. (An instructive example in this respect is ethnomethodology, which is discrepant not only with quantitative but also with most qualitative research, even that of constructionists: see Button, 1991; Button and Sharrock, 1992.) An emphasis upon the practical character of research is certainly of value, then, but one must also recognize that the practice of research often rests upon problematic presuppositions. A pragmatic orientation can easily lead to a failure to recognize this, because it tends to treat the methods used by quantitative and qualitative researchers as given, or as merely technical matters.

I can illustrate this in a concrete way by looking at one example of combining qualitative and quantitative techniques. It is frequently recommended that social survey and case study techniques be combined in such a way that the former provides generalizability while the latter offers detail and accuracy. I do not want to deny that combining these methods can be of value, but it is not as straightforward as is sometimes supposed.

For one thing, the recommendation tends to assume that generalization from a sample of cases to a larger population is always part of the task of research. However, there are two reasons why this need not be so. First, one is sometimes intrinsically interested in particular cases. This is most obviously true with some evaluation research and much action and practitioner research. But, even in more traditional kinds of research, interest occasionally lies in the case studied for itself, because that single case has general social significance. An obvious example would be investigation of the work of a government department or agency, since its decisions have nationwide effects. A second reason why we should not see all research as concerned with empirical generalization is that it is important to distinguish between generalizing from a sample to a finite population, on the one hand, and making inferences about the truth of a theory, on the other. Thus, some research is concerned not with empirical generalization but with theoretical inference.

    Empirical generalization and theoretical inference are often conflated, both
by qualitative researchers and by quantitative researchers. Indeed, there are those
who would reject this distinction, arguing that inferences about the truth of a
theory are one form of generalizing from sample to population. But this neglects
an important difference between the two. Theories apply to all circumstances
where specified conditions hold. For example, labelling theory in the social
psychology of deviance holds that the application of a deviant label by a powerful
agency leads under certain circumstances to changes in the identity and
circumstances of the people labelled, such that their subsequent behaviour
reinforces the labelling. The implication is that this occurs wherever the relevant
conditions obtain: labelling has had these effects in the past, is having them in
the present, and will continue to have them in the future. (This interpretation of
labelling theory is a rational reconstruction that would not be fully accepted by
all of those who were involved in developing it: see Becker's (1973) discussion
of some of the debates surrounding it.)

    In short, theories refer to an infinite population of cases, which we cannot
access in such a way as to be able to draw representative samples. This is different
in significant respects from the situation where we are seeking to generalize to a
finite and accessible population. However, the difference is not just a practical
one: it relates to the manner in which the population is constituted in each
particular instance. Assuming that a theory is true, the population that is defined
by its conditions is causally homogeneous (whereas the populations specified
within empirical generalizations need not be so, and usually are not). Indeed, it
is this causal homogeneity that provides for the possibility of theoretical inference
in the absence of representative sampling. For these reasons, where our concern
is with developing and testing theory, it is not immediately obvious that social
surveys are better than case studies or even that case studies need to be
supplemented by social surveys. Or, at least, any argument to this effect would
have to be more than an appeal to the superiority of surveys as a basis for empirical
generalization.

    Moreover, even if we restrict ourselves to generalizing from samples to finite
populations, we must not assume that case study inquiry is incapable of this. It is
true that within survey research this sort of generalization has come to be almost
entirely identified with the use of statistical sampling techniques, and that these
demand information about relatively large samples. But this is a confusion of
purpose with particular means, very useful though those means are. Rather
surprisingly, some advocates of case study research have accepted criticism of
their work that suggests it is incapable of empirical generalization, meeting this
charge with a denial that it ever relies on such generalization (see, for example,
Yin, 1994, p. 10). They insist that a case study is concerned only with theoretical
inference. And, yet, if one looks at much qualitative research, this is manifestly
not the case. Many case studies draw conclusions that imply empirical
generalization. For example, in the introduction to his study of an English
secondary school, Ball (1981) reports that 'nationally, Beachside appears to be a
fairly typical established comprehensive' (p. 20). In this way he claims that his

findings are representative of many other comprehensive schools. Such claims about typicality are commonplace in qualitative research.

It is important, then, to recognize that statistical sampling is not the *only* method of assessing the representativeness of a sample or a set of cases. Others include comparing the cases studied with the population to be represented, where information is available about relevant features of that population (for example, in official statistics or in other studies in the literature). Another is the use of multi-site investigations, in which sites are selected by means of sampling decisions that are designed to ensure representation of relevant kinds of heterogeneity in the population. Nor is the size of the sample always crucial: where we can be fairly sure a population is homogeneous in relevant respects, a case study or a small number of cases can be an adequate basis for generalization. In this connection, it is worth remembering that most sampling in survey research relies not just upon statistical sampling theory but also upon knowledge about the population, which is used as a basis for stratifying the sample. Furthermore, the validity of generalization is *always* a matter of judgement, even when we use statistical sampling techniques.

Also significant is the fact that, where case studies are concerned with generalizing to a finite population, this is not always to a population that is accessible to statistical sampling. Whenever we are faced with claims about typicality or representativeness, we must ask: 'Typical or representative of what, and in what respects?' In an interesting article concerning generalizability in qualitative research, Schofield (1989) has pointed out that the populations to which we wish to generalize are often populations of cases that *may* occur in the future or even populations of cases that *could* occur. She discusses a number of sampling strategies that qualitative researchers could use to facilitate generalization to such populations. A classic example of research using such a strategy is Cicourel and Kitsuse's (1963) study, *The Educational Decision Makers*. The researchers chose to investigate a school that was markedly atypical at the time they studied it, but which they believed to be representative of how American schools would be in relevant respects in the future, in particular in having a highly developed student counselling system. This is what is sometimes referred to as 'critical case analysis', and what this example illustrates is that it can be an effective strategy for empirical generalization as well as for theoretical inference.

This discussion of generalizability and the relationship between case studies and surveys points to a need to rethink some of the methodological ideas often associated with both qualitative and quantitative research. First, we must question the frequently assumed omni-relevance of empirical generalization: that is, of generalization from a sample to a finite population of extant cases. Second, we must resist the tendency to conflate theoretical inference and empirical generalization. Third, we must recognize that empirical generalization is often a relevant goal in case studies. But, finally, we must not confuse such generalization with the statistical means used to achieve it in survey research. In this respect, and others, simply treating quantitative and qualitative methods as being adequate as they stand and putting them together is unacceptable. It is to ignore the fact that they are not just methods but carry with them particular methodological presuppositions. These may be in conflict with one another, and they are sometimes unreliable.

It is also worth noting that the paradigm view and methodological eclecticism share something in common: treating quantitative and qualitative research as being complementary and of equal value still assumes that the methods of social and psychological research can be neatly assigned to two categories, and that differences within each category are less important than those between them. But this is to neglect the heterogeneity and internal inconsistency to be found within these two rather artificial categories. The diversity of what counts as qualitative research should be all too obvious from the other chapters in this book. Nor is this diversity limited to the use of different methods. There are fundamental disagreements among qualitative researchers at a philosophical and political level. We can see this particularly in the field of educational research, where the main methodological disagreements are no longer between representatives of quantitative and qualitative research, but between those adopting mainstream qualitative approaches and those advocating various radical alternatives, notably constructionists, critical researchers, feminists and post-structuralists (for example, Gitlin *et al.*, 1989; Eisner and Peshkin, 1989; Guba, 1990; see also Denzin and Lincoln, 1994a). And these divisions of opinion are at least as deep as those that had previously been assumed to separate quantitative and qualitative researchers. Moreover, while the differences in approach and perspective to be found among quantitative researchers are perhaps less fundamental, they are by no means insignificant (see, for example, Mook, 1983; Lieberson, 1985; Levine, 1993). Given this heterogeneity, even the methodologically eclectic are in danger of treating the qualitative/quantitative distinction as being more informative than it is.

Conclusion

In conclusion, then, neither of the two views that I have discussed (that quantitative and qualitative research represent competing paradigms; and that they are of equal value and should be used as and when appropriate) is acceptable. This is partly to do with their differences, partly to do with what they share. On the one hand, we have the contrast between two false positions: the idea that research is founded upon philosophical presuppositions that govern or should govern it, versus the idea that the presuppositions associated with particular research strategies can be ignored or taken as they stand. On the other hand, we have the shared, though mistaken, assumption that we are faced with two contrasting but internally homogeneous and consistent approaches. (For a similar critique of these two views about quantitative and qualitative research, see Walker and Evers, 1988.)

The upshot of my argument is that in many respects the quantitative–qualitative distinction is unhelpful. It does not accurately map the differences in practical method or in philosophical position that are actually to be found among researchers. It provides only a crude characterization, and one that can often be misleading. I think that we need to give greater attention to the diversity of methods that is to be found in psychology and the social sciences, and to think through some of the methodological arguments that surround quantitative and qualitative approaches. I recognize of course that this is not easy and that at least for now we cannot simply abandon the qualitative–quantitative distinction.

However, let me give a brief outline of the direction in which I think we need to go. We need a more subtle set of distinctions relating to different facets of the process of doing research. For example, we can distinguish five aspects of the research process: formulating the problems, selecting the cases, producing the data, analysing the data and communicating the findings. (I refer to these as 'aspects', rather than as 'phases' or 'stages', because they are rarely dealt with in strict sequence and usually overlap to some degree.) These apply to all kinds of research, and in respect of each there are several strategies available to researchers. For instance, I am inclined to restrict the terms 'experiment', 'survey' and 'case study' to refer to contrasting ways of selecting cases for investigation, rather than to use them to refer to whole research methods, as they normally tend to be used. In these terms, what is distinctive about an experiment is that the researcher creates the cases to be studied through manipulation of the research situation, controlling both treatment variables and at least some relevant extraneous variables. What is distinctive about a survey is that it involves the simultaneous selection for study of a relatively large number of naturally occurring cases (rather than cases created by the researcher). Finally, from this perspective, what is distinctive about a case study is that it consists of the investigation of a relatively small number of naturally occurring cases (see Hammersley, 1992b, ch. 11). In the same way, we can take each of the other four aspects of the research process and identify various strategies available in relation to them.

While the strategy or strategies we choose for dealing with any one aspect of the research process may sometimes have implications for what we can or should choose in relation to others, the degree of constraint that is involved is nowhere near as great as the quantitative–qualitative distinction implies. Here are some combinations of strategies that the distinction tends to obscure: studying a *single* case can involve the collection of *structured* data and the application to those data of *quantitative* analysis (Hersen and Barlow, 1976; Kratochwill, 1978); *unstructured* data can be collected but subsequently coded and subjected to *quantitative* analysis (see, for example, Scarth and Hammersley, 1988); and it is possible to collect *unstructured* data on a *large* number of cases and to analyse them in *qualitative* terms, especially when the cases are small in scale (see, for instance, Strong, 1979).

Equally important, there is a tendency for both quantitative and qualitative researchers to assume a single model of the research process and its products, as if this exhausted the ways in which research is done and what it produces. Thus, quantitative researchers tend to assume that all research is concerned with hypothesis testing, having been designed to confirm or to disconfirm a theory.

Qualitative researchers, on the other hand, frequently see their work as necessarily exploratory, as concerned with generating theoretical (or 'thick') descriptions or grounded theory. Both these views take the single study as the unit of research, instead of recognizing that both the character and the products of research may need to vary over the course of research programmes in particular fields. The most obvious example of such variation is a more exploratory orientation in the early stages of a programme, followed by a more hypothesis-testing orientation later on. But this is too simplistic: it is more accurate to think in terms of iterative cycles of exploration and testing. Moreover, one must recognize that both structured data collection and statistical analysis can be concerned with exploring patterns in data and developing theoretical ideas, whereas qualitative case studies can be used to test theories. Recognition of both of these points, that the goals of research vary according to the stage that it has reached and that there is no fixed relationship between the use of qualitative or quantitative methods and a particular stage in a research programme, is discouraged by a commitment to the qualitative–quantitative divide.

What is required, then, in my view, is a methodologically aware eclecticism in which the full range of options is kept in mind, in terms of both methods and philosophical assumptions. The practical character of research decisions should be recognized, but this must not lead us to ignore the methodological problems and debates that are involved. And while, for the moment at least, we cannot do without the distinction between quantitative and qualitative approaches, we must remember that it is a poor methodological guide for doing research in the human sciences.

Acknowledgements

Earlier versions of this chapter were presented as talks at the Workshop on Qualitative Research Methods for Psychologists organized by the Department of Human Sciences of Brunel University at Cumberland Lodge in March 1993 and at the Annual Conference of the Education Section of the British Psychological Society held at Easthampton Park in November 1993. A shorter version was published in the BPS *Education Section Review* in January 1995, and some additional material has been reworked from Hammersley (1992b, ch. 9). My thanks go to those who participated in the discussions and to Bob Burden, Tony Cline, Pam Maras and Peter Pumfrey for their responses, which appeared in the *Education Section Review*.

Chapter 13

The use of the self in qualitative research

Estelle King

Qualitative research methods involve procedures that result in rich, descriptive, contextually situated data, based on people's spoken or written words and observable behaviour. Within this context, it is nowadays generally acknowledged (though not frequently discussed in academic journals) that an understanding of the experiences not only of our participants but also of ourselves as researchers constitutes a fundamental part of the research process.

My aim in this chapter is to emphasize the affective aspect of reflexivity. In doing so, the chapter's structure is intended to complement what I perceive as the shifting conceptual terrain associated with a post-structuralist notion of the 'self'. Such a conceptualization recognizes that there is no essentialist 'blueprint' to enable us to understand how we use ourselves as researchers. This is because the self is viewed not as static, but rather as a multiplicity of complex, often contradictory, fragmented or plural identities. In such a context, the self is always in flux (Culler, 1983; Sarup, 1988; Shah, 1994).

What follows is very much bound up with my own experience of carrying out in-depth interviews with older ('non-traditional') students entering higher education. I shall raise a number of issues and ethical concerns relating to the responsibilities of researchers, and this will be followed by a discussion which focuses upon the need to establish appropriate guidelines for both parties to the research interview (and the subsequent debriefing) and to create the necessary boundaries for the interview (including the issue of dealing with disclosure).

Recognizing the need for adequate training in interviewing skills and techniques, I shall then make a comparison between the pertinent aspects of the counselling interview and the research interview. By highlighting the importance of effective listening skills and the power of non-verbal communication in the interview setting, I hope to raise the reader's awareness of how the interviewer can influence the other person's response. Before concluding, I shall consider some of the psychodynamic processes that may operate during the research interview.

The reflexive self

Reflexivity was described by Mead (1934) as 'the turning back of the experience of the individual upon [her- or himself]' (p. 134) and by Delamont (1991) as 'a social scientific variety of self-consciousness' (p. 8). It is a complex concept that takes many forms within the post-modernist or post-structuralist tradition.

The relationships between social constructionism and reflexivity are integral to recent accounts of social epistemology (Soderqvist, 1991). Operating within such a paradigm requires researchers, to the extent of their ability, to analyse and display publicly their history, values and assumptions, as well as the inter-relationship with their participants (see Schwandt, 1994; King, in preparation). In the course of this, the research process becomes anything but straightforward, for the socially situated researcher enters a potentially endless cycle of perceptions, interactions and spiralling dynamics. In an attempt to begin to untangle this sticky, intricate web, interrelated cycles are often planned as part of the emergent research design, with a 'paper trail' that explicates the different perspectives and positions that the work has and has not taken.

Considerable emphasis has been placed on reflexive devices that use different ways of 'telling' (see Woolgar and Ashmore, 1988): examples include treating a dialogue as text, and the construction of a second or alternative voice. In contrast to this, feminist research in particular has highlighted the centrality of affect-ivity, as part both of the social construction of the research encounter and of the production of knowledge (see Roberts, 1981; Reinharz, 1983, 1992; Hollway, 1989; Anderson *et al.*, 1990; Cook and Fonow, 1990; Stanley and Wise, 1993; Maynard and Purvis, 1994). Researchers nowadays are increasingly encouraged to become aware of their feelings, biases and personal peccadilloes and to scrutinize these closely.

This dimension of reflexivity not only acknowledges the affective component of research but can also be used as a source of insight for the purposes of scholarship and innovation (see Fonow and Cook, 1991). Its foremost feature is probably the attempt to redress the power inequalities between the researcher and the researched, in order to construct meaning (Gergen and Gergen, 1991). Opening up the structures and operations that underlie our research and examining how we as researchers are an integral part of the data will amplify rather than restrict the voices of the participants, even when this openness is impeded by the researcher's unrecognized biases and discriminations. As Gergen and Gergen (1991) explained, by means of critical reflection and an examination and exploration of the research process from different positions, the aim of trying to use our reflexivity is to move us outwards to achieve an expansion of understanding. Such a relational approach is in sharp contrast to an introspective one, because it then becomes theoretically possible to transcend the very parameters in which the research is being carried out.

Interviewer responsibility and the nature of the research interview

Many publications cover the methodology of the research interview (for example, Spradley, 1979; Brenner *et al.*, 1985; Lincoln and Guba, 1985; Mishler, 1986; McCracken, 1988; Patton, 1990) and its associated politics (for example, Smith,

1981; Mies, 1983, 1991; Finch, 1986; Gubrium and Silverman, 1989; Bhavnani, 1990; Reinharz, 1992). However, these tend not to focus upon acknowledging and dealing with the researcher's feelings; exceptions are the examples of feminist research cited here, plus the books by Ely *et al.* (1991) and by Kleinman and Copp (1993), and there is brief reference to such issues in the classic text by Bogdan and Taylor (1975). This section therefore briefly considers some of the personal and ethical problems that can be encountered in interview-based research.

Interviewing within an alternative or post-structuralist paradigm can situate both the interviewer and the interviewee in vulnerable positions. Even when they are given clearly presented guidelines, it is unlikely that interviewees will have been in a similar situation before, one in which the focus is almost exclusively on them for a considerable period of time, with the expectation that they should 'tell their story' in depth. Interviewers must decide how to present themselves and their project, and this will be influenced by who is being interviewed and where. Reinharz (1992) argued that interviewers may consciously wish either to 'down play' or to 'play up' their professional status, according to whom they are interviewing. This seems somewhat akin to the traditional view adopted by Riessman (1977, quoted by Mishler, 1986), that interviewers tend to assume mock representations of features taken from ordinary relationships, according to their needs.

Such an approach is in contrast to the model of interviewing advocated by Oakley (1981). This requires on the part of the interviewer an openness or personal responsiveness, an engagement and a striving for intimacy. While 'being yourself' is inherently problematic from a post-structuralist perspective, from the interviewee's point of view adopting an open stance is likely to stand you in good stead when 'slip ups' occur, which will surely happen during the course of a lengthy interview (see Fetterman, 1989). Nevertheless, some decision of how you present yourself still needs to be made, since this leaves a deep impression upon the participants and has considerable influence upon how successful the study will turn out to be (Fontana and Frey, 1994).

An issue central to this is that of trust. Trust has to be earned, and it is likely to be greater when the subject is interviewed several times, as is the depth of interviewing achieved (Reinharz, 1992). If you wish to be trusted, then presumably you need to give considerably of yourself (as I shall discuss in a moment) and appear trusting to the other person. However, the level of trust that interviewees place in the interviewer, possibly enhanced by the assurance of confidentiality, is not the only risk they take. Depending upon the setting of the interview, interviewees may later be ostracized by their peers for having talked (Patton, 1990). Other risks relate to the level of intrusion into their life (after which some issues may be resurrected and seen differently or as recurring patterns), the intellectual as well as the emotional demands of the interview, and the amount of time put into the project. Interviewees may indeed say things that they never intended to tell, as is illustrated by this excerpt from a post-interview debriefing:

> *Neil*: Well, I mean, I find, you know, say particularly, talking about my father very difficult. . . . The only thing that surprised me was be . . . one that I told you in the first place [both laugh], because in talking about it, you see, nobody else particularly would have any motivation or interest in it.

(In this and the following excerpts, the names of the interviewees have of course been changed to protect their anonymity, whereas the interviewer is explicitly identified as myself.)

In the first round of my interviews, while simultaneously wanting to accept responsibility for the creation and conduct of the interview, I was guided by the principle of aiming to treat my participants as autonomous adults. However, this was soon called into question, when a woman being interviewed began to display a considerable amount of emotional distress. I intervened, suggesting that the interview be moved on. In so doing, I assumed a greater degree of control than I was comfortable with, but I also experienced considerable discomfort at having created the situation for this to occur. I had decided that it would have been unethical passively to allow this to continue and thus made an on-the-spot decision that seemed to follow general ethical guidelines, which prioritize the interviewee's wellbeing. I subsequently raised my concern with her as part of the post-interview debriefing:

> *Estelle*: I was concerned about stopping you earlier, you were telling me *your* story, but when I saw you becoming rather upset, I interrupted you and suggested we move on.
> *Enid*: I'm glad you did, actually. . . .

This example illustrates the uneasy balance that can exist between giving participants an opportunity to access and name their world and deciding to intervene in this process. The level of control on the part of the researcher is of central concern to post-structuralists and post-modernists. A considerable degree of control is inevitable, and the interviewer has a responsibility to work with the other person to shape the interview. You need to ask carefully worded, appropriate questions and give verbal and non-verbal feedback cues to support and encourage the other person telling their story. However, this poses a dilemma for the post-structuralist researcher. On the one hand, it is acknowledged that you cannot be neutral; yet, on the other hand, you would probably wish to restrict any direction to a minimum, and usually refrain from interrupting or redirecting the story, despite working within time constraints. The implications of this obviously go beyond the actual interview to affect the analysis and writing up of the project.

Developing appropriate guidelines

The drawing up of interview guidelines is well covered in the literature (see, for instance, McCracken, 1988; Berg, 1989; Patton, 1990) and relates closely to the 'ethics protocol'. However, such guidelines are to a large extent shaped by the paradigmatic features of the proposed project, which will guide the researcher to consider the appropriate ethical obligations and proactively initiate them (Erlandson *et al.*, 1993). For examples of discussions on general ethical issues, readers are referred to Greenwald *et al.* (1982), Kimmel (1988) and Punch (1994).

After going through a relatively short and unambiguous introductory statement with the interviewee, understanding can be enhanced by allowing time for questions and elaboration. Because of the highly personal and interpersonal nature of in-depth interviewing, such inquiry is likely to be more intrusive than most other research methods, and may well open up issues that are highly sensitive for the interviewee. This risk needs to be clearly expressed, and an 'opt out' clause given in order that the interviewees are made aware that they are not obliged to answer all the questions should they prefer not to, and that they can stop the interview should they so wish. They will thereby be offered both some degree of protection and control. A 'contract' to be signed by both parties may also be offered.

If any promises are made by the interviewer (for example, to provide information or a copy of the interview transcript), these ought to be kept. Should this for some reason not prove feasible at a later date, then this should be acknowledged to the interviewee (an example is provided below). This point relates to what Patton (1990) termed 'reciprocity' and Marshall and Rossman (1995) called 'deploying the self': that is, the emergence of an exchange relationship that renders the participant's cooperation and involvement worthwhile. On the face of it, this may seem more relevant to other research methods, such as participant observation. Nevertheless, in my own research the main benefits that were reported by participants were: being given information and feedback; having a sense of being valued and understood as older students; and having the opportunity to reflect upon their past experience to enhance their current understanding. There may be other benefits that depend upon situational and interpersonal factors. For instance, in the case of two participants I acted as childminder when the interviews were unavoidably interrupted, while, for those attending a focus interview, I provided lunch. Subsequent to their interviews, three participants asked me to write references, and one sought me out as a way of negotiating her way back to university after the death of her husband.

Interviewers need to be sensitive to the other commitments of people whom they interview, but also to allow sufficient time for post-interview debriefing (offering another appointment if necessary). This offers both parties an opportunity to clarify or refine aspects that might otherwise cause confusion or concern, but it also offers an opportunity to consider something of the processes that took place. In doing so, the participants may welcome the space to talk through some of the issues that were raised and to 'let go' of some of the 'emotional baggage', rather than having to leave with a sense of burden or emotional overload.

Defining boundaries

Learning how to define and create boundaries in the research interview requires experience, sensitivity, intuition and a strong sense of self. Its importance is often underestimated during the planning phase when the guidelines are established, particularly by novice researchers. At this early stage, it is also desirable that considerable thought be given to the potential difficulties and dilemmas that might be faced later on, when an immediate response is required.

The particular boundaries that I want to address are concerned with the interpersonal quality and nature of the interaction in the interview, rather than its purely physical structure. If researchers display warmth, empathy and genuineness (which I shall discuss later), they can expect to develop close relationships with their participants. However, the extent to which they should do so is hotly debated. For example, Hammersley and Atkinson (1983) argued that there has to be some degree of both social and intellectual distance, for it is this 'space' that creates the opportunity for analytical work; it is, in other words, where the reflexive 'self-as-instrument' process takes place (McCracken, 1988). In fact, the techniques and practice of unstructured interviews vary widely. Even just within feminist research, Reinharz (1992) demonstrated that there are significant variations: she described the practices of feminist interviewers as being situated across a spectrum that ranged from that of the 'interviewer as stranger', through the 'knowledgeable stranger', to the 'interviewer as friend'.

Oakley (1981) was one of the earlier feminist researchers who, guided by feminist ethics concerning commitment and egalitarianism, proposed an interviewing model that included both self-disclosure and the development of a potentially long-lasting relationship with the interviewee. How much emotion the researcher displays and the degree of involvement will vary from one individual to another, but, in my own research, this produced a dilemma. Although during the interviews I felt emotionally close to each of my participants, the level of bonding and sense of 'otherness' that I felt afterwards varied considerably. While I responded positively to any social approach (and there were a number), I refrained from initiating any such approaches myself. This was for two reasons: first, my commitment (albeit somewhat naïve) to egalitarianism; and, second, my concern that anxiety might be raised among other participants (potential 'outsiders') that I might break my assurance of confidentiality. I therefore felt comfortable to develop reciprocal friendships only with those interviewees who had left their courses of study.

Self-disclosure has, for me, been a thorny issue. People may not respond to or trust interviewers who do not take a clear stand (Marshall and Rossman, 1995). Bogdan and Taylor (1975) advocated a 'happy medium' between total disclosure and total detachment, but in my own research I wanted to keep the focus mostly upon the other person. Consequently, I drew the boundary that I would not intentionally disclose anything in the interview that I felt strongly about and would wait to be more open in the post-interview debriefing. With experience, you can recognize a strong reaction in yourself but put the event to one side until what seems to be an appropriate moment. Thus, when two participants talked about their reactions to their father's death, I did not acknowledge until later that my own experience had been similar. I applied the same strategy when my value system was challenged, as it was when a male participant talked of not being able to recognize sexual harassment at work as a significant issue for women. By listening attentively to him, I came to understand his point of view, but I avoided feeling compromised since I voiced my disagreement with him immediately after the interview.

There may well be facets disclosed that you would prefer not to see (Kleinman and Copp, 1993). In my experience, these can take two forms: conflict with your own value system (as just mentioned); or an aspect of the other's experience – for example, disclosure of sexual abuse as a child. This latter example indicates the cumulative power of the interview and the tremendous pressure that can be placed on the interviewer, heightened in my case by my apparently being the first adult to whom this disclosure had been made. I responded to the interviewee by discussing appropriate support agencies and self-help groups, and I offered to provide her with details of the latter. However, I subsequently broke my 'promise' as I felt the responsibility of raising the issue again through correspondence to be too great. Feeling uncomfortable in the intervening period, I waited several months before speaking to her on the telephone, when I explained somewhat indirectly the reason for my inaction.

This example also raises the issue of whether it is appropriate for the interviewer to provide information and advice, a matter discussed by Patton (1990) and by Reinharz (1992). How you manage the interview and the many roles you choose to adopt in it will raise strategic, personal and ethical issues and will also vary according to the focus of the study. However, while much can be learnt from the thought-provoking experiences of previous researchers and from paying careful attention to the planning stage and any subsequent research proposal, personal dilemmas will always arise when carrying out a qualitative research project in which sensitive material is disclosed.

Comparing the research interview to the counselling interview

Much qualitative research is dependent upon the perception of one person (the researcher) of a situation at a given point in time, and that perception will be shaped both by the researcher's personality and by the nature of the interaction between those in the interview (Punch, 1994). In-depth interviewing and the telling of a life history can evoke powerful emotions relating to unresolved past or current events, and these can sensitize interviewees, increase their vulnerability and traumatize them even further (King, 1993; Coyle *et al.*, 1994; Hutchinson and Wilson, 1994; West, 1994). This has ethical implications, and it places considerable responsibility on the interviewer. In particular, it emphasizes the need for adequate training in interviewing skills and techniques, some degree of ongoing supervision and an awareness of some of the psychodynamic processes associated with in-depth interviews. It is in this context that I feel valuable insights can be gained by drawing a comparison between the research interview and the counselling interview, and I want to outline a range of techniques and strategies that can be used. In doing so, I want to take apart the notion that the two types of interview are necessarily distinct. Close scrutiny reveals a number of similarities.

Ostensibly, a research interview does not constitute a counselling situation, for it is not usual to offer therapeutic interventions when conducting research is the primary goal (though for exceptions see Coyle *et al.*, 1994; Hutchinson and Wilson, 1994). As the following excerpt from one of my follow-up interviews indicates, this can become a substantive issue for the interviewer, for the boundaries are not necessarily evident:

> *Estelle*: I was really concerned about how much people were bringing up and whether I was offering any therapeutic intervention, which I didn't want to do. You know, there's a delicate balance to make between offering an interpretation, which I do in order to check out my understanding of what you are saying, and so that I'm not just going along thinking that I understand, I have to check it out, as opposed to offering some sort of intervention, which clearly I am not in a position to do.

This example illustrates the concern I had felt that, by creating a feedback loop and reflecting back what had been said to the other person, I might be construed as potentially offering some level of intervention, whereas my aim had been to enhance my comprehension of the narrative.

In the main, the participants are there to help the researcher, not vice versa. Their reasons for participating may vary, but in the context of health research were characterized by Hutchinson and Wilson (1994) as the desire or intention to achieve self-acknowledgement, self-awareness, catharsis, empowerment or a sense of purpose. Such intentions are likely to vary with the level of interest that the participants have vested in the research topic, but they are also closely related to the fundamental aims of counselling. A knowledge of these aims of counselling and the possession of basic counselling skills that can be used in the research interview are likely to enhance researchers' understanding of themselves as research instruments and their reflexive accounts and analyses and to raise conscious awareness of the choices they make during the interview to effect control and direction.

As outlined by McLeod (1993), the fundamental aims of counselling are threefold: first, to enable the client to develop insight, self-awareness and acceptance; second, to bring about change at a cognitive, behavioural or social level; and, third, to help the client to experience empowerment. The extent to which these apply in the research interview will depend very much on the nature and format of the interview, as well as on the specific individuals involved. However, I want to argue that these aims may often be applicable in the research interview, even if they are a by-product of the research, rather than stated as an explicit goal.

Insight, self-awareness and even acceptance may occur as a result of the evolving narrative during in-depth interviewing. This is demonstrated by my follow-up interview with Liz, in which I asked her to reflect on the interview process as part of the post-interview debriefing:

> *Liz*: In fact in some ways, it's quite useful to reflect [upon the interview], I haven't sat down and really talked about it that much. Erm, I'm aware of my attitude being changed, and I've been surprised at myself. So it's quite useful actually, to have to go over it with you, it actually gets the whole thing together in a way for me.

A consequence of such autobiographical inquiry can be a strengthened sense of self, in which, particularly in longitudinal research, the same issues can be re-explored and commented upon by both parties (West, 1994). Such a strengthened sense of self implies change, as was indicated by Emma in a focus group discussion during the fourth and final year of her degree course. She had been talking about having hated the second year, because of the sense of competitiveness she had experienced, which she felt had put her under extreme pressure:

> *Emma*: When I sat down and analysed things, I thought it's just, I was being silly, really, why don't I go on with the third year, what have I got to lose, you know? And I think Estelle's [follow-up] interview helped me as well to reflect on myself, to bring things back a bit more into balance again.

Within a heated debate on the politics of research interviewing, the re-distribution of power and the attainment of empowerment have recently been very much the focus for academic discussion, both inside and outside feminist debates. For instance, Mishler (1986) equated empowerment with 'being able to speak in one's voice', while according to Bhavnani (1990) the use of direct quotations might convey authenticity, but it could also mask inequalities between the interviewer and the interviewee and hence cause disempowerment. One central point of Bhavnani's argument is that empowerment needs to go beyond the narrative, extending to the possibility of change via action. This and McLeod's (1993) other aims of counselling are features of collaborative research, which, according to Reason (1994), 'is about inquiry as a means by which people engage together to explore some significant aspect of their lives, to understand it better and to transform their action so as to meet their purposes more fully' (p. 9).

However, 'new paradigm' research of this sort (see Reason and Rowan, 1981; Lather, 1986) stands in sharp contrast to a post-structuralist or post-modernist approach, which challenges the notion that the participants will share the same goals as the researcher. Be that as it may, whatever interviewing model or perspective one adopts, the use of basic counselling skills will be valuable in maximizing the interviewer's understanding of the interviewee's experiences and feelings from the latter's perspective, even if the researcher fails to get 'close to the bone', to adopt the expression used by Rennie *et al.* (1988). This is because researchers still have to work within the paradox that they cannot experience the other person's reality. However, I would argue that, even within a person-centred framework, skills of this sort can enhance rather than contradict a post-structuralist approach. Additionally, counselling skills can serve to increase researchers' own awareness of how their responses and mannerisms may affect those of their participants.

I now want to consider briefly some of the fundamental features of a counselling relationship, before indicating how these might be practically employed as active listening skills. These features originated largely in a humanist tradition of the ontology of the self, but the examples I shall give indicate that the skills can be used regardless of any particular persuasion. Rogers (1951) proposed three 'core conditions' that were both necessary and sufficient for a counselling relationship to be successful: empathy; genuineness; and warmth or 'unconditional positive regard'. Empathy, as differentiated from sympathy, is specific and requires that the interviewer should be sensitive from moment to moment to the changing experience of the interviewee, be able to enter the other person's world as far as is possible, and to be able to communicate that understanding to the interviewee. Genuineness involves direct and open communication, a way of being in which the interviewer is explicit about what he or she thinks and feels (but recall the above discussion concerning disclosure), and is closely linked to unconditional positive regard. This third attribute implies acceptance of the other person, of prizing others simply because they are human, regardless of what they might say or of how they behave.

Subsequent work confirmed Rogers' assertion that these three 'core conditions' were necessary for an effective helping relationship, but not his assertion that they were sufficient. For example, Carkhuff (1987) identified three additional, commonly observed features as necessary and basic conditions for helping: concreteness, immediacy and confrontation. However, specifying additional 'core conditions' is a contentious issue, and such features are not necessarily applicable to research interviews. What is pertinent is that the 'core conditions' originally specified by Rogers can be usefully applied in research interviews through employing active listening skills and open questions. Questions can also be used for the purpose of seeking clarification, and these may include probing. In addition to the following suggestions, readers may wish to refer to texts on counselling and helping (such as Tough, 1982; Murgatroyd, 1985; Egan, 1994), which offer further explanation and examples as well as useful exercises. Coyle *et al.* (1994) provided a rationale and examples of how they used counselling interviews as a research method when interviewing people on sensitive issues such as being terminally ill or the experience of bereavement.

Non-verbal communication and active listening skills

Effective attending (for instance, conscious use of physical position, posture and eye contact) places the interviewer in a position to listen carefully to the other person's verbal and non-verbal messages. Part of a researcher's critical awareness includes becoming conscious of how mannerisms and responses can affect the participant (and vice versa), and aware that, in this sense, the story that results is a joint production (Mishler, 1986). The power of suggestion through an 'approving' nod or a 'disapproving' shake of the head can lead to a change in the interviewee's response, so that it no longer represents what that individual originally intended to convey. For instance, in my own research, when an interviewee was describing an emotionally difficult situation with one of her parents, I raised an eyebrow; she took this to indicate my disapproval of her, when in fact I was registering surprise. When I openly acknowledged this with her, she was then able to tell her story as she had seemingly intended.

Listening skills embrace getting in touch with the participants' descriptions of their experiences, behaviour and feelings. This can be conveyed to the interviewees by employing active listening techniques: paraphrasing, reflecting (both content and feeling), summarizing and open questioning. These techniques, along with the communication of empathic understanding, non-critical acceptance and genuineness, comprise those used in the initial exploration stage of Egan's (1994) three-stage skills model of helping. This initial stage involves frequently checking your understanding with the participants, and thus it helps you to construct a mental map of the procedure and content of the interview from the participant's frame of reference, and to focus in depth upon specific areas of interest.

This model contrasts sharply with that proposed by McCracken (1988), who argued that active listening strategies should not be used because they are obtrusive: they violate the 'law' of non-direction and prevent interviewees from telling their story in their own terms. I would argue that such attempts to 'neutralize' the stimulus are artificial. Moreover, they leave the researcher to try to construct the meanings of the data afterwards, rather than checking them out, to some extent at least, during the interview itself.

Paraphrasing can be used throughout an interview and is one way of accurately communicating an empathic understanding of the participant's thoughts, experiences and feelings. It often requires a rich vocabulary on the part of the researcher, since emotions and experiences may often be better expressed by the use of analogy and metaphor. For instance, in his initial life story interview, James had been talking at length about how the death of his father, when he himself was aged 12, had affected him subsequently as a learner:

> *Estelle*: I'm hearing that perhaps his death has had the biggest influence on you and your life so far, certainly as a child, and also at school, he'd had a very big influence on your learning before. . . . I'm hearing you say you lost your sense of purpose, you would have liked this goal, you're talking about a goal to aim for.
> *James*: I don't see how things could have changed really, unless my father had not died.
> *Estelle*: Yeah. So things were as they were, that's the crux of it, really, isn't it?
> *James*: Yeah.

This sense of lost purpose was subsequently picked up a number of times in the interview by both parties, developing a metaphor of James having had a door shut in his face or his shutting it himself in his face.

The interviewer may use reflection of content and often of feelings to mirror to the other person the meaning of what they have said, and it therefore provides further opportunity for the interviewee to confirm, modify or reject the interviewer's understanding of what has been stated. In the life story interview from which I have taken the following extract, Caroline had been talking about her relationship with her parents and how she felt they had not helped her as a young learner:

> *Caroline*: I remember, I used to get really, um, er, I was a bit of a worrier as a young girl, um, er, I used to have like these terrible sort of fed-ups hanging over me.
> *Estelle*: Like a cloud.
> *Caroline*: Yeah, I used to feel very sad, being so young, and I've got memories of sitting in the back of the car and if the weather changed, and it was all grey, I'd feel really grey as well, and er, they didn't pick that up, didn't sense how I felt.
> *Estelle*: So maybe you are saying your Mum could have been closer to you, more sensitive to what you needed.

Reflection can be used either on its own or else in conjunction with paraphrasing or summarizing. Summarizing involves succinctly drawing together the essence of what the other person has said, and it enables the interviewer to check once again with the participant before moving on with the interview. It can thus serve as a memory jogger for anything that the other person has omitted and to highlight important areas. It may include the interviewer contrasting a statement with another one made earlier, and it will focus upon what appears to be the uppermost issue (Inskipp, 1993). Immediately before the following extract, Carly had been talking about what studying and learning meant for her in the second year of her degree course, ending with a description of her sense of feeling different from those in her management seminar:

> *Carly*: I find it very hard to relate to the others in that particular seminar. They've got very different ideas and most of them have come straight from school. That's not usually a problem, but they have very clear ideas, they want to become managers, they want to have power, they want, it's everything that I dislike, really.
> *Estelle*: So you want to sort of strike out against that, don't you, throwing in a job as an administrator and doing something for yourself to find your own direction?
> *Carly*: Yes, yes.

The interviewer's brief summary, here phrased as a question, was an attempt to synthesize and convey the underlying meaning of Carly's conversation over the previous ten minutes or so, and it related to what Carly had said earlier about her reasons for coming to university and to the feelings she expressed about her management seminars. The strength of her reply ('Yes, yes') seemed to confirm the interviewer's interpretation, thus closing that section of the interview. However, the correctness of an interpretation does not necessarily lie in the other person's immediate assent; rather, as Erikson (1958) noted, it lies in the interplay between the two people in which the initial idea is developed, leading to new and perhaps surprising insights. This was the case, for instance, in the interview with James, in which the metaphor of a door being shut in his face was developed.

Psychodynamic processes of the interview

It seems to be only quite recently that psychoanalytic concepts have been applied to in-depth interviewing in psychology or to life history research in the social sciences more generally. As West (1994) commented, writing from outside psychology, considerable suspicion exists of psychoanalytic models of the person, for they are assumed to reflect essentialist (rather than constructionist) tendencies and to offer a conservative view of human nature. However, in-depth interviews can arouse intense emotions for both parties, particularly when participants tell of some past or unresolved trauma and reveal their more vulnerable, 'child' aspects of their self.

The emotions that are experienced by both parties, fuelled by the power dynamics of the interview, are likely to be associated with elements or traces from past social relationships (Winnicott, 1965; Jacobs, 1986). 'Transference' refers to the process by which a client (or an interviewee) reacts emotionally to a therapist (or an interviewer) by associating her or him with previously important relationships. As Wallis (1973) noted, this is largely an unconscious, spontaneous reaction outside the person's control, in which feelings are transferred on to the therapist or the interviewer. Similarly, in countertransference the therapist or the interviewer may experience feelings such as protection, repulsion or attraction towards the interviewee, which will subsequently affect the interview dynamics.

For Jung, transference was not simply the product of psychoanalytic technique, but was rather a general transpersonal or social phenomenon to be regarded as an everyday occurrence (Fordham, 1960; Wallis, 1973). For this reason, the concepts of transference and countertransference, which are central to the practice of psychoanalysis and psychotherapy, become a pertinent area for consideration in the context of qualitative research. In my own work, for example, I was eventually able to recognize that one interviewee, who had expressed a great deal of unresolved anger towards her parents, had apparently transferred something of that on to me during the course of our interview. This in turn had triggered a series of responses in me, leaving me feeling that I had possibly been responsible for disempowering both of us.

Psychodynamic processes of this sort are both complex and powerful, and even highly skilled interviewers may have difficulty recognizing them, let alone detaching themselves from them. A useful concept here is Mies's (1983) idea of 'conscious partiality', that any researcher is likely some of the time to identify with the interviewee. But the dynamics that are associated with partial identification or transference with your research participants can be analysed only so far, especially as the transactional nature of each interview is so different. Elements of interviewer control can of course assume many guises. Here, perhaps, a researcher's greatest resources are honesty and a commitment to review with the participant what has taken place (as far as is wished and as far as both parties are able). In this sense, maintaining a professional attitude need not imply that you assume interpersonal distance. Rather, it becomes a matter of what to do with your own thoughts: of striving to immerse yourself in what the other person is saying and of putting to one side your own feelings until an appropriate moment when they can be sifted through and examined. This is of course easier said than done, especially since most feelings generated in countertransference are unlikely to be very obvious.

Conclusions

It is clear that different types of interviewing are suited to different situations, depending, among other things, on the available resources as well as the researcher's epistemological and political leanings. To pit one type of research interview against another is but a remnant of the now historical paradigmatic debate concerning quantity versus quality (Bryman, 1988). Interviewing is undergoing change not simply at a methodological level but also at a much deeper level, related to the self and others, and in learning about the other, we learn about the self (Fine, 1994; Fontana and Frey, 1994).

The domain of the personal is a difficult and potentially emotionally disturbing area to start to unpack (West, 1994), but to deny our feelings and our constructions would be to shut out one large part of the research experience. Recognizing that we can adopt multiple roles in our relations with others and that we often operate within contradictions involves both extensive examination and also becoming deeply involved with our research material both during and after data collection. At the same time, we need to remain emotionally vital enough to step back and appreciate its general contours and overall significance. This is a rigorous, affective exercise that demands considerable emotional reserves and critical awareness.

Accessing people's lives needs to be handled with great sensitivity, care and skill, and it implies change at some level for all concerned. Reflexively studying ourselves as well as our participants is sometimes excitingly revealing, and sometimes impossible. Yet, as the increasing interest in such research projects would suggest, it is also an exciting and challenging experience and one that can bring considerable rewards.

Chapter 14

Evolving issues for qualitative psychology

Jonathan A. Smith

In this final chapter, I will address a set of current issues for the use of qualitative research methods in psychology. Obviously, the set of concerns that I have identified is selective, and another writer might produce a different list:

(1)   Is qualitative psychology science?
(2)   How can we assess the validity of qualitative research?
(3)   Reflexive research practices
(4)   Software packages for qualitative analysis

Is qualitative psychology science?

I want to address this question, first, by raising the question, 'What is science?' and, then, by suggesting that, according to some conceptions of science, qualitative research in psychology can be at least as scientific as mainstream psychology.

One concern raised about qualitative approaches, either explicitly or implicitly, is that of their scientific status. This obviously reflects academic psychology's long-standing aspiration to claim the status of a respectable 'natural' science. Unfortunately, mainstream psychology tends to have a very narrow conception of what science is. Thus, while it is true that much psychological research has moved beyond the confines of the laboratory experiment, it can be argued that the same positivist logic and empiricist impulse that were at the heart of behaviourist experimentation are still central to the way in which psychological inquiry is nowadays conceived and conducted. Whether it is concerned with mind or behaviour (and whether it is conducted inside or outside the laboratory), research in psychology still tends to be construed in terms of the separation (or reduction) of entities into independent and dependent variables and the measurement of the hypothesized relationships between them.

This assumes a singular view of science and scientific practice, but, if you ask the question 'What is science?', you can find considerable diversity in the literature. In fact, science is a multifaceted activity: there is not just one way of defining what science is and how it should be conducted. For example, Sloman (1976) discussed the definition and aims of science from the perspective of the philosophy of science, and he was critical of the conventional prescriptive concentration on replicability:

> If a phenomenon occurs only once, then it is possible, and its possibility needs explaining. . . . The frantic pursuit of repeatability and statistical correlations is based on a belief that science is a search for laws. This has blinded many scientists to the need for careful description and analysis of what *can* occur and for the explanation of its possibility.
>
> Instead they try to find what *always* occurs – a much harder task – and usually fail. Even if something is actually done by very few persons, or only by one, that still shows that it is possible for a human being, and this possibility needs explanation as much as any other established fact. This justifies elaborate and detailed investigation and analysis of particular cases: a task usually shirked because of the search for statistically significant correlations. Social scientists have much to learn from historians and students of literature.
>
> (p. 17, italics in original)

In arguing that the study of particularity and of single cases can be a part of science, Sloman was challenging the assumptions of universality and replicability that represent central tenets of mainstream psychology. His account was also thereby aligned with many of the theoretical arguments supporting qualitative approaches to psychology. Examples of these include Billig (1985) on the privileging of universality over particularities, Allport (1951) on the validity of personal documents and Smith *et al.* (1995a) on idiography and the case study.

One can go further. Much of the 'new physics' can be said to be critical of, and to be moving beyond, the limited and static premises of the Newtonian scientific paradigm, which academic psychology would seem, at least implicitly, to hold dear (see Graham, 1986). To take one example, part of Heisenberg's uncertainty principle concerns the way in which the measurement of particles at a very fine level cannot be performed without affecting or interfering with the particles themselves. The uncertainty principle can be seen as analogous to the stress placed by 'new paradigm' researchers on the presence of the researcher as an instrument in social scientific inquiry and how that presence can affect the phenomenon being studied. (I shall discuss the idea of reflexivity in more detail below.)

In fact, given their concern with a more dynamic, relational view of the objects of their inquiry, a number of scientists are sympathetic to a new psychology and are looking to psychology to contribute to the projects they are engaged in. Thus, Shotter (1975) cited a passage by Koch where he pointed to a quite different conception of psychology that would be more in tune with many of the currents in the philosophy and practice of contemporary science. Although Koch had been writing in 1964, his words are clearly relevant more than 30 years on:

> Psychology is thus in the unenviable position of standing on foundations which began to be vacated by philosophy almost as soon as the former had borrowed them. The paradox is now compounded: philosophy and more generally the methodology of science are beginning to stand on foundations that only psychology could render secure. [For we need to understand how we understand; the doing of science is itself a human activity and as such an understanding of its conduct is one of the psychologist's tasks.]

A world now in motion towards a more adequate conception begins to perceive that only psychology can implement it. Yet psychology is prevented from doing so because almost alone in the scholarly community it remains in the grip of the old conception. But this state of affairs could lead to a happy consequence: should psychology break out of the circle just described it could at one and the same time assume leadership in pressing towards a resolution of the central intellectual problem of our time and liberate itself for the engagement of bypassed, but important and intensely interesting, ranges of its own subject matter. Moreover, it can find courage to do these things in the circumstance that the very sources upon which it has most leaned for authority – physics and the philosophy of science – are, together with the rest of the scholarly community, urgently inviting them to be done.

(pp. 69–70; sentence in brackets added by Shotter)

This passage asserts that a new psychology can actually have a major role to play in the broader scientific endeavour, and one can argue that qualitative research will have a vital part to play in that process.

So much for science in principle. What about science in practice? Again, we find that it is a much more diverse activity than some of the definitions of science might lead one to think. Mainstream psychology gives particular attention to the scientific method as defined in classic Popperian terms: the establishment of hypotheses that the researcher then attempts to disconfirm. Based on this criterion, most qualitative research would be disqualified from scientific status. However, studies have suggested that practising scientists often show a preference for confirmatory rather than disconfirmatory strategies, and may attempt to stick tenaciously to their theoretical hunches in the face of negative evidence (for example, see Mahoney, 1976). Moreover, much research into the ethnography of laboratory science suggests that science is a messy, much more pragmatic and pluralistic activity than might be suggested by the textbooks (see Chapter 2, by Steve Woolgar). Thus, it cannot be assumed that theoretical models of scientific method correspond with how science is actually conducted.

The point is, therefore, that, while qualitative research has traditionally been criticized by mainstream psychology for failing to meet conventional scientific standards, such criticism assumes a prescriptive view of what science is. In fact, science is a multifaceted activity that is well able to accommodate qualitative approaches to psychology. Indeed, according to some writers and practitioners of science, a psychology that involved a move towards qualitative methodology would be more in keeping with contemporary definitions of what science is and what it can achieve.

How can we assess the validity of qualitative research?

Evaluating the validity of qualitative research is an issue that is beginning to exercise a number of psychologists (see Henwood and Pigeon, 1992; Stiles, 1993). One view is that it is important that qualitative research should be judged against criteria appropriate to that approach. In other words, qualitative research should not be evaluated in terms of the canons of validity that have evolved for the assessment of quantitative research, since these have different epistemological priorities and commitments. This point is linked to the discussion in the previous section. According to the principles of the 'old' paradigm, qualitative research will always be found wanting, but an enlarged definition of 'scientific' psychology will involve amending the criteria for assessing the validity of different types of research.

A number of suggestions have been made, and some of these will be discussed below. I would just like to stress that this is very much an area where work is in progress, and I am presenting these as suggestions for discussion. No criteria have yet been agreed within the community of qualitative researchers, and it is certainly not the intention to provide a definitive checklist for validating qualitative research against which all qualitative studies could be judged to be good or bad.

Internal coherence

There would perhaps be the greatest consensus among different researchers that internal coherence (or the lack of it) would be an appropriate way of assessing qualitative research. The argument is that, rather than being concerned, for example, with the representativeness of the sample used in a qualitative research project, you should concentrate on whether it was internally consistent and coherent. Does it present a coherent argument? For instance, does it deal with loose ends and possible contradictions in the data? This is not to say that contradictions should not be present in written accounts of a project; indeed, they may often provide the richest data. Rather, if ambiguities and equivocations are present in the data, then they should be dealt with in a coherent and ordered way. Additional questions to ask are: Are the interpretations that the researcher makes warranted by the data presented? Does the report deal with alternative readings? Sometimes, it may be considered appropriate for investigators to take into account other ways of interpreting the data and to argue a case for their own reading being more valid. Bromley (1986) invoked a judicial analogy in supporting this way of considering how to evaluate case studies.

Presentation of evidence

This criterion follows quite closely from the previous one. In general, I suggest that a good qualitative research report should present enough of the raw data to allow the reader to interrogate the interpretation that is being made. Or, to put it another way, the reader should be allowed to take part in an interpretative dialogue with the data collected in the study. That would be in contrast to a weaker qualitative report that presented just a single third-person narrative that did not distinguish between raw data and interpretation. Of course, this will apply more to certain types of research than to others. The type of project I have in mind is one that analysed personal documents supplied by a participant or transcripts of interviews. The investigator's field notes obtained in a participant observation study could be treated in a similar way, though obviously the distinction between raw data and interpretation would not be so clear in this case. Research in conversation analysis (Drew, 1995) and discourse analysis (see Chapters 10 and 11, by Jonathan Potter and Rosalind Gill) currently already adopts this strategy, but there is less consistency with other types of qualitative research.

Independent audit

Yin (1989) suggested that one way of checking the validity of a research report would be to file all the data in such a way that somebody else could follow the chain of evidence that led to the final report. Thus, thinking of an interview-based project, the chain might comprise initial notes on research questions, interview schedule, audio tapes, annotated transcripts, codings and initial categorizations, draft reports, and the final report. At a first level, it can be argued that this would be a good discipline for the researcher. By putting yourself in the place of someone else having to make sense of the final report and check that a coherent chain of arguments runs from the initial raw data to the final write up, you are forced to confirm the rigour of your claims. At this level, the notion of an audit is purely hypothetical or personal: the researcher just files the data in such a way that someone else could in principle check through the 'paper trail'.

You could, of course, go further and actually conduct an independent audit, and this was indeed suggested by Lincoln and Guba (1985). In this case, the file of material sequenced as mentioned above is submitted to a researcher who played no part in the project, whose task is to check that the final report is a credible one in terms of the data collected and that a logical progression runs through the chain of evidence. It is, however, important to distinguish between the idea of an independent audit and the more familiar notion of interrater reliability. The independent auditor is attempting to ensure that the account produced is one that is credible and warrantable based on the data collected, but not necessarily the only or definitive account which could be produced. So, an independent audit is not attempting to suppress alternative readings or necessarily to reach a consensus; it is attempting to validate one particular reading.

Triangulation

The idea of triangulation possibly has as much to do with the choice of method-ology as it has to do with validity. The essential rationale is that, if you use a number of different methods or sources of information to tackle a question, the resulting answer is more likely to be accurate. For example, a study of bullying in schools might involve carrying out separate interviews with teachers, the headteacher and the children, and then go on to obtain personal accounts in the form of essays or diaries from the participants as well. Finally, the researchers might attempt to gain access as participant observers and include their own report on the activities within the school as a source of data.

The term 'triangulation' is derived from navigation, where it refers to the notion of fixing an object from two independent locations in order to increase the accuracy of the siting. In fact, the nautical analogy is perhaps unfortunate because it suggests the need for a perfect fix or an absolutely true reading. In general, researchers advocating triangulation would tend to see it as a way of strengthening the claims that they make, of getting a richer or fuller story, and not a route to an absolute truth. At the same time, triangulation can be seen as a viable research strategy whether you subscribe to a realist view or a relativist view of inquiry. Whereas an extreme realist might well support the navigational analogy in terms of pressing the accuracy of claims made from independent sources, a relativist might point to triangulation as a way of capturing the multiple 'voices', and therefore truths, that exist in relation to any phenomenon. The tension that is implicit in these opposing viewpoints of triangulation is well captured in the ambiguity of Levins's claim that 'Our truth is the intersection of independent lies' (quoted by Fielding and Fielding, 1986, p. 23).

Member validation

Member validation has dual roots in a phenomenological epistemology and in a commitment to seeking more democratic research practices. It involves taking the analysis of responses back to the participants (or 'members') to enable them to check or comment upon the interpretation. This can be done at a number of possible stages: for example, after some preliminary analysis has been conducted or once a draft report has been written. From a phenomenological perspective, if you are attempting to record as closely as possible how a particular individual perceives some situation, then it obviously makes sense to check your interpretations of the talk and text that he or she has produced with the individual her- or himself.

My own feeling is that member validation can play a useful role in research, but that it should not be perceived as problem free. However committed the researcher is to democratic research practice, the question of power relations still arises. While the participants may find it easy when they agree with a piece of interpretation, if there is disagreement it may be more difficult for them to question the interpretation of the researcher, who will often be perceived as the more powerful person. This will also be influenced by the local interpersonal dynamics between the researcher and the participants.

As in the case of triangulation, I do not see member validation as an attempt to get at any absolute truth. Rather it is an attempt to gain a fuller understanding of the situation by including multiple viewpoints. Given the right circumstances, it is possible for participants to do much more than just concur with the analysis.

Sometimes their interpretation of a text and their response to the researcher's analysis helps to expand the reading that is given.

Reflexive research practices

The idea of reflexivity has in recent years caught the imagination of a number of different qualitative researchers. Reflexivity was central to Mead's (1934) conception of the person: 'After a self has arisen, it in a certain sense provides for itself its social experiences, and so we can conceive of an absolutely solitary self . . . who still has himself [*sic*] as a companion, and is able to think and to converse with himself as he had communicated with others' (p. 140). Thus, according to Mead, 'there is nothing odd about a product of a given process contributing to, or becoming an essential factor in the further development of that process' (p. 226).

What are the implications of reflexivity for particular research strategies? Orthodox psychological research either neglects reflexivity or considers it a hindrance to the research endeavour. So, for example, the fact that participants or 'subjects' might have a complex and iterative set of views of what the research is about, what their own role in it is and how the researcher is responding to their behaviour would be considered a contaminating factor in traditional experimental design. Furthermore, reflexivity on the part of researchers would be felt to interfere with their own role as a neutral instrument in the project.

However, an alternative position is to recognize that reflexivity is an inevitable consequence of engaging in research with people and that it can be harnessed as a valuable part of the research exercise itself. In fact, two separate groups of qualitative researchers who come from very different theoretical traditions have converged in perceiving reflexivity as a central component in their research practice at both epistemological and methodological levels. One group has emerged from the constructionist perspective in the sociology of science, while the other group comes from a participatory research orientation in the humanistic tradition.

The reflexive focus can be upon the participant, the investigator, or both. Thus, one reading of reflexivity emphasizes an awareness of the researcher's own presence in the research project. So, some writers in the sociology of science (see Woolgar, 1988a) have turned their attention to their own role in the construction of research: 'Any statement which holds that humans necessarily act or believe in particular ways under particular circumstances refers as much to the social scientist as anyone else' (Gruenberg, quoted by Woolgar and Ashmore, 1988, p. 1). This view is often expressed in terms of the relativist position that tends to be adopted by many researchers in this group. Their argument is that it is not consistent for researchers to claim that science is an uncertain, contingent, reflexive activity, and then to pretend that they can stand apart from that activity as a detached observer and make objective, factual statements about it. Rather, researchers need to relativize their own position in relation to the research project,

195

to include an awareness of their own contribution to the exercise; indeed, this can become a research project in its own right. One result of this has been a particular focus upon the way in which the sociology of science is itself written up or constructed as text, and people working on the sociology of scientific knowledge have been attempting to find new, reflexive modes of discourse.

An alternative emphasis can be upon the participant. If your view of a person is that they are a self-reflexive agent, then presumably that holds for the respondent as well as the researcher. Researchers who make use of cooperative inquiry capitalize upon the participants' propensity towards reflection and reflexivity, and they enlist interested parties as co-researchers in a research project. The latter becomes a collaborative activity with, ideally, all of the participants closely involved at every stage of the research project, from its inception and construction, through its execution, to its dissemination (see Reason, 1988).

A 'dialogical' research activity was proposed by Mulkay (1985, p. 76):

> Why not create an analysis in the form of a dialogue with one, or more, of the actual participants? This kind of analysis, as far as I know, has not been tried before. It would be a stringent test of one's analysis to offer it for close scrutiny and comment to those responsible for the original texts. . . . In the course of such an analysis, one could not be continually concerned with one's own textuality. There would be no alternative to projecting one's claims upon participants' own textual products. However, one's analysis would then become a text available to participants for deconstruction and textual analysis. In this way, by abandoning the analyst's usual assumption of interpretative privilege, one could enlist participants' help in revealing one's own textuality, whilst at the same time digging more deeply into their interpretative capacities and your own.

Mulkay used this approach in analysing how scientists talked about their work. His suggestion is an extremely powerful one, partly because it seems to envisage a model of doing research that derives from and corresponds to a theory of persons as reflexive, social and mentating beings. Thus, Mulkay recognized the reflexive work that the researcher and the respondent bring to this encounter, their equal engagement in the activity being reflected in the notion of enlisting the respondent as a co-analyst. Obviously, this attempt at a more negotiated form of analysis will be possible and appropriate only in certain research projects, and questions of power, responsibility and ownership need to be borne in mind.

An example of reflexive practice

I would now like to present some data in order to illustrate one form of reflexive research practice. These data are drawn from a case study of identity change during the transition to motherhood. I visited 'Angela', the participant, at three, six and nine months during her first pregnancy and five months after the birth of her child. At each visit, I interviewed Angela on her thoughts and feelings about her pregnancy and its effect upon her. She also kept a diary throughout the pregnancy, in which she recorded anything associated with the topics discussed in the interviews. When I had carried out some preliminary analysis of Angela's data, I interviewed her again and discussed the material with her. In the following extracts, ellipsis points (. . .) indicate the omission of material, and numbers in square brackets have been added to facilitate my subsequent references to particular remarks. The names of Angela herself and of other people referred to by her have been changed to protect their confidentiality. (For more details of the research project, see Smith, 1994a, 1994b.)

At the beginning of the pregnancy, Angela had been 25 years old and employed as a bank clerk. When I saw her at the three-month stage of her pregnancy, Angela was still adjusting to being pregnant and seemed unsure as to how she felt about it. By the six-month stage, she seemed to be much happier and stated that she was looking forward to the birth of the child. Around about four months, she started writing in her diary about a pregnant neighbour who was three months further ahead in her pregnancy. Angela seemed to be able to use her involvement with this pregnant neighbour as part of her own psychological preparation for mothering. In her diary at about six months, she reported:

> The neighbour over the road had her baby this morning. Her husband came to see us at lunch time to tell us the news. . . . [1] I can't wait to see the baby. I even feel slightly envious that she has had her baby and I have got to wait another 12 weeks.

When I read this diary entry, the sentence [1] ('I can't wait to see the baby') seemed to be ambiguous. Is it that Angela's involvement in her neighbour's excitement meant that she wanted to see her neighbour's baby? Or is it that this earlier birth was making her impatient to see her own child?

A week later, Angela wrote:

> [2] The baby is lovely. [3] I saw her on Monday and Sara came home from hospital on Thursday. . . . [4] I really feel maternal when I hold the baby.

When I read [2], it also struck me as ambiguous. Once again, which baby? This fleeting uncertainty is removed as soon as one reaches [3], which marks the reference as being to the neighbour's child. But why did I feel [2] was ambiguous? In fact, this entry echoed a whole series of previous references by Angela to her own baby as 'the baby', thus cuing anaphoric resonance. Examples of these are shown in Box 14.1. When I read the same abbreviated form in 'The baby is

---

Box 14.1 Examples of previous references to 'the baby' in Angela's diary

I feel very different towards the baby now.
I have not had a scan yet, so I feel a little apprehensive as to whether the baby is developing properly.
We can now see the baby moving.

---

lovely', I was perhaps picking up a reference to Angela again seeing her baby move or to her having now seen it on a scan.

Angela appeared to feel considerable involvement in her neighbour's pregnancy, and this involvement seemed to coincide with an increasing engagement with her own pregnancy, as Angela made explicit in [4]. And perhaps the ambiguities reflected this connection. The manifestation of another baby helped to awaken excitement about her own baby; the close timing meant that her attention was divided between the two pregnancies, and this split attention may have leaked out in the ambiguous references to 'the baby'. Angela may have had both babies in mind, and so reference slipped rapidly between them. This is obviously a speculative reading, and I thought it would be useful to see how Angela herself would respond both to the texts and to my reading of them.

At the feedback meeting, when I returned to see Angela five months after the birth, I first showed her the above diary entries without any comment or interpretation and asked for her reaction. This is what she said:

> Every time I thought 'I don't know what I'm going to do', I could go over there and, you know, that could be my baby for ten minutes. That's how I felt, that if I picked her up she was mine for a little while and it helped me to come to terms with what it was really like.

These remarks suggest that the ambiguous identity referents were even more significant than I had originally considered. While I had suggested that they reflected a splitting of attention on Angela's part, she is pointing here to a stronger identity slippage or fusion. So powerful was her bond with the other family that their baby could, in a sense, become her own. This may help to explain the apparent ambiguity of the previous references to 'the baby'. Angela indeed had access to both babies, and a part of her perceived both as her own.

I then gave some of my interpretation, as outlined above, and I again asked Angela for her reaction:

> *Investigator*: 'The baby is lovely'; I mean, what do you think of what I've said about that?
> *Angela*: Now you've read it out, anyone would assume I was talking about my own. . . . I think it could have been any baby. I felt at that time that any baby was mine. . . . I didn't think of it as being anyone else's when I picked it up. They were completely out of the picture.

This strengthened an 'identity slippage' reading. Although Angela had been literally referring to the neighbour's child, that child in one sense had become her own. Angela went on to make the even stronger claim that not only was ownership of the neighbour's child fluid, but it was almost as if any child could have become hers. And so the apparent ambiguity of a statement such as 'The baby is lovely' became entirely appropriate, since the referent it contains is at the same time both universal and singular. It could have referred to any baby, but by the same token any baby it did refer to was Angela's.

I suggest that this represents a form of reflexive practice. During the first part of my final discussion with Angela, I merely presented some of her account back to her. This then became a stimulus for second-order commentary as she reflected upon what she had written in the diary. Thus, the material was encouraging a natural propensity for reflexivity on the part of the participant. Of course, when I presented her with some of my own interpretation of her data, the field was no longer so neutral, and this part of the interview might be described as being much more like conventional member validation. It is however important to consider the whole context. My own interpretative activity was also reflexive. I did not present my analyses as final or definitive, and indeed my own reading was modified in the light of Angela's comments. I would suggest that, in this exchange, we were engaging in a dialogical form of analysis and, in the terms of Mulkay (1985), 'digging more deeply into our interpretative capacities'. Thus, confronted with such personally relevant material, you are able to encourage additional reflection on the part of the respondent, aspects of which may be captured 'live' in the interview transcript. As suggested by Mulkay and illustrated in this example, the investigator's interpretations are similarly confronted, modified and honed during this process.

Software packages for qualitative analysis

A number of software packages have emerged in the last few years that have been specifically designed for qualitative analysis. There are four main functions these packages can serve: frequency counts; concordance; category selections; and theory building. The first simply provides a frequency count and an alphabetical listing of every word in a text. This produces data in an appropriate form for quantitative content analysis and is likely to be of relatively subordinate interest to most qualitative researchers.

The second software function is performed by 'concordance' programs. These will search for every instance of a selected word or set of words in a text and print out each of the occurrences, embedded within a contextual string. Thus, for example, you can search for every instance of the word 'qualitative' in this chapter, and print these out together with the sentences in which the word had occurred. These programs therefore allow you to look at the different contexts in which a chosen word or phrase is used. This would seem to lend itself well to some of the interests of discourse analysts, for instance to facilitate an examination of the variation in the usage of a particular term. An example of this is the analysis given by Potter and Reicher (1987) of the variable usage of the word 'community' in discussions of an incident in Bristol that has come to be described as 'the St Paul's riot'.

A third software function automates some of the 'cut and paste' tasks involved in qualitative analysis. Here, a 'sort' facility works on codes allocated to chunks of text rather than items within the text itself. If a researcher has allocated a sequence of codes to some file of text, then the program will search through the file and pull out every instance of a particular code. Chunks of text that bear the same code can then appear alongside each other. This would be analogous to the researcher literally cutting up printed versions of the original files and then attempting to cluster together instances sharing a code. This function can obviously be very useful in dealing with large data sets that would prove difficult or even completely impractical to code and sort manually in a comprehensive manner. Further, some of the programs will search and select according to the coexistence of multiple codes. This type of procedure allows you to make analyses that it might be quite inconceivable to carry out manually.

Finally, the fourth function that software can perform is to assist theory building. Programs of this sort look for patterns across codes or category terms themselves (for example, using Boolean logic). See Tesch (1990) for more details.

These software developments can be extremely useful for carrying out qualitative analysis. However, a number of cautions are in order. First, software programs support analysis, they will not do the analysis for the researcher. The complex and multifaceted activities that are involved in interpretative analysis remain human functions. Moreover, these programs have much less to offer in the close reading of small pieces of text that represents one important aspect of qualitative analysis. Thus, while the software can certainly be of enormous benefit to qualitative researchers, the temptation of exaggerating their potential must be avoided. And, just as with all software, the saying 'garbage in, garbage out' remains true. Indeed, at present, I would still recommend researchers to consider using software packages only after they have had some experience of carrying out qualitative analysis in the more traditional way. Finally, there is, in my own experience, considerable variation in the specific tasks that even apparently similar packages can perform and in how they carry them out. If possible, therefore, it is useful to try out a number of sample disks before committing yourself to buying any particular one. Further details on software for qualitative analysis can be found in the books by Tesch (1990), by Fielding and Lee (1991) and by Dey (1993).

Some final thoughts

To end with, I think it might be worth reflecting on the current state of qualitative approaches in psychology. As John Richardson mentioned in Chapter 1, there has clearly been an explosion of interest in qualitative methods among psychologists in recent years, particularly in the UK. This is manifested in, for example, the inclusion of symposia concerning this topic at conferences of the British Psychological Society, the increasing number of postgraduates who are now using qualitative approaches, and a flurry of recent or forthcoming books (including this one) that seek to introduce psychologists to qualitative methods (see, for example, Robson, 1993; Banister *et al.*, 1994; Smith *et al.*, 1995b).

Despite this growth of interest, however, I think that there are some important issues that remain. First, qualitative approaches are still at present relatively marginal to the mainstream discipline. I come to this judgement against two criteria: their appearance in mainstream journals; and their integration within undergraduate syllabuses. Articles describing qualitative research in mainstream psychology journals remain rare. Most qualitative research still appears in book chapters or in dedicated, specialist or interdisciplinary journals. There are some signs of change: for instance, both a special issue of the *Journal of Community and Applied Social Psychology* (Henwood and Parker, 1994b) and a special section of the *Journal of Counselling Psychology* (1994) have recently been devoted to qualitative approaches. However, this is a slow process, and it may take even longer for research studies using qualitative methods to be integrated within undergraduate degree courses on any large scale.

Does this matter? I think this is a point worthy of debate. I suspect that some qualitative researchers would say that they were happy to work outside mainstream psychology and that they defined themselves either in terms of their own sub-field or through cross-disciplinary links (identifying themselves with feminist research, communications studies or, at a broader level, social science, for example). However, for my part, I want to see psychology itself change. I am not an 'anti-psychologist', and I do not think that qualitative research should be peripheral or marginal. Rather, I believe that qualitative research should be at the heart of an expanded and pluralist discipline. This means that getting qualitative research into a range of mainstream journals is important and will remain a major challenge for qualitative researchers.

A connected issue is the relationship between different qualitative approaches. At present, most research is defined in terms of a specific approach (for example, discourse analysis or phenomenology). I think it is important for different approaches not to be watered down or muddied, but I think there is room for more discussion about the interrelationship between them. For example: What are the fundamental differences between the different approaches? Do they differ from each other as much as each does from the mainstream, or can commonalities be identified? Is further integration possible? Discussion of these issues could be very valuable both pragmatically and intellectually. If psychology as a discipline is to be changed, perhaps the challenge can be enhanced by a closer dialogue between the different voices that currently tend to be heard separately.

Acknowledgements

The section on reflexive research practices draws on work that has been previously published and that is cited here as Smith (1994b).

References

Ahlum-Heath, M.E. and Di Vesta, F.J. (1986) The effects of conscious controlled verbalization of a cognitive strategy on transfer in problem solving. *Memory and Cognition, 14*, 281–285.

Allport, G.W. (1951) *The Use of Personal Documents in Psychological Science* (Bulletin No. 49). New York: Social Science Research Council.

Allport, G.W. (1962) The general and the unique in psychological science. *Journal of Personality, 30*, 405–422.

Alton-Lee, A.G. and Nuthall, G.A. (1992) Children's learning in classrooms: Challenges in developing a methodology to explain 'opportunity to learn'. *Journal of Classroom Interaction, 27*(2), 1–7.

Anderson, J.A. (1983) *The Architecture of Cognition*. Cambridge, Massachusetts: Harvard University Press.

Anderson, J.A. (1993) *Rules of the Mind*. Hillsdale, New Jersey: Erlbaum.

Anderson, K., Armitage, S., Jack, D. and Wittner, J. (1990) Beginning where we are: Feminist methodology in oral history. In J.M. Nielsen (Ed.) *Feminist Research Methods: Exemplary Readings in the Social Sciences*. Boulder, Colorado: Westfield Press.

Antaki, C. (Ed.) (1988) *Analysing Everyday Explanation: A Casebook of Methods*. London: Sage.

Antaki, C. (1994) *Arguing and Explaining: The Social Organization of Accounts*. London: Sage.

Antrobus, J.S., Singer, J.L. and Greenberg, S. (1966) Studies in the stream of consciousness: Experimental enhancement and suppression of spontaneous cognitive process. *Perceptual and Motor Skills, 23*, 399–417.

Armistead, N. (Ed.) (1974) *Reconstructing Social Psychology*. Harmondsworth: Penguin.

Ashmore, M. (1993) Behaviour modification of a catflap: A contribution to the sociology of things. *Kennis en Methode, 17*, 214–229.

Ashmore, M., Mulkay, M. and Pinch, T. (1989) *Health and Efficiency: A Sociological Study of Health Economics*. Milton Keynes: Open University Press.

Ashmore, M., Myers, G. and Potter, J. (1995) Seven days in the library: Discourse, rhetoric, reflexivity. In S. Jasanoff, G. Markle, J. Petersen and T. Pinch (Eds) *Handbook of Science and Technology Studies*. London: Sage.

Ashworth, P. (1995) Qualitative methods in psychology. (Book reviews.) *Psychology Teaching Review, 4*, 79–82.

Atkinson, J.M. (1984) *Our Master's Voices: The Language and Body Language of Politics*. London: Methuen.

Atkinson, J.M. and Heritage, J. (1984a) Introduction. In J.M. Atkinson and J. Heritage (Eds) *Structures of Social Action: Studies in Conversation Analysis*. Cambridge: Cambridge University Press.

Atkinson, J.M. and Heritage, J. (Eds) (1984b) *Structures of Social Action: Studies in Conversation Analysis*. Cambridge: Cambridge University Press.

Baddeley, A.D. (1976) *The Psychology of Memory*. New York: Basic Books.

Baldamus, W. (1979) Alienation, anomie and industrial accidents. In M. Wilson (Ed.) *Social and Educational Research in Action*. London: Longman.

Ball, S.J. (1981) *Beachside Comprehensive*. Cambridge: Cambridge University Press.

Banister, P., Burman, E., Parker, I., Taylor, M. and Tindall, C. (1994) *Qualitative Methods in Psychology: A Research Guide*. Buckingham: Open University Press.

Bannister, D. and Mair, J.M.M. (1968) *The Evaluation of Personal Constructs*. London: Academic Press.

Beck, C.T. (1993) Teetering on the edge: A substantive theory of postpartum depression. *Nursing Research, 42*, 42–48.

Becker, H.S. (1973) *Outsiders*, rev. ed. New York: Free Press.

Becker, H.S., Geer, B., Hughes, E.C. and Strauss, A.L. (1961) *Boys in White: Student Culture in Medical School*. Chicago, Illinois: University of Chicago Press.

Becker, S., Horowitz, M. and Campbell, L. (1973) Cognitive responses to stress: Effects of changes in demand and sex. *Journal of Abnormal Psychology, 82*, 519–522.

Bell, D. and Caplan, P. (Eds) (1993) *Gendered Fields: Women, Men, and Ethnography*. London: Routledge.

Benjamin, A.C. (1955) *Operationism*. Springfield, Illinois: Thomas.

Berg, B.L. (1989) *Qualitative Research Methods for the Social Sciences*. Needham Heights, Massachusetts: Allyn and Bacon.

Berk, L.E. (1994) Why children talk to themselves. *Scientific American, 271*(5), 60–65.

Berry, D.C. (1990) Talking about cognitive processes. In K.J. Gilhooly, M.T.G. Keane, R.H. Logie and G. Erdos (Eds) *Lines of Thinking: Reflections on the Psychology of Thought*, vol. 2. Chichester: John Wiley.

Berry, D.C. and Broadbent, D.E. (1984) On the relationship between task performance and associated verbalizable knowledge. *Quarterly Journal of Experimental Psychology, 36A*, 209–231.

Bhavnani, K.-K. (1990) What's power got to do with it? Empowerment and social research. In I. Parker and J. Shotter (Eds) *Deconstructing Social Psychology*. London: Routledge.

Bhavnani, K.-K. and Phoenix, A. (1994) Shifting identities, shifting racisms: An introduction. *Feminism and Psychology, 4*, 5–18.

Billig, M. (1985) Prejudice, categorization and particularization: From a perceptual to a rhetorical approach. *European Journal of Social Psychology, 15*, 79–103.

Billig, M. (1987) *Arguing and Thinking: A Rhetorical Approach to Social Psychology*. Cambridge: Cambridge University Press.

Billig, M. (1988a) Methodology and scholarship in understanding ideological explanation. In C. Antaki (Ed.) *Analysing Lay Explanation: A Case Book*. London: Sage.

Billig, M. (1988b) Rhetorical and historical aspects of attitudes: The case of the British monarchy. *Philosophical Psychology, 1*, 83–103.

Billig, M. (1991) *Ideology and Opinions: Studies in Rhetorical Psychology*. Cambridge: Cambridge University Press.

Billig, M. (1992) *Talking of the Royal Family*. London: Routledge.

Billig, M. (1994) Repopulating the depopulated pages of social psychology. *Theory and Psychology, 4*, 307–335.

Billig, M., Condor, S., Edwards, D., Game, M., Middleton, D.J. and Radley, A.R. (1988) *Ideological Dilemmas: A Social Psychology of Everyday Thinking*. London: Sage.

Blumer, H. (1969a) The methodological position of Symbolic Interactionism. In H. Blumer, *Symbolic Interactionism*. Englewood Cliffs, New Jersey: Prentice-Hall.

Blumer, H. (1969b) *Symbolic Interactionism: Perspective and Method*. Englewood Cliffs, New Jersey: Prentice-Hall.

Bogdan, R. and Taylor, S.J. (1975) *Introduction to Qualitative Research Methods: A Phenomenological Approach to the Social Sciences*. New York: Wiley.

Boring, E.G. (1953) A history of introspection. *Psychological Bulletin, 50*, 169–189.

Borrill, J. and Iljon Foreman, E. (in press) Understanding cognitive change: A qualitative study of the impact of cognitive–behavioural therapy on fear of flying. *Clinical Psychology and Psychotherapy*.

Bowen, E.S. (1964) *Return to Laughter*. New York: Doubleday.

Bowles, G. and Duelli Klein, R. (Eds) (1983) *Theories of Women's Studies*. London: Routledge and Kegan Paul.

Brannigan, A. (1981) *The Social Basis of Scientific Discoveries*. Cambridge: Cambridge University Press.

Brenner, M., Brown, J. and Canter, C. (Eds) (1985) *The Research Interview: Uses and Approaches*. London: Academic Press.

Broadbent, D.E. (1958) *Perception and Communication*. Oxford: Pergamon Press.

Bromley, D.B. (1986) *The Case-Study Method in Psychology and Related Disciplines*. Chichester: Wiley.

Bryman, A. (1988) *Quantity and Quality in Social Research*. London: Unwin Hyman.

Bryman, A. (1992) Quantitative and qualitative research: Further reflections on their integration. In J. Brannen (Ed.) *Mixing Methods: Qualitative and Quantitative Research*. Aldershot: Avebury Press.

Bulbrook, M.E. (1936) An experimental inquiry into the existence and nature of 'insight'. *American Journal of Psychology*, *44*, 409–453.

Bulmer, M. (1979) Concepts in the analysis of qualitative data. In M. Bulmer (Ed.) *Sociological Research Methods*. London: Macmillan.

Burck, C. and Frosh, S. (1994) Research process and gendered reflexivity. *Human Systems*, *5*, 109–122.

Burgess, R.G. (1982) *Field Research: A Sourcebook and Field Manual*. London: Allen and Unwin.

Burgess, R.G. (1984) *In the Field: An Introduction to Field Research*. London: Allen and Unwin.

Burman, E. and Parker, I. (Eds) (1993) *Discourse Analytic Research: Repertoires and Readings of Texts in Action*. London: Routledge.

Button, G. (Ed.) (1991) *Ethnomethodology and the Human Sciences*. Cambridge: Cambridge University Press.

Button, G. and Lee, J.R.E. (1987) *Talk and Social Organisation*. Clevedon: Multilingual Matters.

Button, G. and Sharrock, W. (1992) A disagreement over agreement and consensus in constructionist sociology. *Journal for the Theory of Social Behaviour*, *23*, 1–25.

Carkhuff, R.R. (1987) *The Art of Helping*, 6th ed. Amherst, Massachusetts: Human Resource Development Press.

Charmaz, C. (1990) 'Discovering' chronic illness: Using grounded theory. *Social Science and Medicine*, *30*, 1161–1172.

Charmaz, C. (1995) Grounded theory. In J. A. Smith, R. Harré and L. Van Langenhove (Eds) *Rethinking Methods in Psychology*. London: Sage.

Cicourel, A.V. (1964) *Method and Measurement in Sociology*. New York: Free Press.

Cicourel, A.V. and Kitsuse, J.I. (1963) *The Educational Decision Makers*. New York: Bobbs-Merrill.

Claparède, E. (1934) Genèse de l'hypothèse. *Archives de Psychologie*, *24*, 1–155.

Clifford, J. and Marcus, G.E. (Eds) (1986) *Writing Culture: The Poetics and Politics of Ethnography*. Berkeley, California: University of California Press.

Clough, P.T. (1992) *The End(s) of Ethnography: From Realism to Social Criticism*. Newbury Park, California: Sage.

Collins, H.M. and Pinch, T.J. (1982) *Frames of Meaning: The Social Construction of Extraordinary Science*. London: Routledge and Kegan Paul.

Condor, S. (1986) Sex role beliefs and traditional women: Feminist and intergroup perspectives. In S. Wilkinson (Ed.) *Feminist Social Psychology: Developing Theory and Practice*. Milton Keynes: Open University Press.

Cook, J.A. and Fonow, M.M. (1990) Knowledge and women's interests: Issues of epistemology and methodology in feminist sociological research. In J.M. Nielsen (Ed.) *Feminist Research Methods: Exemplary Readings in the Social Sciences*. Boulder, Colorado: Westfield Press.

Coulter, J. (1979) *The Social Construction of Mind*. London: Macmillan.

Coulter, J. (1983) *Rethinking Cognitive Theory*. London: Macmillan.

Coulter, J. (1989) *Mind in Action*. Cambridge: Polity Press.

Coulter, J. and Parsons, E.D (1991) The praxiology of perception: Visual orientations and practical action. *Inquiry*, *33*, 251–272.

Coyle, A. (1995) Discourse analysis. In G.M. Breakwell, S. Hammond and C. Fife-Schaw (Eds) *Research Methods in Psychology*. London: Sage.

Coyle, A., Good, A. and Wright, C. (1994) *The Counselling Interview as Research Method*. Paper presented at the Annual Conference of the British Psychological Society, Brighton, 24–27 March.

Croll, P. (1986) *Systematic Classroom Observation*. Lewes: Falmer.

Crowle, A. (1976) The deceptive language of the laboratory. In R. Harré (Ed.) *Life Sentences: Aspects of the Social Role of Language*. London: Wiley.

Crutcher, R.J., Ericsson, K.A. and Wichura, C.A. (1994) Improving the encoding of verbal reports using MPAS, a computer-aided encoding system. *Behavior Research Methods, Instruments, and Computers*, *26*, 167–171.

Csordas, T. (1990) Embodiment as a paradigm for anthropology. *Ethos*, *18*, 5–47.

Culler, J. (1983) *On Deconstruction: Theory and Criticism after Structuralism*. London: Routledge and Kegan Paul.

Currie, D. (1988) Re-thinking what we do and how we do it: A study of reproductive decisions. *Canadian Review of Sociology and Anthropology, 25*, 231–253.

Curt, B.C. (1994) *Textuality and Tectonics: Troubling Social and Psychological Science*. Buckingham: Open University Press.

Deffner, G. (1983) *Lautes Denken: Untersuchung zur Qualität eines Datenerhebungsverfahrens*. Doctoral dissertation, University of Hamburg, Hamburg, Germany.

Deffner, G. (1984) *Think Aloud: An Investigation of the Validity of a Data Collection Procedure*. Frankfurt-am-Main, Germany: Peter Lang.

Deffner, G. (1989) Interaction of thinking aloud, solution strategies and task characteristics? An experimental test of the Ericsson and Simon model. *Sprache und Kognition, 9*, 98–111.

De Groot, A.D. (1965) *Thought and Choice in Chess*. The Hague: Mouton.

Delamont, S. (1991) *Fieldwork in Educational Settings: Methods, Pitfalls and Perspectives*. London: Falmer Press.

Delamont, S. and Hamilton, D. (1984) Revisiting classroom research: A continuing cautionary tale. In S. Delamont (Ed.), *Readings on Interaction in the Classroom*. London: Methuen.

Denscombe, M., Szulc, H., Patrick, C. and Wood, A. (1986) Ethnicity and friendship: The contrast between sociometric research and fieldwork observation in primary school classrooms. *British Educational Research Journal, 12*, 221–235.

Denzin, N.K. (1990) The spaces of postmodernism: Reading Plummer on Blumer. *Symbolic Interaction, 13*, 145–154.

Denzin, N.K. (1994) The art and politics of interpretation. In N.K. Denzin and Y.S. Lincoln (Eds) *Handbook of Qualitative Research*. Thousand Oaks, California: Sage.

Denzin, N.K. and Lincoln, Y.S. (Eds) (1994a) *Handbook of Qualitative Research*. Thousand Oaks, California: Sage.

Denzin, N.K. and Lincoln, Y.S. (1994b) Introduction: Entering the field of qualitative research. In N.K. Denzin and Y.S. Lincoln (Eds) *Handbook of Qualitative Research*. Thousand Oaks, California: Sage.

Der Derian, J. and Shapiro, M. (Eds) (1989) *International/Intertextual Relations as Political Theory: Postmodern Readings of World Politics*. Lexington, Virginia: Lexington Books.

Derrida, J. (1978) *Writing and Difference*. Chicago, Illinois: University of Chicago Press.

Dey, I. (1993) *Qualitative Data Analysis: A User Friendly Guide for Social Scientists*. London: Routledge.

Dilthey, W. (1977) *Descriptive Psychology and Historical Understanding* (R.M. Zaner and K.L. Heiges, Trans.). The Hague: Martinus Nijhoff. (Original work published 1894.)

Dipboye, R.L. and Flanagan, M.F. (1979) Research settings in industrial and organizational psychology: Are findings in the field more generalizable than in the laboratory? *American Psychologist, 34*, 141–150.

Dominowski, R.L. and Jenrick, R. (1972) Effects of hints and interpolated activity on solution of an insight problem. *Psychonomic Science, 26*, 335–338.

Drew, P. (1992) Descriptions in legal settings. In P. Drew and J. Heritage (Eds) *Talk at Work: Interaction in Institutional Settings*. Cambridge: Cambridge University Press.

Drew, P. (1995) Conversation analysis. In J.A. Smith, R. Harré and L. Van Langenhove (Eds) *Rethinking Methods in Psychology*. London: Sage.

Drew, P. and Holt, E. (1989) Complainable matters: The use of idiomatic expressions in making complaints. *Social Problems, 35*, 501–520.

Duelli Klein, R. (1983) How to do what we want to do: Thoughts about feminist methodology. In G. Bowles and R. Duelli Klein (Eds) *Theories of Women's Studies*. London: Routledge and Kegan Paul.

Duncker, K. (1945) On problem solving. *Psychological Monographs, 58*, 1–113.

Economic and Social Research Council (1992) *Corporate Plan 1992–1997*. Swindon, UK: Economic and Social Research Council.

Edwards, D. (1994) Script formulations: An analysis of event descriptions in conversation. *Journal of Language and Social Psychology, 13*, 211–247.

Edwards, D. (1995) Two to tango: Script formulations, dispositions, and rhetorical symmetry in relationship troubles talk. *Research on Language and Social Interaction, 28*, 319–350.

Edwards, D. (1996) *Discourse and Cognition*. London: Sage.

Edwards, D., Ashmore, M. and Potter, J. (1995) Death and furniture: The rhetoric, politics and the theology of bottom line arguments against relativism. *History of the Human Sciences, 8*, 25–49.

Edwards, D. and Potter, J. (1992) *Discursive Psychology*. London: Sage.

Edwards, D. and Potter, J. (1993) Language and causation: A discursive action model of description and attribution. *Psychological Review, 100*, 23–41.

Egan, G. (1994) *The Skilled Helper: A Problem-Management Approach to Helping*, 5th ed. Pacific Grove, California: Brooks-Cole Publishing.

Eisner, E. and Peshkin, A. (Eds.) (1989) *Qualitative Inquiry in Education*. New York: Teachers College Press.

Ellen, R.F. (1984) *Ethnographic Research: A Guide to General Conduct*. London: Academic Press.

Elstein, A.S., Schulman, L.S. and Sprafka, S.A. (1978) *Medical Problem Solving: An Analysis of Clinical Reasoning*. Cambridge, Massachusetts: Harvard University Press.

Ely, M., Anzul, M., Friedman, T., Garner, D. and Steinmetz, A.M. (1991) *Doing Qualitative Research: Circles within Circles*. London: Falmer Press.

Erickson, B. and Nosanchuk, T. (1979) *Understanding Data: An Introduction to Exploratory and Confirmatory Data Analysis for the Social Sciences*. Milton Keynes: Open University Press.

Ericsson, K.A. (1975) *Instruction to Verbalize as a Means to Study Problem Solving Processes with the 8-Puzzle: A Preliminary Study* (Report No. 458). Stockholm: University of Stockholm, Department of Psychology.

Ericsson, K.A. and Simon, H.A. (1980) Verbal reports as data. *Psychological Review, 87*, 215–251.

Ericsson, K.A. and Simon, H.A. (1983) *Protocol Analysis: Verbal Reports as Data*. Cambridge, Massachusetts: MIT Press.

Ericsson, K.A. and Simon, H.A. (1993) *Protocol Analysis: Verbal Reports as Data*, rev. ed. Cambridge, Massachusetts: MIT Press.

Erikson, E. (1958) The nature of clinical evidence. In D. Lerner (Ed.) *Evidence and Inference*. Glencoe, Illinois: Free Press of Glencoe.

Erlandson, D.A., Harris, E.L., Skipper, B.L. and Allen, S.D. (1993) *Doing Naturalistic Inquiry*. Newbury Park, California: Sage.

Evans, J.St.B.T. (in press) Implicit learning, consciousness and the psychology of thinking. *Thinking and Reasoning*.

Festinger, L., Riecken, H. and Schachter, S. (1964) *When Prophecy Fails*. London: Harper and Row.

Fetterman, D.M. (1989) *Ethnography: Step by Step*. Newbury Park, California: Sage.

Feyerabend, P. (1975) *Against Method*. London: New Left Books.

Fielding, N.G. and Fielding, J.L. (1986) *Linking Data*. Beverly Hills, California: Sage.

Fielding, N.G. and Lee, R.M. (1991) *Using Computers in Qualitative Research*. London: Sage.

Filmer, P., Phillipson, M., Silverman, D. and Walsh, D. (1973) *New Directions in Sociological Theory*. London: Routledge and Kegan Paul.

Filstead, W.J. (Ed.) (1970) *Qualitative Methods*. Chicago, Illinois: Markham.

Finch, J. (1986) *Research and Policy: The Uses of Qualitative Methods in Social and Educational Research*. London: Falmer Press.

Fine, M. (1994) Working the hyphens: Reinventing self and other in qualitative research. In N.K. Denzin and Y.S. Lincoln (Eds) *Handbook of Qualitative Research*. Thousand Oaks, California: Sage.

Fodor, J.A. and Pylyshyn, Z.W. (1988) Connectionism and cognitive architecture: A critical analysis. *Cognition, 28*, 3–71.

Fonow, M.M. and Cook, J.A. (Eds) (1991) *Beyond Methodology: Feminist Scholarship as Lived Research*. Bloomington, Indiana: Indiana University Press.

Fontana, A. and Frey, J.H. (1994) Interviewing: The art of science. In N.K. Denzin and Y.S. Lincoln (Eds) *Handbook of Qualitative Research*. Thousand Oaks, California: Sage.

Fordham, M. (1960) Counter-transference: 1. *British Journal of Medical Psychology, 33*, 1–8.

Fox-Keller, E. (1985) *Reflections on Gender and Science*. New Haven, Connecticut: Yale University Press.

Freud, S. (1900) The interpretation of dreams. In *Standard Edition*, vols IV and V. London: Hogarth Press.

Fulgosi, A. and Guilford, J.P. (1968) Short term incubation in divergent production. *American Journal of Psychology, 81*, 241–246.

Gantt, L.T. (1992) Growing up heartsick: The experiences of young women with congenital heart disease. *Health Care for Women International, 13*, 241–248.

Garfinkel, H. (1967) *Studies in Ethnomethodology*. Englewood Cliffs, New Jersey: Prentice Hall.

Geertz, C. (1973) *The Interpretation of Cultures: Selected Essays*. New York: Basic Books.

Geertz, C. (1979) From the native's point of view: The nature of anthropological understanding. In K.H. Basso and H. Selby (Eds) *Meaning and Anthropology*. Albuquerque, New Mexico: University of New Mexico Press.

Gephart, R.P. (1988) *Ethnostatistics: Qualitative Foundations for Quantitative Research*. London: Sage.

Gergen, K.J. (1985) The social constructionist movement in modern psychology. *American Psychologist, 40*, 266–275.

Gergen, K.J. (1994a) *Realities and Relationships: Soundings in Social Construction*. Cambridge, Massachusetts: Harvard University Press.

Gergen, K.J. (1994b) *Toward Transformation in Social Knowledge*, 2nd ed. London: Sage.

Gergen, K.J. and Gergen, M.M. (1991) Toward reflexive methodologies. In F. Steier (Ed.) *Research and Reflexivity*. London: Sage.

Gergen, M. (1988) Narrative structures in social explanation. In C. Antaki (Ed.) *Analysing Everyday Explanation: A Casebook of Methods*. London: Sage.

Gergen, M. (1992) Life stories: Pieces of a dream. In G. Rosenwald and R. Ochberg (Eds) *Storied Lives*. New Haven, Connecticut: Yale University Press.

Gergen, M.M. and Gergen, K.J. (1993) Narratives of the gendered body in popular autobiography. In R. Josselson and A. Lieblich (Eds) *The Narrative Study of Lives*. Newbury Park, California: Sage.

Gherardi, S. and Turner, B.A. (1987) *Real Men Don't Collect Soft Data* (Quaderno 13). Trento: Università di Trento, Dipartimento di Politica Sociale.

Gilbert, G.N. and Mulkay, M.J (1984) *Opening Pandora's Box: A Sociological Analysis of Scientists' Discourse*. Cambridge: Cambridge University Press.

Gilhooly, K.J. and Green, C. (1989) A suite of computer programs for use in verbal protocol analysis. *Literary and Linguistic Computing, 4*, 1–5.

Gilhooly, K.J. and Gregory, D.J. (1989) Thinking aloud performance: Individual consistencies over tasks. *Current Psychology: Research and Reviews, 8*, 179–187.

Gilhooly, K.J., Wood, M., Kinnear, P.R. and Green, C. (1988) Skill in map reading and memory for maps. *Quarterly Journal of Experimental Psychology, 40A*, 87–107.

Gilhooly, K.J., McGeorge, P., Hunter, J., Rawles, J., Kirby, I., Green, C.A. and Wynn, V. (1995) *Biomedical Knowledge in Diagnostic Thinking: The Case of Electrocardiogram (ECG) Interpretation*. Unpublished manuscript, Department of Psychology, University of Aberdeen. Copies available on request from the first author.

Gill, R. (1993a) Ideology, gender and popular radio: A discourse analytic approach. *Innovation, 6*, 323–339.

Gill, R. (1993b) Justifying injustice: Broadcasters' accounts of inequality in radio. In E. Burman and I. Parker (Eds) *Discourse Analytic Research: Repertoires and Readings of Texts in Action*. London: Routledge.

Gill, R. (1995) Relativism, reflexivity and politics: Interrogating discourse analysis from a feminist perspective. In S. Wilkinson and C. Kitzinger (Eds) *Feminism and Discourse: Psychological Perspectives*. London: Sage.

Gillett, G. (1995) The philosophical foundations of qualitative psychology. *The Psychologist, 8*, 111–114.

Gitlin, A.D., Siegel, M. and Boru, K. (1989) The politics of method: From leftist ethnography to educative research. *Qualitative Studies in Education, 2*, 237–253.

Glaser, B.G. (1992) *Basics of Grounded Theory Analysis*. Mill Valley, California: Sociology Press.

Glaser, B.G. and Strauss, A.L. (1965) *Awareness of Dying*. Chicago, Illinois: Aldine.

Glaser, B.G. and Strauss, A.L. (1967) *The Discovery of Grounded Theory: Strategies for Qualitative Research*. Chicago, Illinois: Aldine.

Gloersen, B., Kendall, J., Gray, P. and McConnell, S. (1993) The phenomenon of doing well in people with AIDS. *Western Journal of Nursing Research, 15*, 44–54.

Goethals, G.R. and Reckman, R.F. (1973) The perception of consistency in attitudes. *Journal of Experimental Social Psychology, 9*, 491–501.

Graham, H. (1986) *The Human Face of Psychology*. Milton Keynes: Open University Press.

Green, A. (1995) Verbal protocol analysis. *The Psychologist, 8*, 126–129.

Greenwald, R.A., Ryan, M.K. and Mulvihill, J.E. (Eds) (1982) *Human Subjects Research: A Handbook for Institutional Review Boards*. New York: Plenum.

Greemwood, J.D. (1982) On the relation between laboratory experiments and social behaviour: Causal explanation and generalization. *Journal for the Theory of Human Behaviour, 12*, 225–250.

Griffin, C. (1986) Qualitative methods and female experience. In S. Wilkinson (Ed.) *Feminist Social Psychology: Developing Theory and Practice*. Milton Keynes: Open University Press.

Griffin, C. (1995) Feminism, social psychology and qualitative research. *The Psychologist, 8*, 119–121.

Griffin, C. and Phoenix, A. (1994) The relationship between qualitative and quantitative research: Lessons from feminist psychology. *Journal of Community and Applied Social Psychology, 4*, 225–238.

Guba, E. (Ed.) (1990) *The Paradigm Dialog*. Newbury Park, California: Sage.

Guba, E.G. and Lincoln, Y.S. (1994) Competing paradigms in qualitative research. In N.K. Denzin and Y.S. Lincoln (Eds) *Handbook of Qualitative Research*. Thousand Oaks, California: Sage.

Gubrium, J.F. and Silverman, D. (Eds) (1989) *The Politics of Field Research: Beyond Enlightenment*. Newbury Park, California: Sage.

Hammersley, M. (1985) From ethnography to theory. *Sociology, 19*, 244–259.

Hammersley, M. (1989) *The Dilemma of Qualitative Method: Herbert Blumer and the Chicago Tradition*. London: Routledge.

Hammersley, M. (1991) A myth of a myth: An assessment of two ethnographic studies of option choice schemes. *British Journal of Sociology, 42*, 61–94.

Hammersley, M. (1992a) The paradigm wars: Reports from the front. *British Journal of Sociology of Education, 13*, 131–143.

Hammersley, M. (1992b) *What's Wrong with Ethnography?* London: Routledge.

Hammersley, M. and Atkinson, P. (1983) *Ethnography: Principles in Practice*. London: Routledge.

Hammersley, M. and Atkinson, P. (1995) *Ethnography: Principles in Practice*, 2nd ed. London: Routledge.

Haraway, D. (1989a) The biopolitics of postmodern bodies: Determinations of self in immune system discourse. *Differences, 1*, 2–43. Haraway, D. (1989b) *Primate Visions: Gender, Race, and Nature in the World of Modern Science*. New York: Routledge.

Haraway, D. (1991) *Simians, Cyborgs, and Women: The Reinvention of Nature*. New York: Routledge.

Harding, S. (1986) *The Science Question in Feminism*. Milton Keynes: Open University Press.

Harding, S. (Ed.) (1987) *Feminism and Methodology*. Milton Keynes: Open University Press.

Harding, S. (1991) *Whose Science? Whose Knowledge? Thinking From Women's Lives*. Milton Keynes: Open University Press.

Harré, R. (1979) *Social Being: A Theory for Social Psychology*. Oxford: Blackwell.

Harré, R. (Ed.) (1992a) New methodologies: The turn to discourse. (Special issue.) *American Behavioural Scientist, 36*(1).

Harré, R. (1992b) *Social Being: A Theory for Social Psychology*, 2nd ed. Oxford: Blackwell.

Harré, R. (1993) Rules, roles and rhetoric. *The Psychologist, 6*, 24–28.

Harré, R. and Secord, P.F. (1972) *The Explanation of Social Behaviour*. Oxford: Blackwell.

Hayes, N. (Ed.) (in press) *Qualitative Analysis in Psychology*. Hove: Erlbaum.

Henriques, J., Hollway. W., Urwin, C., Venn C. and Walkerdine, V. (1984) *Changing the Subject: Psychology, Social Regulation and Subjectivity*. London: Methuen.

Henwood, K.L. (1993) Women and later life: The discursive construction of identities within family relationships. *Journal of Ageing Studies, 7*, 303–319.

Henwood, K. and Nicolson, P. (1995a) Qualitative research. *The Psychologist, 8*, 109–110.

Henwood, K. and Nicolson, P. (Eds) (1995b) Qualitative research. (Special issue.) *The Psychologist, 8*(3).

Henwood, K. and Parker, I. (1994a) Introduction: Qualitative social psychology. *Journal of Community and Applied Social Psychology, 4*, 219–224.

Henwood K. and Parker, I. (Eds) (1994b) Qualitative social psychology. (Special issue.) *Journal of Community and Applied Social Psychology, 4*(4).

Henwood, K.L. and Pidgeon, N.F. (1992) Qualitative research and psychological theorising. *British Journal of Psychology, 83*, 97–111.

Henwood, K. and Pidgeon, N. (1994) Beyond the qualitative paradigm: A framework for introducing diversity within qualitative psychology. *Journal of Community and Applied Social Psychology, 4*, 225–238.

Henwood, K. and Pidgeon, N. (1995a) Grounded theory and psychological research. *The Psychologist, 8*, 115–118.

Henwood, K.L. and Pidgeon, N.F. (1995b) Remaking the link: Qualitative research and feminist standpoint theory. *Feminism and Psychology, 5*, 7–30.

Henwood, K.L. and Pidgeon, N.F. (1995c) *Theory, Grounding and Reflexivity: Another Route to Constructivist Psychology?* Unpublished manuscript, Brunel University and Birkbeck College. Copies available from the authors.

Heritage, J. (1984) *Garfinkel and Ethnomethodology*. Cambridge: Polity Press.

Heritage, J. (1988) Explanations as accounts: A conversation analytic perspective. In C. Antaki (Ed.) *Analysing Everyday Explanation: A Case Book of Methods*. London: Sage.

Heritage, J. (1995) Conversation analysis: Methodological aspects. In V. Quasthoff (Ed.) *Aspects of Oral Communication*. Berlin: De Gruyter.

Heritage, J. and Greatbatch, D. (1991) On the institutional character of institutional talk. In D. Boden and D. Zimmerman (Eds) *Talk and Social Structure: Studies in Ethnomethodology and Conversation Analysis*. Cambridge: Polity Press.

Hersen, M. and Barlow, D.H. (1976) *Single-Case Experimental Designs*. Oxford: Pergamon.

Hewitt, J.P. (1994) *Self and Society: A Symbolic Interactionist Social Psychology*, 6th ed. Boston, Massachusetts: Allyn and Bacon.

Hewitt, J.P. and Stokes, R. (1975) Disclaimers. *American Sociological Review, 40*, 1–11.

Heydemann, M. (1986) The relationship between eye-movements and think aloud for Raven's Matrices. *Psychologische Beitrage, 28*, 76–87.

Hine, C. (1994) *Virtual Ethnography* (CRICT Discussion Paper No. 43). Uxbridge, Middlesex: Brunel University, Centre for Research into Innovation, Culture and Technology.

Holland, J.H., Holyoak, K.J., Nisbett, R.E. and Thagard, R.R. (1986) *Induction: Processes of Inference, Learning and Discovery*. Cambridge, Massachusetts: MIT Press.

Hollway, W. (1989) *Subjectivity and Method in Psychology: Gender, Meaning and Science*. London: Sage.

Hutchinson, S. and Wilson, H. (1994) Research and therapeutic interviews: A poststructuralist perspective. In J.M. Morse (Ed.) *Critical Issues in Qualitative Research Methods*. Thousand Oaks, California: Sage.

Inskipp, F. (1993) *Counselling: The Trainer's Handbook*. Cambridge: National Extension College Trust.

Jacobs, M. (1986) *The Presenting Past*. London: Harper and Row.

Jaeger, M.E. and Rosnow, R.L. (1988) Contextualism and its implications for psychological inquiry. *British Journal of Psychology, 79*, 63–75.

Jasanoff, S., Markle, G.E., Petersen, J.C. and Pinch, T. (Eds) (1995) *Handbook of Science and Technology Studies*. London: Sage.

Jefferson, G. (1985) An exercise in the transcription and analysis of laughter. In T. van Dijk (Ed.) *Handbook of Discourse Analysis*, vol. 3. London: Academic Press.

Johnson, A. and Johnson, O. (1990) Quality into quantity. In R. Sanjek (Ed.) *Fieldnotes: The Makings of Anthropology*. Ithaca, New York: Cornell University Press.

Journal of Counselling Psychology (1994) Special section on qualitative research in counselling process and outcome. *Journal of Counselling Psychology, 41*, 427–512.

Keat, R. and Urry, J. (1975) *Social Theory as Science*. London: Routledge and Kegan Paul.

Kelle, U. (Ed.) (1995) *Computer-Aided Qualitative Data Analysis: Theories, Methods and Practice*. London: Sage.

Kelly, A. (1978) Feminism and research. *Women's Studies International Quarterly, 1*, 225–232.

Kidder, L.H. (1981) Qualitative research and quasi-experimental frameworks. In M.B. Brewer and B.E. Collins (Eds) *Scientific Inquiry and the Social Sciences*. San Francisco, California: Jossey-Bass.

Kimmel, A.J. (1988) *Ethics and Values in Applied Social Research*. Newbury Park, California: Sage.

King, E. (1993) Power versus empowerment as part of the research process. *Psychology of Women Newsletter*, No.11, pp. 16–19.

Kirk, J. and Miller, M.L. (1986) *Reliability and Validity in Qualitative Research*. Newbury Park, California: Sage.

Kleinman, S. and Copp, M.A. (1993) *Emotions and Fieldwork*. Newbury Park, California: Sage.

Kline, P. (1988) *Psychology Exposed, or the Emperor's New Clothes*. London: Routledge.

Knorr Cetina, K.D. (1981) *The Manufacture of Knowledge: An Essay on the Constructivist and Contextual Nature of Science*. Oxford: Pergamon.

Knorr Cetina, K.D. (1995) Laboratory studies: The cultural approach to the study of science. In S. Jasanoff, G. Markle, T. Pinch and J. Petersen (Eds) *Handbook of Science, Technology and Society*. London: Sage.

Kolakowski, L. (1972) *Positivist Philosophy*. Harmondsworth: Penguin.

Kratochwill, T.R. (Ed.) (1978) *Single Subject Research*. London: Academic Press.

Krippendorf, K. (1980) *Content Analysis: An Introduction to Its Methodology*. London: Sage.

Kuhn, T.S. (1970) *The Structure of Scientific Revolutions*, 2nd ed. Chicago, Illinois: University of Chicago Press.

Kvale, S. (1986) Psychoanalytic therapy as qualitative research. In P.D. Ashworth, A. Giorgi and A.J.J. De Koning (Eds) *Qualitative Research in Psychology*. Pittsburgh, Pennsylvania: Duquesne University Press.

Lamberts, K. (1990) A hybrid model of learning to solve physics problems. *European Journal of Cognitive Psychology, 2*, 151–170.

Lamberts, K. and Pfeifer, R. (1992) Computational models of expertise. In K. Gilhooly and M.T. Keane (Eds) *Advances in the Psychology of Thinking*. London: Harvester Wheatsheaf.

Lather, P. (1986) Research as praxis. *Harvard Educational Review, 56*, 257–277.

Latour, B. (1987) *Science in Action*. Milton Keynes: Open University Press.

Latour, B. (1988) The politics of explanation. In S. Woolgar (Ed.) *Knowledge and Reflexivity: New Directions in the Sociology of Knowledge*. London: Sage.

Latour, B. (1990) Drawing things together. In M. Lynch and S. Woolgar (Eds) *Representation in Scientific Practice*. Cambridge, Massachusetts: MIT Press.

Latour, B. and Woolgar, S. (1979) *Laboratory Life: The Social Construction of Scientific Facts*. Beverly Hills, California: Sage.

Latour, B. and Woolgar, S. (1986) *Laboratory Life: The Construction of Scientific Facts*, rev. ed. Princeton, New Jersey: Princeton University Press.

Layder, D. (1993) *New Strategies in Social Research*. Cambridge: Polity Press.

Levine, J. (1993) *Exceptions are the Rule: An Enquiry into the Methods of the Social Sciences*. Boulder, Colorado: Westview.

Levinson, S. (1983) *Pragmatics*. Cambridge: Cambridge University Press.

Lévi-Strauss, C. (1969) *The Elementary Structures of Kinship* (J.H. Bell, J.R. von Sturmer and R. Needham, Trans.). London: Eyre and Spottiswoode. (Original work published 1949.)

Lewis, G. (1980) *Day of Shining Red*. Cambridge: Cambridge University Press.

Lieberson, S. (1985) *Making it Count: The Improvement of Social Research and Theory*. Berkeley, California: University of California Press.

Lincoln, Y.S. and Guba, E.G. (1985) *Naturalistic Inquiry*. Beverly Hills, California: Sage.

Lofland, J. (1967) Notes on naturalism. *Kansas Journal of Sociology, 3*(2), 45–61.

Lofland, J. and Lofland, L.H. (1983) *Analyzing Social Settings*. Belmont, California: Wadsworth.

Lundberg, G. (1933) Is sociology too scientific? *Sociologus, 9*, 298–322.

211

Lynch, M. (1985) *Art and Artifact in Laboratory Science: A Study of Shop Work and Shop Talk in a Research Laboratory*. London: Routledge and Kegan Paul.

Lynch, M. (1993) *Scientific Practice and Ordinary Action: Ethnomethodology and Social Studies of Science*. Cambridge: Cambridge University Press.

Lynch, M. and Bogen, D. (in press-a) *The Ceremonial of the Truth at the Iran-Contra Hearings*. Durham, North Carolina: Duke University Press.

Lynch, M. and Bogen, D. (in press-b) Reinventing cognitive sociology. In *Proceedings of the 1994 Conference on Ethnomethodology/Conversation Analysis*. Urbino, Italy: Centro Internazionale de Semiotica e Linguistica.

Madill, A. and Doherty, K. (1994) 'So you did what you wanted to then': Discourse analysis, personal agency, and psychotherapy. *Journal of Community and Applied Social Psychology*, *4*, 261–274.

Mahoney, M. (1976) *Scientist as Subject: The Psychological Imperative*. Cambridge, Massachusetts: Ballinger.

Mangabeira, W. (1995) Qualitative analysis and micro-computer software: Some reflections on a new trend in sociological research. In R. Burgess (Ed.) *Studies in Qualitative Methodology*, vol. 5. Greenwich, Connecticut: JAI Press.

Marsh, P., Rosser, E. and Harré, R. (1978) *The Rules of Disorder*. London: Routledge.

Marshall, C. and Rossman, G.B. (1995) *Designing Qualitative Research*, 2nd ed. Thousand Oaks, California: Sage.

Marshall, H. and Raabe, B. (1993) Political discourse: Talking about nationalization. In E. Burman and I. Parker (Eds) *Discourse Analytic Research: Repertoires and Readings of Texts in Action*. London: Routledge.

Matza, D. (1969) *Becoming Deviant*. Englewood Cliffs, New Jersey: Prentice Hall.

Maynard, M. and Purvis, J. (Eds) (1994) *Researching Women's Lives from a Feminist Perspective*. London: Taylor and Francis.

McCracken, G.D. (1988) *The Long Interview*. Newbury Park, California: Sage.

McDonald, M. (1989) *We are Not French: Language, Culture and Identity in Brittany*. London: Routledge.

McLeod, J. (1993) *An Introduction to Counselling*. Buckingham: Open University Press.

Mead, G.H. (1934) *Mind, Self and Society*. (Edited by C.W. Morris.) Chicago, Illinois: University of Chicago Press.

Mies, M. (1983) Towards a methodology for feminist research. In G. Bowles and R. Duelli Klein (Eds) *Theories of Women's Studies*. London: Routledge.

Mies, M. (1991) Women's research or feminist research? The debate surrounding feminist science and methodology. In M.M. Fonow and J.A. Cook (Eds) *Beyond Methodology: Feminist Scholarship as Lived Research*. Bloomington, Indiana: Indiana University Press.

Miles, M.B. and Huberman, A.M. (1984) *Qualitative Data Analysis: A Sourcebook of New Methods*. Beverly Hills, California: Sage.

Miles, M.B. and Huberman, A.M. (1994) *Qualitative Data Analysis: An Expanded Sourcebook*, 2nd ed. Thousand Oaks, California: Sage.

Mishler, E.G. (1986) *Research Interviewing: Context and Narrative*. Cambridge, Massachusetts: Harvard University Press.

Moerman, M. (1974) Who are the Lue? In R. Turner (Ed.) *Ethnomethodology*. Harmondsworth: Penguin.

Mook, D.G. (1983) In defense of external invalidity. *American Psychologist*, *38*, 379–387.

Mulkay, M. (1979) *Science and the Sociology of Knowledge*. London: Allen and Unwin.

Mulkay, M. (1985) *The Word and the World*. London: Allen and Unwin.

Murgatroyd, S. (1985) *Counselling and Helping*. London: British Psychological Society and Methuen.

Murray, H.G. and Denny, J.P. (1969) Interaction of ability level and interpolated activity in human problem solving. *Psychological Reports*, *24*, 271–276.

Nairn, R. and McCreanor, T.N. (1991) Race talk and common sense: Patterns of discourse on Maori/Pakeha relations in New Zealand. *Journal of Language and Social Psychology*, *10*, 245–262.

Neisser, U. (1963a) The imitation of man by machine. *Science*, *139*, 193–197.

Neisser, U. (1963b) The multiplicity of thought. *British Journal of Psychology*, *54*, 1–14.

Newell, A. (1962) Some problems of basic organization in problem solving programs. In M.C. Yovits, G.T. Jacobi and G.D. Goldstein (Eds) *Self-Organizing Systems*. Washington, DC: Spartan Books.

Newell, A. (1990) *Unified Theories of Cognition*. Cambridge, Massachusetts: Harvard University Press.

Newell, A. and Simon, H.A. (1972) *Human Problem Solving*. Englewood Cliffs, New Jersey: Prentice-Hall.

Nicolson, P. (1991) *Qualitative Psychology*. Report prepared for the Scientific Affairs Board of the British Psychological Society, Leicester, UK.

Nisbett, R.E. and Wilson, T.D. (1977) Telling more than we can know: Verbal reports on mental processes. *Psychological Review, 84*, 231–259.

Nofsinger, R.E. (1991) *Everyday Conversation*. London: Sage.

Norman, D.A. (1981) Categorization of action slips. *Psychological Review, 88*, 1–15.

Norman, D.A. (1986) Reflections on cognition and parallel distributed processing. In D.E. Rumelhart, J.L. McClelland and the PDP Research Group (Eds) *Parallel Distributed Processing*, vol. 2. Cambridge, Massachusetts: MIT Press.

Oakley, A. (1981) Interviewing women: A contradiction in terms. In H. Roberts (Ed.) *Doing Feminist Research*. London: Routledge and Kegan Paul.

Obeyesekere, G. (1981) *Medusa's Hair*. Chicago, Illinois: Chicago University Press.

Ochs, E. (1979) Transcription as theory. In E. Ochs and B. B. Schieffelin (Eds) *Developmental Pragmatics*. New York: Academic Press.

Ohlsson, S. (1992) Information processing explanations of insight and related phenomena. In K.J. Gilhooly and M.T. Keane (Eds) *Advances in the Psychology of Thinking*. London: Harvester Wheatsheaf.

Olson, J.R. and Biolsi, K.J. (1991) Techniques for representing expert knowledge. In K.A. Ericsson and J. Smith (Eds) *Towards a General Theory of Expertise: Prospects and Limits*. Cambridge: Cambridge University Press.

Olton, R.M. and Johnson, D.M. (1976) Mechanisms of incubation in creative problem solving. *American Journal of Psychology, 89*, 617–630.

Opie, A. (1992) Qualitative research, appropriation of the 'other' and empowerment. *Feminist Review, 40*, 52–69.

Ots, T. (1990) The angry liver, the anxious heart and the melacholy spleen: The phenomenology of perceptions in Chinese culture. *Culture, Medicine and Psychiatry, 14*, 21–58.

Parker, I. (1988) Deconstructing accounts. In C. Antaki (Ed.) *Analysing Everyday Explanation: A Casebook of Methods*. London: Sage.

Parker, I. (1989) *The Crisis in Modern Social Psychology and How to End It*. London: Routledge.

Parker, I. (1992) *Discourse Dynamics: Critical Analysis for Social and Individual Psychology*. London: Routledge.

Parker, I. (1994) Reflexive research and the grounding of analysis: Social psychology and the psy-complex. *Journal of Community and Applied Social Psychology, 4*, 239–252.

Patrick, C. (1937) Creative thought in artists. *Journal of Psychology, 4*, 35–73.

Patton, M.Q. (1990) *Qualitative Evaluation and Research Methods*, 2nd ed. Newbury Park, California: Sage.

Payne, J.W. (1994) Thinking aloud: Insights into information processing. *Psychological Science, 5*, 241–247.

Perelman, C. and Olbrechts-Tyteca, L. (1971) *The New Rhetoric*. Notre Dame, Indiana: University of Notre Dame Press.

Phoenix, A. (1990) Social research in the context of feminist psychology. In E. Burman (Ed.) *Feminists and Psychological Practice*. London: Sage.

Pickering, A. (Ed.) (1992) *Science as Practice and Culture*. Chicago, Illinois: Chicago University Press.

Pidgeon, N.F., Blockley, D.I. and Turner, B.A. (1988) Site investigations: Lessons from a late discovery of hazardous waste. *The Structural Engineer, 66*, 311–315.

Pidgeon, N.F., Turner, B.A. and Blockley, D.I. (1991) The use of grounded theory for conceptual analysis in knowledge elicitation. *International Journal of Man–Machine Studies, 35*, 151–173.

Poincaré, H. (1908) *Science et Méthode*. Paris: Flammarion.

Popper, K. R. (1959) *The Logic of Scientific Discovery*. London: Hutchinson. (Original work published 1934.)

Porter, S. (1993) Critical realist ethnography: The case of racism and professionalism in a medical setting. *Sociology, 27*, 591–609.

Porter Poole, F.J. (1981) Transforming 'natural' woman: Female ritual leaders and gender ideology among Bimin-Kuskusmin. In S.B. Ortner and H. Whitehead (Eds) *Sexual Meanings*. Cambridge: Cambridge University Press.

Potter, J. (1996) *Representing Reality: Discourse, Rhetoric and Social Construction*. London: Sage.

Potter, J. and Collie, S. (1989) 'Community care' as persuasive rhetoric: A study of discourse. *Disability, Handicap and Society, 4*, 56–64.

Potter, J. and Mulkay, M. (1985) Scientists' interview talk: Interviews as a technique for revealing participants' interpretative practices. In M. Brenner, J. Brown and D. Canter (Eds) *The Research Interview: Uses and Approaches*. London: Academic Press.

Potter, J. and Reicher, S. (1987) Discourses of community and conflict: The organization of social categories in accounts of a 'riot'. *British Journal of Social Psychology, 26*, 25–40.

Potter, J. and Wetherell, M. (1987) *Discourse and Social Psychology: Beyond Attitudes and Behaviour*. London: Sage.

Potter, J. and Wetherell, M. (1988) Accomplishing attitudes: Fact and evaluation in racist discourse. *Text, 8*, 51–68.

Potter, J. and Wetherell, M. (1994) Analysing discourse. In A. Bryman and R.G. Burgess (Eds) *Analysing Qualitative Data*. London: Routledge.

Potter, J. and Wetherell, M. (1995) Discourse analysis. In J. Smith, R. Harré and L. van Langenhove (Eds) *Rethinking Methods in Psychology*. London: Sage.

Potter, J., Wetherell, M. and Chitty, A. (1991) Quantification rhetoric: Cancer on television. *Discourse and Society, 2*, 333–365.

Potter, J., Wetherell, M., Gill, R. and Edwards, D. (1990). Discourse: Noun, verb or social practice? *Philosophical Psychology, 3*, 205–217.

Powdermaker, H. (1966) *Stranger and Friend: The Way of an Anthropologist*. New York: Norton.

Psathas, G. (1990) Introduction. In G. Psathas (Ed.) *Interactional Competence*. Washington, DC: University Press of America.

Psathas, G. (1995) *Conversation Analysis: The Study of Talk-in-Interaction*. Thousand Oaks, California: Sage.

Psathas, G. and Anderson, T. (1990) The 'practices' of transcription in conversation analysis. *Semiotica, 78*, 75–99.

Punch, M. (1994) Politics and ethics in qualitative research. In N.K. Denzin and Y.S. Lincoln (Eds) *Handbook of Qualitative Research*. Thousand Oaks, California: Sage.

Quinlan, P. (1991) *Connectionism and Psychology*. London: Harvester Wheatsheaf.

Rachel, J. and Woolgar, S. (1995) The discursive structure of the social–technical divide: The example of information systems development. *Sociological Review, 43*, 251–273.

Radke, H.L. and Stam, H.J. (1994) *Power/Gender: Social Relations in Theory and Practice*. London: Sage.

Reason, J. (1979) Actions not as planned: The price of automatization. In G. Underwood and K. Stevens (Eds) *Aspects of Consciousness*, vol. 1. London: Academic Press.

Reason, P. (Ed.) (1988) *Human Inquiry in Action*. London: Sage.

Reason, P. (1994) *Participation in Human Inquiry*. London: Sage.

Reason, P. and Rowan, J. (Eds) (1981) *Human Inquiry: A Sourcebook of New Paradigm Research*. Chichester: Wiley.

Reicher, S. (1994) Particular methods and general assumptions. *Journal of Community and Applied Social Psychology, 4*, 299–304.

Reinharz, S. (1983) Experiential analysis: a contribution to feminist research. In G. Bowles and R. Duelli Klein (Eds) *Theories of Women's Studies*. London: Routledge.

Reinharz, S. (1992) *Feminist Methods in Social Research*. New York: Oxford University Press.

Rennie, D.L., Phillips, J.R. and Quartaro, G.K. (1988) Grounded theory: A promising approach to conceptualization in psychology? *Canadian Psychology, 29*, 139–150.

Rhenius, D. and Heydemann, M. (1984) Think aloud during the administration of Raven's Matrices. *Zeitschrift für experimentelle und angewandte Psychologie, 31*, 308–327.

Riessman, C.K. (1977) *Interviewer Effects in Psychiatric Epidemiology: A Study of Medical and Lay Interviewers and their Impact on Reported Symptoms*. Unpublished doctoral thesis, Columbia University, New York.

Riessman, C.K. (1993) *Narrative Analysis*. Newbury Park, California: Sage.

Roberts, H. (1981) *Doing Feminist Research*. London: Routledge.

Robson, C. (1993) *Real World Research: A Resource for Social Scientists and Practitioner-Researchers*. Oxford: Blackwell.

Rogers, C. (1951) *Client-Centered Therapy*. London: Constable.

Rosnow, R.L. (1981) *Paradigms in Transition: The Methodology of Social Inquiry*. New York: Oxford University Press.

Rosnow, R.L. and Georgoudi, M. (Eds.) (1986) *Contextualism and Understanding in Behavioral Science*. New York: Praeger.

Rottenberg, C.J. and Searfoss, L.W. (1992) Becoming literate in a preschool class: Literacy development of hearing-impared children. *Journal of Reading Behavior, 24*, 463–479.

Rumelhart, D.E., McClelland, J.L. and the PDP Research Group (Eds) (1986a) *Parallel Distributed Processing*, vol.1. Cambridge, Massachusetts: MIT Press.

Rumelhart, D.E., Smolensky, P., McClelland, J.L. and Hinton, G.E. (1986b) Schemata and sequential thought processes in PDP models. In J.L. McClelland, D.E. Rumelhart and the PDP Research Group (Eds) *Parallel Distributed Processing*, vol. 2. Cambridge, Massachusetts: MIT Press.

Russo, J.E., Johnson, E. and Stephens, D.L. (1989) The validity of verbal protocols. *Memory and Cognition, 17*, 759–769.

Sacks, H. (1992) *Lectures on Conversation* (2 vols). Oxford: Blackwell.

Sampson, E.E. (1989) The deconstruction of the self. In J. Shotter and K.J. Gergen (Eds) *Texts of Identity*. London: Sage.

Sanjek, R. (Ed.) (1990) *Fieldnotes: The Makings of Anthropology*. Ithaca, New York: Cornell University Press.

Sarup, M. (1988) *Poststructuralism and Postmodernism*. London: Harvester Wheatsheaf.

Scarth, J. and Hammersley, M. (1988) Examinations and teaching: An exploratory study. *British Educational Research Journal, 14*(3), 231–249.

Schegloff, E.A. (1988) Presequences and indirection: Applying speech act theory to ordinary conversation. *Journal of Pragmatics, 12*, 55–62.

Schegloff, E.A. (1992) Repair after next turn: The last structurally provided defence of intersubjectivity in conversation. *American Journal of Sociology, 97*, 1295–1345.

Schegloff, E.A. (1993) Reflections on quantification in the study of conversation. *Research on Language and Social Interaction, 26*, 99–128.

Schenkein, J. (1978) Sketch of the analytic mentality for the study of conversational interaction. In. J. Schenkein (Ed.) *Studies in the Organization of Conversational Interaction*. New York: Academic Press.

Schofield, J. (1989) Increasing the generalizability of qualitative research. In E. Eisner and A. Peshkin (Eds) *Qualitative Inquiry in Education*. New York: Teachers College Press.

Schooler, J.W., Ohlsson, S. and Brooks, K. (1993) Thoughts beyond words: When language overshadows insight. *Journal of Experimental Psychology: General, 122*, 166–183.

Schutz, A. (1962) *Collected Papers*, Vol 1. The Hague: Martinus Nijhoff.

Schwandt, T.A. (1994) Constructivist, interpretivist approaches to human inquiry. In N.K. Denzin and Y.S. Lincoln (Eds) *Handbook of Qualitative Research*. Thousand Oaks, California: Sage.

Shah, S. (1994) Kaleidoscope people: Locating the 'subject' of paedagogic discourse. *Journal of Access Studies, 9*, 257–270.

Shapin, S. (1994) *A Social History of Truth: Civility and Science in Seventeenth-Century England*. Chicago, Illinois: University of Chicago Press.

Shapin, S. and Schaffer, S. (1985) *Leviathan and the Air-Pump: Hobbes, Boyle, and the Experimental Life*. Princeton, New Jersey: Princeton University Press.

Sharrock, W.W. and Anderson, R.J. (1982) On the demise of the native: Some observations on and a proposal for ethnography. *Human Studies, 5*, 119–136.

Shotter, J. (1975) *Images of Man in Psychological Research*. London: Methuen.

Shotter, J. and Gergen, K.J. (Eds) (1989) *Texts of Identity*. London: Sage.

Shotter, J. and Gergen, K. (1994) Inquiries in social construction. (Series editors' introduction.). In T.R. Sarbin and J.I. Kitsuse (Eds) *Constructing the Social*. London: Sage.

215

Sieber, S.D. (1973) The integration of fieldwork and survey methods. *American Journal of Sociology, 78*, 1335–1359.

Silverman, D. (1985) *Qualitative Methodology and Sociology*. Aldershot: Gower.

Silverman, D. (1993) *Interpreting Qualitative Data: Methods for Analysing Talk, Text and Interaction*. London: Sage.

Simon, H.A. (1966) Scientific discovery and the psychology of problem solving. In R.G. Colodny (Ed.) *Mind and Cosmos: Essays in Contemporary Science and Philosophy*. Pittsburg, Pennsylvania: University of Pittsburg Press.

Simon, H.A. (1967) Motivational and emotional controls of cognition. *Psychological Review, 74*, 29–39.

Simon, H.A. and Kaplan, C.A. (1989) Foundations of cognitive science. In M.I. Posner (Ed.), *Foundations of Cognitive Science*. Cambridge, Massachusetts: MIT Press.

Singer, J.L. (1975) Navigating the stream of consciousness: Research in daydreaming and related inner experience. *American Psychologist, 30*, 727–738.

Sloboda, J. and Newstead, S. (1995) *Guidelines for Assessment of the PhD in Psychology and Related Disciplines*. Sheffield: Universities' and Colleges' Staff Development Agency.

Sloman, A. (1976) What are the aims of science? *Radical Philosophy*, spring, 7–17.

Smith, D. (1978) K is mentally ill: The anatomy of a factual account. *Sociology, 12*, 23–53.

Smith, D.E. (1981) *The Everyday World as Problematic*. Saskatoon, Saskatchewan: University of Saskatchewan Press.

Smith, J.A. (1994a) Reconstructing selves: an analysis of discrepancies between women's contemporaneous and retrospective accounts of the transition to motherhood. *British Journal of Psychology, 85*, 371–392.

Smith, J.A. (1994b) Towards reflexive practice: Engaging participants as co-researchers or co-analysts in psychological inquiry. *Journal of Community and Applied Social Psychology, 4*, 253–260.

Smith, J.A. (1995) Qualitative methods, identity and transition to motherhood. *The Psychologist, 8*, 122–125.

Smith, J.A., Harré, R. and Van Langenhove, L. (1995a) Idiography and the case study. In J.A. Smith, R. Harré & L. Van Langenhove (Eds) *Rethinking Psychology*. London: Sage.

Smith, J.A., Harré, R. and Van Langenhove, L. (Eds) (1995b) *Rethinking Methods in Psychology*. London: Sage.

Smith, J.K. (1984) The problem of criteria in judging interpretive inquiry. *Educational Evaluation and Policy Analysis, 6*, 379–391.

Smith, J.K. (1989) *The Nature of Social and Educational Inquiry: Empiricism versus Interpretation*. Norwood, New Jersey: Ablex.

Smith, J.K. and Heshusius, L. (1986) Closing down the conversation: The end of the quantitative–qualitative debate among educational inquirers. *Educational Researcher, 15*, 4–12.

Soderqvist, T. (1991) Biography or ethnobiography or both? Embodied reflexivity and the deconstruction of knowledge-power. In F. Steier (Ed.) *Research and Reflexivity*. London: Sage.

Sperling, G.A. (1960) The information available in brief visual presentation. *Psychological Monographs, 74* (whole no. 498).

Spradley, J.P. (1979) *The Ethnographic Interview*. New York: Holt, Rinehart and Winston.

Squire, C. (1994) Empowering women: The Oprah Winfrey Show. *Feminism and Psychology, 4*, 63–80.

Stanley, L. and Wise, S. (1993) *Breaking Out Again: Feminist Epistemology and Ontology*, 2nd ed. London: Routledge.

Steier, F. (Ed.) (1991) *Research and Reflexivity*. Newbury Park, California: Sage.

Stern, P.N. (1994) Eroding grounded theory. In J.M. Morse (Ed.), *Critical Issues in Qualitative Research Methods*. Thousand Oaks, California: Sage.

Stiles, W. (1993) Quality control in qualitative research. *Clinical Psychology Review, 13*, 593–618.

Stinessen, L. (1985) The influence of verbalization on problem solving. *Scandinavian Journal of Psychology, 26*, 342–347.

Strauss, A.L. (1987) *Qualitative Analysis for Social Scientists*. Cambridge: Cambridge University Press.

Strauss, A.L. and Corbin, J. (1990) *Basics of Qualitative Research: Grounded Theory Procedures and Techniques*. Newbury Park, California: Sage.

Strauss, A.L. and Corbin, J. (1994) Grounded theory methodology: An overview. In N.K. Denzin and Y.S. Lincoln (Eds) *Handbook of Qualitative Research*. Thousand Oaks, California: Sage.

Strong, P. (1979) *The Ceremonial Order of the Clinic*. London: Routledge and Kegan Paul.

Tesch, R. (1990) *Qualitative Research: Analysis Types and Software Tools*. Basingstoke: Falmer.

Thomas, W.I. and Znaniecki, F. (1927) *The Polish Peasant in Europe and America* (5 vols). Chicago, Illinois: University of Chicago Press.

Thorndyke, P.W. and Stasz, C. (1980) Individual differences in procedures for knowledge acquisition from maps. *Cognitive Psychology, 12*, 137–175.

Titchener, E.B. (1909) *A Text-Book of Psychology*, vol. 1. New York: Macmillan.

Toren, C. (1990) *Making Sense of Hierarchy: Cognition as Social Process in Fiji*. London: Athlone Press.

Toren, C. (1994) Transforming love: Representing Fijian hierarchy. In P. Gow and P. Harvey (Eds) *Sex and Violence: Issues in Representation and Experience*. London: Routledge.

Tough, A. (1982) *Intentional Changes: A Fresh Approach to Helping People Change*. Chicago: Follett Publishing.

Traweek, S. (1988) *Beam Times and Life Times: The World of Particle Physics*. Cambridge, Massachusetts: Harvard University Press.

Turner, B.A. (1981) Some practical aspects of qualitative data analysis: One way of organizing the cognitive processes associated with the generation of grounded theory. *Quality and Quantity, 15*, 225–247.

Turner, B.A. (1994) Patterns of crisis behaviour: A qualitative inquiry. In A. Bryman and R.G. Burgess (Eds) *Analyzing Qualitative Data*. London: Routledge.

Van Maanen, J. (1988) *Tales of the Field: On Writing Ethnography*. Chicago, Illinois: University of Chicago Press.

Vaughan, D. (1992) Theory elaboration: The heuristics of case analysis. In H. Becker and C. Ragin (Eds) *What is a Case?*. Cambridge: Cambridge University Press.

von Borstel, G. (1982) *Experimentelle Überprüfung einiger Annahmen zur Methode des Lauten Denkens* [*An Experimental Test of an Assumption of the Think Aloud Method*]. Unpublished diploma thesis, University of Hamburg, Hamburg.

Walker, J.C. and Evers, C.W. (1988) The epistemological unity of educational research. In J.P. Keeves (Ed.) *Educational Research, Methodology and Measurement: An International Handbook*. Oxford: Pergamon.

Wallas, G. (1926) *The Art of Thought*. London: Jonathan Cape.

Wallis, J.H. (1973) *Personal Counselling: An Introduction to Relationship Therapy*. London: Allen and Unwin.

Watson, J.B. (1920) Is thinking merely the action of language mechanisms? *British Journal of Psychology, 11*, 87–104.

Watts, F.N. (1992) Is psychology falling apart? *The Psychologist, 5*, 489–494.

Weber, R.P. (1990) *Basic Content Analysis*, 2nd ed. Newbury Park, California: Sage.

Weeden, C. (1987) *Feminist Practice and Poststructuralist Theory*. Oxford: Blackwell.

Wegner, D.M. (1994) Ironic processes of mental control. *Psychological Review, 101*, 34–52.

Wegner, D.M., Schneider, D.J, Carter, S.R. and White, T.L. (1987) Paradoxical effects of thought suppression. *Journal of Personality and Social Psychology, 53*, 5–13.

Weitzman, E.A. and Miles, M.B. (1995) *Computer Programs for Qualitative Data Analysis: A Software Sourcebook*. Thousand Oaks, California: Sage.

Wertsch, J.V. (1991) *Voices of the Mind: A Sociocultural Approach to Mediated Action*. London: Harvester Wheatsheaf.

West, L. (1994) Whose story, whose terms? Some problems of reflectivity in life history research. In *Life Histories and Learning: Language, the Self and Education*. Falmer: Centre for Continuing Education, University of Sussex, and Canterbury: School of Continuing Education, University of Kent.

Westcott, M. (1979) Feminist criticism of the social sciences. *Harvard Educational Review, 49*, 422–430.

Wetherell, M. (1994) The knots of power and negotiation, blank and complex subjectivities. *Journal of Community and Applied Social Psychology, 4*, 305–308.

Wetherell, M. and Potter, J. (1988) Discourse analysis and the identification of interpretative repertoires. In C. Antaki (Ed.) *Analysing Everyday Explanation: A Casebook of Methods*. London: Sage.

Wetherell, M. and Potter, J. (1992) *Mapping the Language of Racism: Discourse and the Legitimation of Exploitation*. London: Harvester Wheatsheaf.

Wetherell, M., Stiven, H. and Potter, J. (1987) Unequal egalitarianism: A preliminary study of discourses concerning gender and employment opportunities. *British Journal of Social Psychology, 26*, 59–71.

White, P.A. (1988) Knowing more about what we can tell: 'Introspective access' and causal report accuracy 10 years later. *British Journal of Psychology, 79*, 13–46.

White, P.A. (1989) Evidence for the use of information about internal events to improve the accuracy of causal reports. *British Journal of Psychology, 80*, 375–382.

Whyte, W.F. (1967) *Street Corner Society: The Social Structure of an Italian Slum*. Chicago, Illinois: Chicago University Press.

Widdicombe, S. (1992) Subjectivity, power and the practice of psychology. *Theory and Psychology, 2*, 487–499.

Widdicombe, S. (1993) Autobiography and change: Rhetoric and authenticity of 'Gothic' style. In E. Burman and I. Parker (Eds) *Discourse Analytic Research: Readings and Repertoires of Texts in Action*. London: Routledge.

Widdicombe, S. and Wooffitt, R. (1995) *The Language of Youth Subculture*. London: Harvester Wheatsheaf.

Wieder, D.L. (Ed.) (1993) Colloquy: On issues of quantification in conversation analysis. *Research on Language and Social Interaction, 26*, 151–226.

Wilde, B., Starrin, B., Larsson, G. and Larsson, M. (1993) Quality of care from a patient perspective: A grounded theory study. *Scandinavian Journal of Caring Sciences, 7*, 113–120.

Wilkinson, S. (Ed.) (1986) *Feminist Social Psychology*. Milton Keynes: Open University Press.

Willis, P. (1977) *Learning to Labour: How Working Class Kids Get Working Class Jobs*. Farnborough: Saxon House.

Wilson, T.D. (1994) The proper protocol: Validity and completeness of verbal reports. *Psychological Science, 5*, 249–252.

Wilson, T.D. and Nisbett, R.E. (1978) The accuracy of verbal reports about the effects of stimuli on evaluations and behavior. *Social Psychology, 41*, 118–131.

Winnicott, D.W. (1965) *The Maturational Process and the Facilitating Environment*. London: Hogarth Press.

Wolf, M. (1990) Chinanotes: Engendering anthropology. In R. Sanjek (Ed.) *Fieldnotes: The Makings of Anthropology*. Ithaca, New York: Cornell University Press.

Wolf, M. (1992) *A Thrice-Told Tale: Feminism, Postmodernism, and Ethnographic Responsibility*. Stanford, California: Stanford University Press.

Woodworth, R.S. and Schlossberg, H. (1954) *Experimental Psychology*, 3rd ed. London: Methuen.

Wooffitt, R. (1990) On the analysis of interaction: An introduction to conversation analysis. In P. Luff, D. Frohlich and G.N. Gilbert (Eds) *Computers and Conversation*. New York: Academic Press.

Wooffitt, R. (1992a) Analyzing accounts. In N. Gilbert (Ed.) *Researching Social Life*. London: Sage.

Wooffitt, R. (1992b) *Telling Tales of the Unexpected: The Organization of Factual Discourse*. London: Harvester Wheatsheaf.

Woolgar, S. (1983) Irony in the social study of science. In K.D. Knorr-Cetina and M.J. Mulkay (Eds) *Science Observed: Perspectives on the Social Study of Science*. London: Sage.

Woolgar, S. (Ed.) (1988a) *Knowledge and Reflexivity*. London: Sage.

Woolgar, S. (1988b) Reflexivity is the ethnographer of the text. In S. Woolgar (Ed.) *Knowledge and Reflexivity: New Directions in the Sociology of Knowledge*. London: Sage.

Woolgar, S. (1988c) *Science: The Very Idea*. London: Tavistock.

Woolgar, S. (1989) Representation, cognition and self. In S. Fuller, M. de Mey and S. Woolgar (Eds) *The Cognitive Turn: Sociological and Psychological Perspectives on Science*. Dordrecht: Kluwer.

Woolgar, S. (1991) Configuring the user. In J. Law (Ed.) *A Sociology of Monsters: Essays on Power, Technology and Domination*. London: Routledge.

Woolgar, S. (1994) Rethinking agency: New moves in science and technology studies. *Mexican Journal of Behavior Analysis, 20*, 213–240.

Woolgar, S. and Ashmore, M. (1988) The next step: An introduction to the reflexive project. In S. Woolgar (Ed.) *Knowledge and Reflexivity: New Frontiers in the Sociology of Knowledge*. London: Sage.

Wootton, A. (1989) Remarks on the methodology of conversation analysis. In D. Roger and P. Bull (Eds) *Conversation*. Clevedon: Multilingual Matters.

Wright, H.F. (1960) Observational child study. In P.Mussen (Ed.), *Handbook of Research Methods in Child Development*. New York: Wiley.

Yin, R. (1989) *Case Study Research: Design and Methods*, rev. ed. Newbury Park, California: Sage.

Yin, R. (1994) *Case Study Research: Design and Methods*, 2nd ed. Thousand Oaks, California: Sage.

Young, P. and Wilmott, M. (1957) *Family and Kinship in East London*. New York: Penguin Books.

Zelditch, M. (1962) Some methodological problems of field studies. *American Journal of Sociology*, 67, 566–576.

Zimbardo, P.G., Cohen, A., Weisenberg, M., Dworkin, L. and Firestone, L. (1969a) The control of experimental pain. In P.G. Zimbardo (Ed.) *The Cognitive Control of Motivation*. Glenview, Illinois: Scott, Foresman.

Zimbardo, P.G., Weisenberg, M., Firestone, I. and Levy, B. (1969b) Changing appetites for eating fried grasshoppers with cognitive dissonance. In P.G. Zimbardo (Ed.) *The Cognitive Control of Motivation*. Glenview, Illinois: Scott, Foresman.

Index